Unpacking Sensitive Research

The term 'sensitive research' is applied to a wide range of issues and settings. It is used to denote projects that may involve risk to people, stigmatising topics, and/or require a degree of sensitivity on behalf of the researcher. Rather than take the notion of 'sensitive research' for granted, this collection unpacks and challenges what the term means.

This book is a collective endeavour to reflect on research practices around 'sensitive research', providing in-depth explorations about what this label means to different researchers, how it is done – including the need to be sensitive as a researcher – and what impacts this has on methods and knowledge creation. This book includes chapters from researchers who have explored a diverse range of research topics, including sex and sexuality, death, abortion, and learning disabilities, from several disciplinary perspectives, including sociology, anthropology, health services research, and interdisciplinary work. The researchers included here collectively argue that current approaches fail to adequately account for the complex mix of emotions, experiences, and ethical dilemmas at the heart of many 'sensitive' research encounters. Overall, this book moves the field of 'sensitive research' beyond the genericity of this label, showing ways in which researchers have in practice addressed the methodological threats that are triggered when we uncritically embark on 'sensitive research'.

The chapters in this book were originally published in the *International Journal of Social Research Methodology* and the journal *Mortality*.

Erica Borgstrom is Senior Lecturer in Medical Anthropology and End-of-life Care, The Open University, UK. Her work focuses on death and dying, with a focus on end-of-life care, care delivery, and research methods.

Sharon Mallon is Senior Lecturer in Mental Health, The Open University, UK. Her teaching includes critical approaches to mental health. Her research includes suicide prevention and postvention, and the impact of sensitive research on researchers.

Sam Murphy is Senior Lecturer in Health Studies, The Open University, UK. Her background is in medical sociology, especially the study of reproductive loss.

Unpacking Sensitive Research

Epistemological and Methodological Implications

Edited by
Erica Borgstrom, Sharon Mallon
and Sam Murphy

LONDON AND NEW YORK

First published 2022
by Routledge
4 Park Square, Milton Park, Abingdon, Oxon, OX14 4RN

and by Routledge
605 Third Avenue, New York, NY 10158

Routledge is an imprint of the Taylor & Francis Group, an informa business

© 2022 Taylor & Francis

All rights reserved. No part of this book may be reprinted or reproduced or utilised in any form or by any electronic, mechanical, or other means, now known or hereafter invented, including photocopying and recording, or in any information storage or retrieval system, without permission in writing from the publishers.

Trademark notice: Product or corporate names may be trademarks or registered trademarks, and are used only for identification and explanation without intent to infringe.

British Library Cataloguing-in-Publication Data
A catalogue record for this book is available from the British Library

ISBN13: 978-1-032-17220-0 (hbk)
ISBN13: 978-1-032-17221-7 (pbk)
ISBN13: 978-1-003-25232-0 (ebk)

DOI: 10.4324/9781003252320

Typeset in Minion Pro
by codeMantra

Publisher's Note
The publisher accepts responsibility for any inconsistencies that may have arisen during the conversion of this book from journal articles to book chapters, namely the inclusion of journal terminology.

Disclaimer
Every effort has been made to contact copyright holders for their permission to reprint material in this book. The publishers would be grateful to hear from any copyright holder who is not here acknowledged and will undertake to rectify any errors or omissions in future editions of this book.

Contents

Citation Information   vii
Notes on Contributors   ix
Preface   xii

1 Introduction: Unpacking sensitive research: a stimulating
   exploration of an established concept   1
   Sharon Mallon, Erica Borgstrom and Sam Murphy

PART ONE
Unpacking 'sensitivity': the tyranny of established definitions

2 What is 'sensitive' about sensitive research? The sensitive
   researchers' perspective   9
   Sharon Mallon and Iris Elliott

3 Relatively normal? Navigating emergent sensitivity in generating
   and analysing accounts of 'normality'   22
   Tom Witney and Peter Keogh

4 Involving young people with life-limiting conditions in research on sex: the
   intersections of taboo and vulnerability   29
   Sarah Earle and Maddie Blackburn

PART TWO
'Sensitive' Ethics in action: Research encounters and 'Whose research is this anyway'?

5 Reflecting on asynchronous internet mediated focus groups for researching
   culturally sensitive issues   39
   Noirin MacNamara, Danielle Mackle, Johanne Devlin Trew,
   Claire Pierson and Fiona Bloomer

CONTENTS

6 'Working together is like a partnership of entangled knowledge': exploring the sensitivities of doing participatory data analysis with people with learning disabilities — 52
Elizabeth Tilley, Iva Strnadová, Sue Ledger, Jan Walmsley, Julie Loblinzk, Paul Anthoney Christian and Zara Jane Arnold

7 Difficult data: reflections on making knowledge claims in a turmoil of competing subjectivities, sensibilities and sensitivities — 65
Lesley Hoggart

PART THREE
'The ideal sensitive researcher': reflexivity, internalisation and the cost to self?

8 Internalising 'sensitivity': vulnerability, reflexivity and death research(ers) — 75
Erica Borgstrom and Julie Ellis

9 Researching perinatal death: managing the myriad of emotions in the field — 89
Kerry Jones and Sam Murphy

10 'Men, we just deal with it differently': researching sensitive issues with young men — 102
Martin Robb

11 The performance of researching sensitive issues — 111
Carol Komaromy

Index — 125

Citation Information

The following chapters, except chapter 11, were originally published in the *International Journal of Social Research Methodology*, volume 24, issue 5 (2021). Chapter 11 was originally published in the journal *Mortality*, volume 25, issue 3, (2020). When citing this material, please use the original citations and page numbering for each article, as follows:

Chapter 1
Unpacking sensitive research: a stimulating exploration of an established concept
Sharon Mallon, Erica Borgstrom and Sam Murphy
International Journal of Social Research Methodology, volume 24, issue 5 (2021) pp. 517–521

Chapter 2
What is 'sensitive' about sensitive research? The sensitive researchers' perspective
Sharon Mallon and Iris Elliott
International Journal of Social Research Methodology, volume 24, issue 5 (2021) pp. 523–535

Chapter 3
Relatively normal? Navigating emergent sensitivity in generating and analysing accounts of 'normality'
Tom Witney and Peter Keogh
International Journal of Social Research Methodology, volume 24, issue 5 (2021) pp. 537–543

Chapter 4
Involving young people with life-limiting conditions in research on sex: the intersections of taboo and vulnerability
Sarah Earle and Maddie Blackburn
International Journal of Social Research Methodology, volume 24, issue 5 (2021) pp. 545–551

Chapter 5
Reflecting on asynchronous internet mediated focus groups for researching culturally sensitive issues
Noirin MacNamara, Danielle Mackle, Johanne Devlin Trew, Claire Pierson and Fiona Bloomer
International Journal of Social Research Methodology, volume 24, issue 5 (2021) pp. 553–565

Chapter 6
'Working together is like a partnership of entangled knowledge': exploring the sensitivities of doing participatory data analysis with people with learning disabilities
Elizabeth Tilley, Iva Strnadová, Sue Ledger, Jan Walmsley, Julie Loblinzk, Paul Anthoney Christian and Zara Jane Arnold
International Journal of Social Research Methodology, volume 24, issue 5 (2021) pp. 567–579

Chapter 7
Difficult data: reflections on making knowledge claims in a turmoil of competing subjectivities, sensibilities and sensitivities
Lesley Hoggart
International Journal of Social Research Methodology, volume 24, issue 5 (2021) pp. 581–587

Chapter 8
Internalising 'sensitivity': vulnerability, reflexivity and death research(ers)
Erica Borgstrom and Julie Ellis
International Journal of Social Research Methodology, volume 24, issue 5 (2021) pp. 589–602

Chapter 9
Researching perinatal death: managing the myriad of emotions in the field
Kerry Jones and Sam Murphy
International Journal of Social Research Methodology, volume 24, issue 5 (2021) pp. 603–615

Chapter 10
'Men, we just deal with it differently': researching sensitive issues with young men
Martin Robb
International Journal of Social Research Methodology, volume 24, issue 5 (2021) pp. 617–625

Chapter 11
The performance of researching sensitive issues
Carol Komaromy
Mortality, volume 25, issue 3, (2020) pp. 364–377

For any permission-related enquiries please visit:
http://www.tandfonline.com/page/help/permissions

Notes on Contributors

Zara Jane Arnold is actor and member of Access All Areas. She was a researcher on the MADHOUSE re:exit Evaluation.

Maddie Blackburn is (semi-retired) qualified lawyer, senior health professional, clinician, and Lecturer with extensive background in policy development, research, management, law, and performance auditing and inspection. Her particular expertise includes academic, policy research, and management related to young people with life-limiting and/or life-threatening conditions, high level reviews and regulatory inspections of health, social care and youth offending institutions and health care law and ethics.

Fiona Bloomer is Senior Lecturer in Social Policy at Ulster University, Ireland. She has written extensively on abortion policy and is co-author of a newly published book *Reimagining Global Abortion Politics*.

Erica Borgstrom is Lecturer in Medical Anthropology and End-of-life Care, The Open University, UK. Erica has published on a variety of issues relating to end-of-life care and death studies. Erica is the co-editor for *Mortality* and sits on the council of the Association for the Study of Death and Society.

Paul Anthoney Christian is qualified performer and trustee from Access All Areas, a UK-based theatre company for people with learning disabilities. Paul was also a researcher on the MADHOUSE re:exit Evaluation.

Sarah Earle is sociologist with a qualitative research background and extensive experience of in-depth interviewing and focus groups, grounded theory methods, thematic analysis, and narrative synthesis. She has worked inclusively on research with young people and adults with life-limiting or life-threatening conditions and with people with learning disabilities.

Iris Elliott is Visiting Scholar at the School of Social Sciences, Education and Social Work, Queens University Belfast, Northern Ireland. Her research interests have focused on the vernacularization of human rights in everyday life. She is particularly interested in embedding mental health within conflict prevention and peacebuilding.

Julie Ellis is Senior Lecturer in Sociology of Health and Illness, University of Huddersfield, UK. Her research interests include personal relationships, death, dying and bereavement, materiality, and the everydayness of illness experience.

Lesley Hoggart is Professor of Social Policy Research and Research Director of the School of Health, Wellbeing and Social Care, The Open University, UK. Her research projects are focused on reproductive health, abortion policy and politics, and sexual health, and she has published widely in these areas. Her recent outputs include the award-winning *MyBodyMyLife* abortion story-telling exhibition.

Kerry Jones is Lecturer in end-of-life care at the School of Health and Social Care, The Open University, UK.

Peter Keogh is Deputy Associate Dean for Research Excellence and Senior Lecturer in the Faculty of Well-being, Education and Language Studies, The Open University, UK. He is interested in how people with HIV and those at risk for HIV manage their sexual, intimate, and social lives as the epidemic unfolds.

Carol Komaromy has worked as academic in death studies for over 20 years. She has a practitioner background.

Sue Ledger is Visiting Research Fellow in Health and Social Care of the School of Health, Wellbeing and Social Care at the Faculty of Wellbeing, Education and Language Studies, The Open University, UK. Sue has a background in social work and is particularly interested in supporting the inclusion of people with complex learning disabilities in research and the co-development of support services.

Julie Loblinzk is self-advocate at Self Advocacy Sydney, Inc., Australia, and Adjunct Lecturer at the School of Education at the Faculty of Arts and Social Sciences, University of New South Wales Sydney, Australia.

Danielle Mackle is Lecturer in Social Work at the School of Applied Social and Policy Sciences at Ulster University, Ireland. Danielle's research interests include the human development and well-being of the LGBTQ+ community, separated young people and refugee and asylum seeking people.

Noirin MacNamara is Data Analyst in Technological University Dublin, Ireland. Her research focuses on reproductive justice and feminist political theory.

Sharon Mallon is Senior Lecturer in Mental Health at The Open University, UK. Her research interests span a number of areas of sensitive research related to mental health. She has focused on suicide prevention and postvention. She is particularly interested in the impact of suicide on young people.

Sam Murphy is Associate Head of the School for Health, Social Care, and Social Work at The Open University, UK.

Claire Pierson is Lecturer in Gender Politics, University of Liverpool, UK. She specialises in reproductive rights and activism, and women, peace and security.

Martin Robb is Senior Lecturer at the Faculty of Wellbeing, Education and Language Studies, The Open University, UK, where he leads the MA in Childhood and Youth Studies. His research has focused on issues of gender and care, including studies of fatherhood, men working in childcare, and young masculinities.

Iva Strnadová is Professor in Special Education and Disability Studies in the School of Education at the Faculty of Arts and Social Sciences, University of New South Wales Sydney, Australia, and Academic Lead Research at UNSW Disability Innovation Institute, University of New South Wales Sydney, Australia.

Elizabeth Tilley is Senior Lecturer in Health and Social Care of the School of Health, Wellbeing and Social Care at the Faculty of Wellbeing, Education and Language Studies, The Open University, UK, and chairs the Social History of Learning Disability Research Group, The Open University, UK.

Johanne Devlin Trew is Course Director of Social Policy, Ulster University, Ireland. Her research focuses on migration, racism, and digital applications of qualitative methodologies.

Jan Walmsley is Visiting Professor, The Open University, UK, and a researcher with a particular interest in inclusive methodology.

Tom Witney completed a PhD researching the lived experiences of gay/bisexual men in serodiscordant relationships in the UK.

Preface

As social scientists, across the course of our academic careers, each of us, in our way, has become acutely aware that the word 'sensitive' is 'loaded'. In our personal and professional lives, we have experienced it both as an insult ("you are too sensitive") and as a compliment ("thank you for being sensitive to my needs"). Thus, like many of the words that we encounter in our daily lives, it is multifaceted, and its use reflects the complex nature of communication and interaction. And, like many other things, we have become accustomed to its imperfect presence.

However, it is the blanket and unquestioned application of the term 'sensitive' to our research topics that has caused us to pause, reflect, and ultimately to act by collating this book. In these contexts, we experienced and witnessed the consequences of this word on research participants, researchers, and on knowledge production in general. In many cases, the term 'sensitive' was used by those within academia, ethics committees, and research funders in an attempt to protect vulnerable populations. Yet it was our experience that this was not always the outcome, and at times, research participants even challenged such framings of their lives. Moreover, the application of this generic term did little to reflect the multiplex nature of social research or researcher-participant interactions.

Attending to these concerns, we use this collection to interrogate the term 'sensitive' from a range of perspectives. Highlighting that what makes something sensitive is often bound up with people's experiences of the phenomenon of interest and crucially that it may also be influenced by their perceptions and of it. For example, morticians might not feel that death is a sensitive subject where they are concerned but will be aware that those who are not in the business of death may find it an extremely challenging topic. Similarly, as academic researchers there is a risk we may become immune or blasé about the sensitivity of our topic. Conversely, for those who have little or no experience of challenging issues, assumptions may be made about how it *might* feel, or how we *should* react.

As academic researchers then, we became mindful of the need not only to prioritise the needs of the people we are asking to participate in our research but to also examine our own sensitivities, or lack thereof, around particular subjects. In turn, contributors also examine those of the gatekeepers who have the power to grant us permission to undertake this research, be that through providing funding, ethical permission, or access to participants. This collection is our response to challenging established notions and our own experiences of 'sensitive' when it comes to research. It is a book that has been created from a special issue of the *International Journal of Social Research Methodology*. As you can read in the special issue introduction entitled *Unpacking sensitive research: a stimulating exploration of an established concept*, it sought to challenge the unquestioned ways in which 'sensitive research' is used in academia, during research, and even by research ethics committees.

As editors and researchers who have worked in fields that are considered 'sensitive', we are acutely aware how this framing of particular research endeavours impact upon the methods that people use and the forms of knowledge that are produced and considered as legitimate within different fields.

At The Open University, we have a long, established history of conducting research on topics which may be considered 'sensitive' in a range of settings – from research on sexuality and gender, to topics related to death including abortion and suicide, to co-produced research with participants who have learning disabilities. These topics are considered 'sensitive' for a variety of reasons and have brought issues of consent, researcher support, and publishing to the fore for many of us over the years. As a way of starting the process to envision a potential collaborative publication, we held several workshops within our department to share people's experiences and 'takes' on sensitive research. This was beneficial for many reasons, not least for this book, but also to make connections between and across our varied research projects and careers.

The resulting collection is therefore predominately from people who have a connection to The Open University. Not only does it showcase the collective expertise that the university has in the field of 'sensitive research', it also highlights how the university's unique stance on being open to ideas and methods has enabled us to interrogate this taken-for-granted term. Indeed, we acknowledge here that we have benefitted from working in an institution that has provided academic staff stable employment in a supportive environment, allowing people to conduct the type of research which is included in this edition. We have also taken this opportunity within the edited collection to add a paper written by one of our retired colleagues – Carol Komaromy – who has written on the performance of researching sensitive issues.

As editors, we would like to thank our colleagues – both at The Open University and at other institutions – who have made this collection possible through writing, feedback, collaborative research, their own work, and many times, being a listening ear or providing peer-support. We also thank the many research participants who have been part of these studies. Their contributions and interactions with us (and other authors in this collective) have helped us question and reframe what 'sensitive research' is and can be, sometimes even actively and vocally resisting the label or illustrating how it can be helpful and/or hurtful. Without these exchanges, we would not be able to draw out the epistemological, methodological, relational, and emotional elements that are present within this collection of papers.

Erica Borgstrom, Sharon Mallon, and
Sam Murphy – September 2021

INTRODUCTION

Unpacking sensitive research: a stimulating exploration of an established concept

Sharon Mallon, Erica Borgstrom and Sam Murphy

We are living in turbulent times. The hashtag #MeToo went viral in 2017; the death of George Floyd propelled the Black Lives Matter movement back into international headlines; and the emergence of COVID-19 has brought to the fore issues around illness, death, dying and bereavement, it seems that emotions and sensitivities are running high for many people, if not for everyone.

In 2018, when we conceived this special issue, we noted in our proposal that since the term 'sensitive research' first emerged, there has been a growing acceptance that many research topics are 'sensitive' in nature (De Laine, 2000; Lee, 1993; Lee & Renzetti, 1990). Writing this, in late 2020, it now feels as if all topics are 'sensitive' in ways we have only begun to consider, and the emergence and ongoing debate about 'cancel culture' has added a new and highly controversial element to these sensitivities. It seems therefore that this special issue is more important than ever, given our overarching objective was to critique and challenge some of the presuppositions that have emerged around 'sensitive' topics of research.

This special issue emerges from a perspective that proposes that affording the moniker of 'sensitive' to a research project has wide-reaching epistemological implications and dictates the basic methodological parameters under which much 'sensitive' social science research is undertaken. Indeed, at the core of this special issue is the theoretical argument that the assumed nature of the term 'sensitive research', including how it is normatively and routinely applied to a range of topics, uncritically reproduces ways of categorising the social world and sets of relationships. From ethics committees presuming what harms research may present and who needs protecting, to implicit practices in academia that promote research that is deemed less socially or politically 'risky'. Yet, attempting to contain sensitive research in this way fails to adequately account for the experiences and complex mix of emotions at the heart of many research encounters and across research careers. We acknowledge that the recent turn towards emotional aspects of such research is helpful. However, we also feel it is about much more than *'just'* emotions. It is our suggestion that broader experiences, including the reactions of others to our research, *and* complex emotions that fundamentally affect how researchers make knowledge claims about all sorts of divergent issues.

Consequently, the articles which follow have emerged from a collective endeavour to reflect upon a range of research practices around 'sensitive research' and to provide in-depth explorations about what this label means to different researchers; how the research is undertaken, including the need to be 'sensitive' as a researcher; the sensitivities engendered and required by the research; and thus the impacts this all has on methodologies and knowledge creation. As such, we do not seek to offer a unifying definition of what sensitive research is or how to best undertake it. Indeed, the overall aim has been to enable researchers from all sectors to critically engage with what it means to do 'sensitive research' in the twenty-first century and to reflect on their own research practices. As such the inclusion of articles which are drawn from a range of disciplinary backgrounds from researchers who have explored a diverse range of research topics, has been entirely purposeful.

Cross-cutting themes in the special issue

The authors who have contributed to this issue argue that current approaches fail to adequately account for the complex mix of emotions, experiences and ethical dilemmas which lie at the heart of many 'sensitive' research encounters. There are several themes that intersect across each of the articles. One of these is the issue of emotions and emotional affect. Although there is now widespread acknowledgement of the presence of emotions in the research encounter, their effect on the research and processes of knowledge creation is poorly understood and rarely routinely discussed. Loosely, we can understand how emotion tends to refer to the way in which feelings are expressed while 'affect' refers to the biological experiences of them.

When exploring sensitive topics, much attention is paid, rightly, to mitigating the possible deleterious feelings the process may give rise to in participants. But, as social scientists, our tools are not only our voice or image recorders and the pen, but also our bodies. Across the articles presented here, it is clear that the researcher and the researched are not unattached and objective instruments; rather research is personal, emotional and reflective, and situated in existing cultural and structural contexts (Coffey, 1999). Paying attention to the embodied experience of our emotions during the research process has been important to all these researchers. It was their reactions – emotional and embodied – to the experiences they were exploring, that had enormous potential to impact, both positively and negatively, on their (and our) understanding of the subjects at hand, and thus on the production of knowledge. For example, the articles here show how complex these reactions can be in sensitive research when the topic encourages the researcher to make assumptions and emotional investments that were prohibitive or disruptive (Witney and Keogh, Mallon and Elliott, Jones and Murphy, Hoggart) while others found it to be key to their understanding (Borgstrom and Ellis). Similarly, research can be made sensitive when participants evoke responses in us that are not expected such as anger (Jones and Murphy, Hoggart) and guilt (Jones and Murphy, Borgstrom and Ellis, Mallon and Elliott) which can result in some accounts being privileged over others.

When considering 'sensitive research', sensitivity is often thought of in terms of two key elements: firstly, the inherent sensitive or taboo qualities of the research topic itself and secondly the methodological and practical means of sensitively addressing such 'sensitive' issues. All of the articles here engage with both issues, and show how we need to think about the techniques of data collection and what this means for conducting research sensitively (Bloomer et al., Blackburn and Earle, Tilley et al.). A facet of this is an engagement with critically thinking about the sensitivity of, and experienced by, the researcher across the entire research journey. The examples in this special issue illustrate how the power of the researcher is of paramount importance in contextualizing any research scenario because it determines how sensitivity is navigated and resisted across the practice of social science research. For example, the sensitive nature of the research was apparent not only during data collection (as has traditionally transfixed ethics committees) but during analysis and dissemination (see Mallon & Elliott, Tilley et al., Jones and Murphy, and Hoggart). Researchers may find sensitivity arises unexpectedly in themselves, or the participants, in otherwise uncontroversial research (Robb, Tilley et al., Witney and Keogh). Several of the articles discuss what it means and how researchers navigate their own, and their participants' emotions unexpectedly through a research project where such issues had not previously been considered. Research can also be made sensitive when participants don't behave as researchers might hope (Hoggart, Mallon and Elliott) thus reducing or challenging the power of the researcher and the underlying (but often unspoken research agenda) and leading to practices in the research that feel deceptive (Hoggart, Witney and Keogh). Moreover, simplistic conceptualisations of the 'insider versus outsider' debate, such as those set out by Bourdieu (1996) who argues that reducing the social and cultural distance through subject familiarity, are repeatedly challenged in this special issue (see Jones and Murphy, Borgstrom and Ellis).

As well as the cross cutting intersections between articles, we also view the special issue as having three parts, each of which tackles a particular thematic area. Part One is **Unpacking 'sensitivity': the tyranny of established definitions**, with articles challenging the terminology of sensitive research from different perspectives by examining the processes involved in the practice of sensitive researchers. The overall commentary of these pieces provides an insightful acknowledgement of the lack of certainty that questioning the definition of 'sensitive' and 'sensitivity' can create in the research encounter. This, by its unique nature, makes a contribution to the intellectual field and has the potential to reduce the problems associated with such research; showing how researchers may be guided in their future application of this term to their research. For example, Mallon and Elliott explore how researchers' motivations, combined with their personal and professional investment, can heighten their sensitivity to aspects of the research that remain underexplored in methodological texts on the issue of sensitive research. Conversely, Witney and Keogh's article is a revealing account of the unexpected consequences of how broad stroke approaches and assumptions of the heightened sensitivity of research topics and research subjects can also limit one's approaches to research. This article, in combination with Blackburn and Earle's account of the intersection of multiple 'sensitivities', shows how the ethics review processes can encourage us to make unhelpful assumptions about the ways in which a topic might be 'sensitive'. Both articles provide insightful details that illustrate how, as researchers, we can then set ourselves, and our participants, up to experience the topic as sensitive, whether the participants do or not. The articles also provide valuable critique of how researchers can work towards limiting and challenging these discourses of 'normality' and 'taboo' subjects.

This theme, of challenging the very basis of how we refer to a subject as sensitive, giving rise to a self-fulfilling prophecy of sensitivity is carried through to the second part that covers **'sensitive' ethics in action**. The authors in this section provide timely methodological insight into emerging areas associated with collaborative and innovative practices within research. For example, Bloomer et al.'s online research shows how 'sensitive processes' can be experienced in groups on a culturally sensitive issue (abortion). In doing so, they show how 'sensitive' and 'sensitivities' can be reshaped, repackaged, and how they can be resisted across the research lifecycle. Tilley et al. explore another highly topical area by examining the impact of societal assumptions about inclusive research and the complex sensitivities of analytic interpretation involved in co-productive research with people with intellectual disability. Hoggart takes this analysis one step further by delving into her personal sensitivities, exploring how the emotional underpinning and subjective position of the researcher can cause challenges during analysis and tensions in representation of the research.

Authors in the final section – **'The ideal sensitive researcher'** – address the issue of sensitivity as it applies directly to researchers involved in the research process. They consider the implications for 'performed roles' and knowledge production, examining how researchers might respond to these issues. For example, while sensitive subjects are often considered to be ones in which strong and potentially distressing emotions are likely to be unleashed, here the authors show the value in reconsidering methodologies in terms of the study of the emotions and emotional affects. The definition offered by Lee (1993) acknowledged that areas of research had the potential to be threatening for those involved but fell short of explicitly acknowledging the ways in which researchers *themselves* can be made to feel threatened or vulnerable. Instead, it is widely assumed that researchers operate in a context where, while the research is seen as 'risky' and participants are positioned as 'vulnerable'. These concepts and identities, and the protection that can be afforded because of them through ethics and governance procedures, are not routinely applied to the position occupied by the researcher. As a result, the care of the participant becomes paramount and to a certain extent, it is claimed that self-care for the researcher is now also well attended to. However, Borgstrom and Ellis take debates on researcher sensitivity beyond their usual boundaries to reimagine how it can get underneath the skin of the researcher re-emerging within their everyday lives. Following this, Jones and Murphy address some of the lesser discussed sensitive aspects of the process by considering emotions such as anger and guilt. Using the theoretical concept of emotional labour, they consider the consequences of this during the lifecycle of research. Indeed, unexpected emotions have the potential to result in a privileging of one account over another. Such an impact on knowledge creation may result in some participants being marginalised in the research findings. In the final article, Robb provides new insight into the challenges of mitigating and responding to 'performative' aspects of sensitivity as they intersect with the gender of researcher and the researched.

The discussion within and inspired by the articles in this special issue indicate that there is a need to rethink some of the practical structures and support that are in place for 'sensitive' research across the entire life course of the research project, and even research careers. As several of the articles indicate, how researchers deal appropriately with sensitive research has to some extent been allocated to the deliberations of ethics committee and demanding individual research reflexivity. Whilst these procedures have been useful in thinking through potential harm to the participant and researcher subjectivities, they are not sufficient in themselves nor fully supportive of the researcher. Here is a non-exhaustive collection of the practical implications raised by the discussions within this special issue:

- Researchers should have access to support – both in terms of research design and emotional – within their organisations from an early stage in the research process and beyond. This is particularly pertinent for, postgraduate students, early career researches, and those otherwise marginalised within academic settings. Examples can include peer-support groups, expert supervision or mentoring, and counselling.
- Funding bodies should be invested in knowing about and financially supporting such activities before committing to research projects. Organisations that regularly fund research that they class as 'sensitive' should consider what practical support they offer the researchers they fund both during and after the lifecycle of a project.
- All funders should consider what biases they may have towards research topics that may be considered as sensitive and how this inadvertently affects funding decisions, and by implication, what groups of researchers may be excluded (e.g. those with lived experiences seeking to study topics of personal and professional interest).
- Postgraduate supervisors should receive training on how to support students conducting 'sensitive research'. Encounters during supervisions can greatly impact how researchers feel about their own work and worth, and influence decision-making around research design, analysis and representation.
- The nature of relationships in research teams can impact the ability to conduct research sensitively. Teams need to make time and energy for developing relationships that generate a level of trust and psychological safety, especially if there is the potential for research topics to reactivate trauma for those involved.
- Research ethics committees and researchers should not classify all projects related to certain topics as 'sensitive' by default. Instead there should be a consideration of why, when and from whose perspective a topic may be sensitive and the implications this has for the research and all stakeholders.
- Research ethics committees should also be willing to consider the implications for the research on the researcher when conducting 'sensitive' research, but not use this as a reason not to provide a favourable opinion on a proposed project.
- Projects can incorporate practices that support researchers and participants, depending on the context, such as safeguarding procedures within projects and/or operational plans for when a researcher is unwell or for extended periods of leave.
- As academics, we can be more committed in making academia a safe space in which the complexities and emotionality of 'sensitive' research and its related sensitivities are discussed. This can be at workshops, conferences, and within journals, as well as day-to-day in our workspaces and online.

Conclusion

Overall, the methodological contribution of this special issue rests on the collective critique of the ways in which the term 'sensitive' have increasingly been deployed as shorthand for a range of very different research encounters. Labelling a research study as 'sensitive' can be considered to be an important methodological step but simply doing so does not avoid ethical problems and dilemmas or provide readymade answers for their resolution – this requires a more in-depth analysis of the issues. Across all the articles, it is apparent that two methodological threats result from the easy acceptance and ready application of the terms 'sensitive' and 'sensitivity' within social science research. The first relates to the perfunctory practices that have formed around sensitive research that provide a rather simplistic set of processes by which it appears such research should be carried out. These processes are significant in responding to a potentially unsatisfactory definition of what defines 'sensitivity', as they provide unreliable assumptions of what is fundamentally involved in undertaking 'sensitive' forms of research. They also determine how those involved in the research; the participant, the researcher, ethical reviewers, and funders will perform during the research process. The second threat comes from the assumed emotional context which the researched and researcher are placed within much of 'sensitive research', and the consequences this has for the knowledge which is produced, as it disempowers or marginalises the resistance of those exposed to particular experiences. Collectively, we hope in drawing together research from a variety of areas to examine the consequences of its use for knowledge production, the articles move the field of 'sensitive research' beyond the genericity of this label, showing ways in which researchers have in practice addressed the methodological threats that are triggered when we uncritically embark on 'sensitive research'.

Acknowledgments

This special issue has been collated during exceptional times, both within HE generally and globally as we have all had to adjust to new ways of working. We wish to thank all the reviewers who gave their time to peer review these articles, without their critical and reflective views this would not have been possible.

References

Bourdieu, P. (1996). Understanding. *Theory, Culture & Society*, *13*(2), 17–37. https://doi.org/10.1177/026327696013002002

Coffey, A. (1999). *The ethnographic self*. Sage.

De Laine, M. (2000). *Fieldwork, participation and practice: Ethics and dilemmas in qualitative research*. Sage Publications.

Lee, R., & Renzetti, C. (1990). The problems of researching sensitive topics: An overview and introduction. *American Behavioral Scientist*, *33*(5), 510–528. https://doi.org/10.1177/0002764290033005002

Lee, R. M. (1993). *Doing research on sensitive topics*. Sage Publications.

Part One

Unpacking 'sensitivity'

The tyranny of established definitions

What is 'sensitive' about sensitive research? The sensitive researchers' perspective

Sharon Mallon and Iris Elliott

ABSTRACT
There is growing consensus in the literature about the emotional consequences for researchers involved in sensitive research. There is also concern about the support provided to these researchers. Such concerns are amplified by a lack of discussion on what exactly researchers themselves consider is 'sensitive' about their involvement in this type of research. This paper draws on data from a roundtable with 12 researchers working across a range of 'sensitive' research areas. It presents an examination of their views on these issues presented in themes that emerged from our analysis of these data. These themes are interconnected with examples from the literature that contextualises and add to our methodological understanding of the issue of sensitivity. Our analysis suggested these researchers' sensitivities were closely linked to the context of the research. In addition, they described how issues of identity, as well as political motivations, meant there was a strong personal and professional investment in the research. We conclude by reflecting on these sensitivities, arguing that although they are supported by current definitions of sensitivity, they are more nuanced than broader discussions of sensitivity allow.

Introduction

"I would have assumed that if you are doing (research about) a traumatic subject ... that the topic itself is where the emotion comes from, but what I am hearing is that's not at all really where the emotional risks come from ... " (Author 1)

These are the opening words from a roundtable discussion convened by both the authors of this paper to discuss the issue of sensitivity in sensitive research. We had spent many years working on sensitive topic research studies and were aware of the extensive literature and governance procedures that provide guidance on how to conduct sensitive research. For example, the published literature can give some indication of the likely areas of sensitivity that may arise (Powell et al., 2018). Ethics committees may give some direction on where particular issues of vulnerability may occur, and how these might be managed (Powell et al., 2018). In addition, supervisors may provide support and guidance as the research progresses.

However, it was our sense that the guidance available to researchers was based on presumptive notions of sensitivity that failed to reflect the 'true' sensitivity involved in 'sensitive' research. Over a number of years, we had conversed about our experiences of undertaking qualitative fieldwork on sensitive topics, as well as the concerns that emerged from our roles managing other researchers.

The concept of holding an event emerged from these informal discussions. In short, we wanted to re-examine how sensitive research is experienced by those working as researchers at the front line. Thus, in May 2015, we held a roundtable discussion designed to facilitate an intellectual debate among sensitive topic researchers, providing them with a safe space in which they could share their experiences. Our intention was to explore the issue of sensitive research from their perspective, examining in detail the issues they were 'sensitive' about. We were keen to use these experiences productively, to create guidance that could take this issue forward in practical way (see Mallon & Elliott, 2019 for more details). However, the aim of this paper is to shift the analytic gaze from these practical concerns, towards a theoretical analysis of the data that reflects upon how the issue of sensitivity was constructed and enacted by researchers. Lee and Lee's (2012) systematic review of sensitive research highlighted the need for further conceptual work in this area, that was focused on the definition of sensitivity and the emotional demands of fieldwork aspects. It is these aspects that are the subject here.

The paper begins with a brief summary of the literature's approach to defining sensitive research and researcher's reactions to this work. It then outlines the 'research sensitivities' described by the UK researchers who participated in the roundtable. By drawing upon this data, we explore the tensions that exist for researchers undertaking this type of research. In doing so, we reveal that the particular areas of sensitivity they identified were connected not only to the nature of the topics themselves (Lee & Lee, 2012) but were also closely linked to the context of the research. Our approach here is to combine brief extracts from the roundtable with established views from the literature. This allows us to reflect upon, contribute to and challenge our current methodological understandings of the work involved in undertaking 'sensitive' research. In doing so, this article will contribute to the knowledge about the complexities inherent in this type of research for researchers and their supervisors.

What defines a 'sensitive' topic?

Exactly what defines a research topic as being 'sensitive' varies. Sieber and Stanley (1988 p. 49) defined 'socially sensitive' research as 'studies in which there are potential consequences, either for the participants in the research or the class of individuals represented by it.'. Lee (1993) argued this definition was too broad and offered a definition of sensitive research in which the topic under investigation, the situation, as well as any other issues, posed a threat to the individuals involved with it. Later, Dickson-Swift et al. (2008) highlighted the impact of the research as being the focus of the 'sensitivity'; identifying areas like murder, suicide and domestic violence as sensitive, since they bring to the fore upsetting emotions for the participant. More recently, Lee and Lee's (2012) systematic review identified various aspects such as the topic of the research as being sensitive. However, methodological techniques, such as interviewing and documentary analysis also featured. The review also identified two emerging areas of sensitivity; internet use in research, and the emotional wellbeing of researchers.

The importance of understanding the 'sensitivities' of researchers

Historically, the literature on the broader issue of sensitivity has tended to focus on the practical and ethical considerations of undertaking this type of research (Lee & Lee, 2012). In part, these ethical concerns have emerged because research on sensitive topics includes an array of topics with participants who may be defined as 'vulnerable'. However, there is growing consensus within the literature of the considerable emotional consequences for researchers who are involved in social research on sensitive topics; with one paper declaring that despite some progress, the demands on those who undertake this type of research are now 'difficult to ignore' (Lee & Lee, 2012, p. 47).

The issue of vulnerability, has been discussed from both an individual researcher's perspective (Komaromy, 2020) and more infrequently from the perspective of groups of researchers (Dickson-

Swift et al., 2007). Some awareness has been drawn to the emotional demands placed on the researcher, with an emphasis on the emotional risks of this type of work (Dickson-Swift et al., 2009) and the ways in which researchers can respond to these risks (Johnson & Clarke, 2003). There has also been a turn in the literature towards using the emotional labour theory to contextualise researchers' responses to their fieldwork (Dickson-Swift, 2017; Komaromy, 2020). Many of those who have published on these issues, have expressed concern about the support that is provided to researchers (Dickson-Swift, 2017; Mallon & Elliott, 2019). However, such concerns are amplified by confusion on what exactly is sensitive about the researcher's involvement in social research on sensitive issues. The lack of a robust examination of the issue of sensitivity, especially in relation to how it presents itself to the researchers themselves, potentially renders any discussion of the issue an incomplete and ineffectual exercise. This article uses data gathered from UK researchers during a roundtable to contribute towards addressing this gap in our methodological understanding of sensitive research.

Research Methodology

The roundtable was planned in early 2015 and took place in May of that year. We invited 20 researchers from across the UK to participate in the event. Potential participants were initially selected by contacting colleagues who were identified from the literature as working in areas of research that could be loosely defined as 'sensitive'. Those who declined the invitation were asked to pass their invitation to a colleague who was working in the same area of research. Those eventually in attendance at the roundtable had undertaken research into topics such as death and dying, stillbirth, homelessness, abortion, suicide, drug addiction, lived experience of mental health issues and those who had worked with peer researchers. In total, 12 researchers attended the event, eleven were female and one male. Participants crossed disciplinary boundaries, some being social workers and sociologists, while others were from psychology or nursing backgrounds. In addition, they ranged from those who were currently undertaking a PhD (n = 1) or had just a few years' experience researching sensitive topics (n = 2), to those who had been involved in multiple studies (n = 6) and were currently operating as principal investigators (n = 3). All of the researchers were from the UK.

The authors acted as the convenors of the discussion. Although we had a plan of topics to be covered, participants were free to talk about whatever issues they felt were relevant to them and a natural flow emerged in the proceedings with little formal direction. The overall tone and direction of the discussion that ensued thus came to reflect the whole spectrum of issues that the researchers found were 'sensitive' about their area of sensitive research. Here, our analysis focuses on how the issue of sensitivity itself was enacted from the researcher's perspective. We have collectively labelled these here as 'research sensitivities'; by this we mean those issues the roundtable discussion revealed researchers were attuned or sensitive to as they emerged during the process of undertaking all aspects of the research. A broad approach to the issue of 'sensitivity' was adopted in our analysis, in that we considered it to be something that has the potential to arouse an emotional reaction (Johnson & Clarke, 2003).

During the roundtable, we used digital recorders to capture the researchers' discussion; participants were asked to consent to the use of these recordings in the production of research publications. These recordings were subsequently transcribed and analysed by both authors. The intention of this study was to provide an overview of the sensitive aspects reported by these researchers; therefore, what follows is a thematic synthesis of the key points. For similar reasons to Powell et al. (2018), the 'treatment of quotes in this article is methodological' in the sense that we 'allow (them) to speak for themselves' (p. 652). Our intention in this is to allow the participants voices to speak clearly to the reader, avoiding undue interpretation to be placed upon their words. This is important because the issue of sensitivity is not straightforward, but we have similarly found that it is regularly rolled out in a manner which is under evaluated (Richards et al., 2015). However, we diverge slightly from Powell et al.'s (2018) approach by interspersing quotes with commentary based on the literature and authors reflections. In doing so, we take our understanding of the issue of sensitivity to a new methodological level. All quotes are anonymised and for the purpose of confidentiality, we have mostly tried to avoid linking participant quotes to specific topics.

What are researchers 'sensitive' about when undertaking sensitive research?

In this section, we turn our attention to data from the roundtable, highlighting aspects of the discussion that were identified as being integral to the overall emergence of researchers' sensitivities. We demonstrate that the 'sensitivity' was multi-layered, being more than just about the actual topic of research or the potential impact on the participants. Items under discussion include: the researchers' motivations for undertaking the research and sense of identification with the people they interviewed; the emotional reaction evoked by the research, as well as those of the individuals with whom they attempted to discuss these emotions. Finally, we discuss the sensitivities they expressed in relation to the power dynamics that emerged during the research process.

Motivation and identification

In this section, we explore how some of the sensitivities discussed by the researchers emerged from their original motivation for undertaking the research. We will also examine how in some cases this emotional connection to the topic did not pre-exist their work, but rather it emerged for some researchers during the research, in response to a shared sense of identity that developed after meeting participants.

(i) Motivations for entering the field. Schostak and Schostak (2013, p. viii) have suggested that 'no research is ever undertaken without a motive'. Despite its clear relevance to the research process, the motivation of the researcher and its potential impact on the research has been infrequently examined in the literature. Here, the topic of motivation emerged naturally during the roundtable in relation to the tensions that researchers reported in relation to their experiences of undertaking fieldwork. The motivations reported by researchers for undertaking work into their area of sensitive research fell into two groups; the first group had connected with the topic personally, and whether they initially realized it or not, this came to drive their overall experience of the research; sometimes in powerful, constraining ways. The second group described how a broad curiosity had initially motivated them, but a subsequent sense of identification with the participants, emerged and heightened during the research, combining to mean the topic affected them more than they had expected. In this section, we will explore how these two groups described their experiences of sensitivity in the field.

Identification through past personal experiences. Personal experience has long been accepted in the literature as a valid reason for entering a sensitive field of research (Etherington, 2005). The limited material that tangentially examines the issue of motivation and personal experience among researchers, tends to accept personal experience as a positive feature, arguing that it adds insight to the analysis and may make research participants feel more comfortable, and thus likely to reveal more intimate details (Kleinman & Copp, 1993). However, the examples provided by researchers at the round table identified particular tensions in these assumptions, with those who had personal knowledge of the topic they were researching, reporting that in the field these experiences intersected with that of their participants, to shape the overall feel of undertaking the research.

Some researchers admitted that to colleagues they tended to portray their personal connection to the topic in a positive manner, reporting to them that as the literature suggests, it allowed them greater insight into a topic. However, privately they held reservations about it; acknowledging that in practice it was more complicated than their professional position would allow them to comfortably reveal. Those who did reveal a personal connection sometimes felt judged by supervisors, as the following quote illustrates:

> ... I think my supervisors probably felt I had gone native, in that I would probably, I was not being objective enough with the stories that I was listening to, now whether or not that is to do with my own experience which actually although I was encouraged to reflect on my research, they didn't want to know anything about what had happened to me. (P2)

It is also worth noting that upon entry into their chosen field of research, these individuals were not aware that this would become an issue for them, some felt they had previously achieved a sense of emotional peace that was subsequently challenged by the process of undertaking the research. Overall, the roundtable data suggested that the emotional state of researchers as they enter the field, and how this affects their subsequent reactions to it, were perhaps not always as straightforward as has sometimes previously been acknowledged.

Identification through shared characteristics. It was not only those who had previous experience of the topic who were sensitive to it; in some cases, even if the researcher had no personal experience of the circumstances but could empathize closely with them, they experienced distressing emotions. Researchers who fell into this second group described how they had been motivated to take part in the research because of a broad sense of curiosity rather than personal experience. However, as the research progressed, they found that this initial 'naive' curiosity came to be mixed in with a whole range of emotions that subverted their original neutrality, and heightened their emotional sensitivity to the issue:

> ... you are listening to stuff that was so close to your heart that it was just really distressing to sort of see people that you identify with having gone through really tough situations... Then when I was out in the world it made me much more emotional when those issues just came up. (P1)

Prior to undertaking this research, this researcher had no direct experience of the specific topic she was exploring. As this quote suggests, however, the material she was exposed to was *close to the heart* because she shared particular characteristics with the participant. These meant she empathised more closely with their experiences. In this case, it was sexuality. However, in other instances, the characteristic was gender or shared childhood experiences. This maps with other authors who have pointed out that when one is reminded of a personal circumstance, even one that connects with us only tangentially, our emotional reaction may be more powerful (Bloor et al., 2010).

Consequences of shared identification. It was notable that in both groups these changes were not confined to the research encounter itself, or indeed the field work stage, but instead resulted in heightened emotional sensitivity that continued for some considerable time after the research had concluded:

> ... if I look at an interview now, a few years later, I can imagine myself right back in that room and I can see the person, I can hear them... So we are talking about going in once but actually we revisit these stories many times... through the course of data analysis. (P2)

This new-found emotional sensitivity and its long-lasting nature was concerning to the researchers, who felt it made them more receptive to being affected by the emotions of the other participants they were continuing to interview. This was worrying not only because of the need to protect themselves, but also because of an awareness that they may not be able to protect later participants in ways they had been able to when they first entered the fieldwork phase of their research. As this quote succinctly illustrates:

> ... it is not only ourselves but it is also participants in the research as well, like an emotional risk for them if we are not really grounded... (P3)

As set out at the beginning of this section, these issues of motivation and shared identification were not a direct focus of our discussion, thus we have only been able to brush the surface of these issues. In preparation for leading the roundtable discussion, we had undertaken a broad scoping review of the published literature. In a rare publication, Roberts (2007) determined that interest in a topic, relevance to work, gaps in literature and personal experience all contributed to a researchers' reasons for entering the field. However, we found that motivation for undertaking research has achieved little critical attention within the literature on sensitive issues; those that have commented on it have assumed that motivation based on personal experience is a positive thing which promotes engagement and revaluation (Etherington, 2005). The lack of critical exploration of this issue is notable; in areas of comparable work, in which an individual enters similarly emotional arenas with vulnerable individuals, such as counselling and psychotherapy, therapists are required by professional bodies to expressly undertake initial personal therapy and ongoing supervision. The purpose of this therapy is, at least in part, to facilitate the critical examination of how this motivation might impact upon the clients and themselves (BACP, 2018). Similarly, social workers are now encouraged to reflect upon their past experiences as part of their ongoing professional development (Houston, 2015). Our data shows there is clearly a need for more in-depth work to explore the emotional state of researchers as they enter the field; as well as issues related to motivation and identification, and how this affects their subsequent emotional reaction to the work.

To sum up this section on motivation and identification, we conclude that the literature as it currently stands contains a potentially irreconcilable tension; for while there is wide acceptance of both the positive and negative emotions that may result for those who are participants in research, little attention has paid to the vulnerability and reaction of the researcher, both to entering the field and their subsequent reaction to data that is collected. An enhanced vulnerability is particularly apparent when aspects of the researcher's life or identity connects with aspects of the lives under investigation, either through past experiences or an emotional connection with the lives of those being researched. We explore these emotional reactions in greater detail in the next section.

(ii) The emotional reaction evoked by the research. It has been suggested that interview encounters will inevitably be emotional (Powell et al., 2018). Certainly, feelings of sadness that result from undertaking sensitive research are widely supported by the literature (Dickson-Swift et al., 2009). However, our data also showed that researchers were sensitive to other emotions they experienced during the research; these included feelings such as guilt, anger, fear and states of hopelessness. It is these emotional reactions we turn to in this section.

One of the emotions reported by researchers was guilt, this focused around the passivity of the research role and as this researcher pointed out, the very process of turning the encounters they had with their research participants into data:

> *you are supposed to turn these experiences and stories into data but they are not, they are still stories and experiences with you, but if you are working with these things day to day then you could have a very direct relationship to the processing of those experiences into strategies of care plans whatever else but we don't do we, they just sit with us for years and then we mind them every now and again and then feel guilty about it. (P4)*

Other researchers discussed powerful feelings of anger. These feelings have already been discussed in the literature on sensitive topics. For example, researchers such as Hubbard et al. (2010) have commented on experiencing anger that was directed at the participants of the research. At our roundtable, this emotion emerged as a feeling of generalised anger about the situation faced by the research participants, rather than directly at them as an individual:

> *to sort of see people that you identify with, having gone through really tough situations but I think then that it was a real, just very angry and frustrated (P1)*

In several cases, this anger was connected to frustration at not being able to do more to change the situation faced by those they were interviewing. Thus, it was not just the direct content of participants' testimonies that affected the researchers, but the broader discourse the research takes place within, as well as the perceived passivity of the role of the researcher in the encounter. We discuss this again in the final section.

An additional emotion experienced by researchers that is rarely mentioned in the literature was that of fear. As this researcher summed up:

I was quite scared of telling people the reaction I was having because I didn't want to lose my PhD or my job (P5)

Later the same participant expanded on the reasons for this fear:

How do you as a contract researcher admit that you are struggling because it is your job, you can't, you need to not be signed off, you need to not damage your career, your reputation, so that nobody will employ you to do that job again, these are all reality (P5)

In these quotes, we see the inherent and multilayered vulnerability in being a contract researcher, Early Career Researcher or PhD student. It is notable that the emerging and powerful emotion of fear is not, as is so often made the case in the literature, connected to the content of interviews or the physical context in which they take place, all of which are often carefully governed in lone worker and debriefing polices (Kenyon & Hawker, 2010). Rather the fear is connected to the *consequences* of sharing the details of the emotional reaction the researcher is experiencing. In this sense, it is connected to the professional expectations and working conditions imposed upon the researcher. This seems particularly significant as Visser (2017) has pointed out that debriefing opportunities are too often absent from social researchers. In the next quote, we see how the risk associated with sharing emotions was also closely linked to the researcher's personal sense of professional identity:

... some of the interviews we were doing, I found them very emotionally affecting and then I had all the dilemmas about (it) because I want to be seen as a professional researcher, I don't want to risk being signed off sick, I don't want to risk losing my job, all those things, but sometimes I just couldn't help it because you know hearing other women's stories I just found, they were very moving, I couldn't help it (P6)

We have already discussed how recent literature has tended to focus on the emotional reaction of the researchers. Here, and elsewhere in the roundtable discussion, it was apparent that researchers were not always sensitive to the nature of their emotional response. For example, this researcher is clear in stating she was aware that she '*just couldn't help*' this reaction. Instead, the concerns of this researcher and others at the roundtable were centred around the reaction of *others* to these emotions, and the consequences for their job and professional identity. We have found limited commentary on these vulnerabilities in the literature, or of the fear that was associated with them. Behar's (1996) work is one example in which concern about sharing experiences in relation to these types of reaction is referenced. In it, Behar suggests the power/gender structures of academia, especially in oral presentations where one is publicly open to immediate criticism, is a key prohibitive factor in revealing such emotions. Another example can be found in Woodthorpe (2011) in which it is argued that some of the more demanding emotional components of social research are kept 'firmly in the closet' (p. 107).

Fear about events which *may* happen, relating to job security and professional image, are notable and in part speak to the precarious nature of many sensitive topic researchers. However, it is worth noting that these fears were not always based on hypothetical summations of what might happen. Rather, some researchers became fearful after they had attempted to talk through their emotional reactions to their research with their supervisors. There was sense in the room, from almost all the researchers, that attempts to share the types and intensity of the emotions they had experienced were met with reactions that led them to believe they were inappropriate and unprofessional. As the quote earlier demonstrated, the deep-rooted adage of '*going native*' was prevalent for those who already had an experience of the topic they were researching. However, it was not confined to this group. Instead, other researchers also reported feeling judged when they revealed they had emotional reactions to the research with supervisors suggesting this meant they were not undertaking '*proper research*':

people have a very particular narrative around what is proper research, what is robust research that sense of objectivity being claimed and that sense of distance you got ... judgement of you talking about your emotional content of your research. (P1)

This went even further for some participants, who felt that the judgment levelled at them by their supervisors about the emotions experienced in response to the research, extended beyond them, towards the people they had interviewed:

... you feel emotionally attached to these people so when your supervisors start to critique what they have told you, that is a problem, you know and I found that really, really, quite difficult to deal with .....But you are not in a position where you can say actually hold on a minute you know, who are you say that .... (P2)

As this quote shows, researchers were sensitive about the perceived insensitivity of other members of the research team, towards the participants to whom they had formed a bond. The desire to protect these participants was closely connected to the final area of sensitivity we identified at the roundtable, that of the power dynamics the researchers experienced during the research process, and those they tried to resist. We explore these in the next section.

(iii) Sensitive about the power dynamics in the research process. The power dynamics in research, particularly sensitive research, have been the subject of much attention. For example, it has been claimed that sensitive research methodology was developed partly in response to research on taboo topics (Faberbow, 1963). Sensitive topic research has also been particularly dominated by qualitative approaches. However, the use of qualitative methodologies in these areas has tended to be uncritical. For example, feminist researchers have been forthright in suggesting sensitive subjects particularly lend themselves to investigation via qualitative methodology because these methods have the ability to empower the researched (Kleinman & Copp, 1993). However, we found that the issue of power within the research process remained highly problematic for many of the researchers who attended the round table; the majority of whom had almost exclusively used qualitative approaches. As this next quote shows, there was a continuing sense of concern about the potential exploitation inherent in the research process:

it's that sense of exploitation isn't it, that is involved in the research process and the disparity ... the power in the relationship (P6)

There were repeated references during the roundtable to this sense that there was a '*disparity of giving*' when undertaking research on sensitive topics. Overall, researchers felt there was a lack of acknowledgment in the literature about the true imbalance of power within the interview situation. They reported that although it was helpful to think of the process of interviewing as being the key to the empowerment of the research participants, it was sometimes experienced by researcher as a troublesome undertaking.

it became a real kind of burden and tension because you are going in and watching and coming out (P5)

It is particularly interesting that the process of undertaking a qualitative interview was experienced here as '*watching*', as this links with a significant theme that ran through the data about the passivity of the role of the researcher, which for most researchers was a source of tension and frustration. As the broader discussion from this researcher alluded to, this sensitivity was heightened when the impact of the research, in the form of changing practice or opinions, was less assured.

Self-gain from the research was a pertinent issue for some researchers who described how the research was '*almost a bit selfish*' because the use of the stories had ultimately led some of these researchers towards a PhD qualification or enhanced their academic career:

because you know, it was about finding out about what had happened to them ... and hopefully changing practice through dissemination but there is always that worry that actually it was almost a bit selfish to go in there and sort of use a story which would get me a PhD and then would later get me a job (P2)

Some researchers found the interviews themselves to be emotionally charged because of the power imbalance. However, imbalances in power that were 'sensitive' emerged across the whole research process, not just the interview encounter itself. Some emerging once again in arguably a more sustained way, during analysis and dissemination. In these cases, it was often about the lack of power of the researcher to make change happen:

> ... I struggle sometimes with the change that I am hoping to see at the end of that research project that is ... going to happen well after I have been involved so this idea that I am not going to help the person that I interviewed, you know they are still going to carry on, in the conditions that they are living in ... (P7)

As this quote indicates, researchers were particularly sensitive about their role as an intermediary and their lack of control over implementing changes which could bring about an end in suffering for the people they had interviewed and formed a connection with.

Some researchers recognised that in the longer term through the research, they could contribute to the empowerment of these individuals. However, they also reported feeling like they were not helping the person in the immediate encounter was sometimes tough to deal with:

> ... ultimately then our relationship is severed and then it goes back to the service to make those changes, we don't have any kind of control in that situation (P2)

The sensitive nature of the types of topics these researchers were exploring meant special consideration had often been given to the vulnerability of the participants. Ethics committees, concerned about the impact of this type of research on participants, now require researchers to carefully consider the consequences of this type of research on those being studied (Lee-Treweek & Linkogle, 2000). In addition, trends within research funding have resulted in an increased involvement of peer researchers in the research process, with some associated concern about the impact of this on the mental health of those involved (Brett et al., 2014). The discussion at the roundtable suggested these changes between the interaction between the researcher and the participants were not without consequences for the researchers themselves. For example, some of the sensitivities reported in relation to the interview process itself, came from the sense that researchers were being encouraged to reduce the power inequity that is inherent in the process, with a lack of support or direction on how to manage the consequences of this:

> ... there is sort of stuff about power, there is stuff about equalising relationships ... and opening yourself up but not necessarily then a conversation about how might that be for you and how are you going to manage it ... (P8)

Notably, researchers at the roundtable were less sensitive to this impact if the involvement of their participants was carried out in a meaningful way:

> I think maybe that is why the more action type research projects or where you are involved people (researchers) might find a little easier to deal with because you feel that you are actually helping in some way or having an impact. (P6)

All of the researchers, without exception, described being sensitive to the potential lack of meaningful impact of their research. This was described by one researcher as bringing about a deep feeling of *'discomfort'*. The idea of justice was also prevalent here, as was the desire to give something back to their participants. This broad issue was compounded by the sense among researchers that research was rarely designed from the outset as an endeavour in which the meaning of the study would come directly from the participants and benefit their lives. As this quote suggests:

> ... I am all for knowledge production that is great but I am also for the deployment of that knowledge and if you build that into the research design from the outset it makes it a lot easier to then remind people, and also just normalising the fact that you are going to feel not so cool sometimes when you are doing research in uncool areas (P4)

As authors, we had been particularly struck at the roundtable by the remarkable sense of commitment researchers had shown towards the projects they had worked on. They valued the contribution that was made to the research by each of the participants they worked with and were deeply invested in ensuring their voices were heard. Our sense, from the discussion, was that much of the sensitivity they experienced in relation to the topic emerged from a sense of responsibility connected to this commitment. However, while this was not inherently problematic, feeling they had not been taught how to develop and manage the emotions experienced in relation to this responsibility, was problematic:

> ...actually that clarity of objective I have found really useful, but it was never taught; we were never really taught that (P4)

The '*clarity of objective*' described here was important to all of the researchers, as the following quote demonstrates, research was less emotionally challenging when it was perceived to be part of something bigger, even when the subject was itself, emotionally troubling:

> that was probably one of the most emotionally raw areas of research I have done actually, there was so much satisfaction in the ways that it travelled or the sense that it was part of something bigger, so it wasn't just research it was part of a bigger part of my life. (P1)

Researchers repeatedly described the protective impact of well-planned outcomes and campaigning research, which in some sense diminished some of the sensitivities they felt around collecting the data:

> ... I am much more involved outside in campaigning and political activity as well and I think rather than make that more emotionally challenging for me, I think it makes it somehow easier because you feel as though you are doing something as well rather than just go in, get the job done, take the data, leave them alone never bother them again. [...] if you are helping, or you are hoping to help to do something that will make a difference... (P6)

Similarly, another researcher reported how it felt like being '*a member of a social movement*', as the research could be a valuable and empowering resource to the people that were affected by the issues they were researching.

Conclusions

In their systematic review, Lee and Lee (2012) identified that the methodological literature on sensitive topics showed a continuing lack of interest in developing the core concept of what is 'sensitive' in meaningful, practical ways. In responding to this, we sensed there was a pressing need for us to understand more about how the issue was constructed and enacted by researchers. As reported here, we collected data from a roundtable discussion in which researchers undertaking work on sensitive topics were invited to talk about their experiences. Elsewhere, we have discussed how researchers responded to emotional sensitivity within the interview setting, how they managed the consequences of it in the longer term, alongside practical recommendations for supporting these researchers (Mallon & Elliott, 2019). Here, we have developed and deepened our understanding of these issues, focusing our analytic lens more directly on the researchers' overall experiences, in order to report upon those issues they were particularly attuned or sensitive to. Consequently, the experiences described here represent those of a group of researchers, each of whom had been working in an area that could be described as 'sensitive'. The quotes included here indicate their sensitivities, and in conjunction with those reported in the literature to date, comparisons and key discussion points have already been made in the text. There are a number of limitations to the data presented. Firstly, the experiences represented here are of a small number of researchers from the UK. As a result, it cannot be assumed that they are representative of a unified 'sensitive researcher' perspective. In addition, the authors convened and contributed to the discussion analysed here. While every effort has been taken to maintain a critical distance in the analysis, it is inevitable that our role and presence in the discussion will have influenced the type of topics discussed as well as their selection and emphasis here.

A number of the themes included here relate to the emotions the researchers experienced, thus reflecting some of the current trends in the published literature (Vincett, 2018). However, our analysis goes further, in describing not only the emotions themselves but in revealing how rather than the emotions being a source of discomfort for the researchers; much of the associated sensitivity came from the reaction of others to them, and in some cases their unexpected origins. Furthermore, our sense from the discussion was that much of the sensitivity they experienced emerged not from the topic itself, but from a strong sense of responsibility connected to their commitment to the research participants. This has previously been under acknowledged in the literature. It leads us to commence our concluding remarks with our primary insight, that based on our analysis it appears that the 'sensitivity' of a sensitive topic research is not just connected to the actual topic under investigation. Instead, the discussion of sensitivity encountered here shows that it was multi-layered. It was connected to the overall context of the lives that were examined in these studies. It was also influenced by the research environment in which the researchers operated, both institutionally, professionally and more broadly, as they struggled to create research that could impact on societal values and attitudes. Perhaps most crucially, our discussion demonstrates how the reaction researchers' received when admitting to their supervisors they were having emotional challenges in response to their work, were instrumental in shaping their experiences of undertaking sensitive topic research.

We conclude by highlighting a number of points that are worthy of further consideration. Firstly, our findings illuminate how researchers described being motivated to study sensitive topics because of personal, ideological and political motivations. This analysis provides considerable insight into how these connections brought with them sensitivities that affected their experience across the whole research process. In some cases, this was connected to a pre-existing emotional connection to the topic under discussion, and in others to identifications that emerged through the process of undertaking the research. For too long, the issue of motivation and personal investment in sensitive research has been either ignored or straightforwardly reported as a positive feature. In the literature, it is frequently suggested that the consequences of identification can be positive, in the sense that the researcher's experiences and emotions can add context to the subject under investigation. Such is the strength of the argument that personal experience is beneficial to the research, that some writers have suggested it can be challenging for those who do not have such experience to find their 'voice' and position within an area of sensitive research (Mallon, 2019). The overall flow of the roundtable discussion showed that enhanced emotions can be experienced when the researcher's personal experience, or identification with, a phenomenon intersect with the topic they are researching. This intersection has hitherto been both underplayed and under-explored in the literature. Of course, researchers have a right to choose their own research interests, including those topics they personally connect with. However, the roundtable demonstrated there were drawbacks to this enhanced sense of connection. This connection does not need to be problematic; as Woodthorpe (2011) has pointed out, acknowledging that we are not neutral or objective can allow us to find ways to scrutinise the impact of the topic more closely. It is notable, that over the past few decades, a range of safeguarding procedures have been established to protect the participants of such research, with a number of gatekeepers including ethics committees, service organisations, professionals, practitioners and occasionally parents or caregivers determining whether vulnerable groups can participate in research (Powell et al., 2018). However, little consideration is given within the formal governance framework, to examine the suitability of researchers, or preparing and supporting them in the work they undertake. As Robinson (2020) has pointed out, ethics tends to be focused on procedural elements, or 'paper ethics', rather than real-world research. We suggest more thought could be given to the impact of researcher experiences on their choice of research topic and the sensitivities this may bring. This is crucial if researchers are to be adequately supported and protected from the harm that can result from their engagement in research.

Additionally, as has been increasingly acknowledged in the literature, these sensitivities went beyond the fieldwork phase of the research and continued into broad concerns about how the data of the participants were handled, published and disseminated. Lee's (1993, p. 4) original definition of sensitive research, pointed out that it was not only the collection of data that was 'sensitive' but that the 'holding and/or dissemination of research data' was also inherently sensitive. Overall, our data support this assertion, suggesting that the emergent nature of the researchers' sensitivities are poorly accommodated in the definitions that are currently used for sensitive research. In fact, as our data also showed, one of the main issues researchers were sensitive to was the reactions and guidance of their supervisors. Additionally, and arguably more crucially, the sensitivities of the researcher is an aspect of sensitive research that needs to be managed more carefully by supervisors, because it is the front-line workers who witness and hold the sensitivity across all the coal-face aspects of the research process.

As a final point, we turn to Lee and Lee's question 'is there a simple relationship between sensitivity and stress, such that the more sensitive a topic studied, the more likely there is to be emotional consequences?' (2012, p. 46). Our data suggest not, but shows that what makes a topic sensitive, certainly from the researcher's perspective, cannot be reduced to a single factor. Rather, it is underpinned by the researcher's relationship with the topic, both as it exists when they enter the field, and as it develops throughout the fieldwork and into analysis. In addition, it is affected by complex relationships between the researcher, their immediate peers, supervisors and the overall institutional environment in which the research takes place. Sensitive research is thus uniquely 'sensitive' to the researcher in ways the literature currently fails to fully acknowledge but which are worthy of further examination. The benefits of refining our understanding of this are widespread. Helping to protect not only potentially vulnerable participants, but also in providing protection for researchers and helping supervisors and managers be better prepared to respond to the potential vulnerabilities that may emerge during such research. Ethics committees and reviewers will also be in a better position to advise on the ethical conduct of such studies.

Disclosure statement

No potential conflict of interest was reported by the authors.

References

BACP. (2018). *Ethical framework for good practice in counselling and psychotherapy.*
Behar, R. (1996). *The vulnerable observer: Anthropology that breaks your heart.* Beacon Press.
Bloor, M., Fincham, B., & Sampson, H. (2010). Unprepared for the worst: Risks of harm for qualitative researchers. *Methodological Innovations Online, 5*(1), 45–55. https://doi.org/10.4256_mio.2010.0009
Brett, J., Staniszewska, S., Mockford, C., Herron-Marx, S., Hughes, J., Tysall, C., & Suleman, R. (2014). Mapping the impact of patient and public involvement on health and social care research: A systematic review. *Health Expectations : An International Journal of Public Participation in Health Care and Health Policy, 17*(5), 637–650. https://doi.org/10.1111/j.1369-7625.2012.00795.x
Dickson-Swift, V. (2017). Emotion and sensitive research. In P. Liamputtong (Ed.), *Handbook of research methods in health social sciences.* Springer, 1–18.
Dickson-Swift, V., James, E. L., & Liamputtong, P. (2008). Undertaking Sensitive Research in the Health and Social Sciences: Managing Boundaries, Emotions and Risks. Cambridge: Cambridge University Press.

Dickson-Swift, V., James, E., Kippen, S., & Liamputtong, P. (2007). Doing sensitive research: What challenges do qualitative researchers face?:. *Qualitative Health Research*, *7*(3), 327–353. https://doi.org/10.1177_1468794107078515

Dickson-Swift, V., James, E., Kippen, S., & Liamputtong, P. (2009). Researching sensitive topics: Qualitative research as emotion work. *Qualitative Research*, *9*(1), 61–79. https://doi.org/10.1177/1468794108098031

Etherington, K. (2005). *Becoming a reflexive researcher: Using ourselves in research*. Jessica Kingsley.

Faberbow, N. L. (1963). *Taboo topics*. Atherton Press.

Houston, S. (2015). Enabling others in social work: Reflexivity and the theory of social domains. *Critical and Radical Social Work*, *3*(2), 245–260. https://doi.org/10.1332/204986015X14302240420229

Hubbard, G., Backett-Milburn, K., & Kemmer, D. (2010). Working with emotion: Issues for the researcher in fieldwork and teamwork. *International Journal of Social Research Methodology*, *4*(2), 119–137. https://doi.org/10.1080/13645570116992

Johnson, B., & Clarke, J. M. (2003). Collecting sensitive data: The impact on researchers. *Qualitative Health Research*, *13*(3), 421–434. https://doi.org/10.1177/1049732302250340

Kenyon, E., & Hawker, S. (2010). 'Once would be enough': Some reflections on the issue of safety for lone researchers. *International Journal of Social Research Methodology*, *2*(4), 313–327. https://doi.org/10.1080/136455799294989

Kleinman, S., & Copp, M. A. (1993). *Emotions and fieldwork: Qualitative research methods*. Sage Publications.

Komaromy, C. (2020) The performance of researching sensitive issues, Mortality, *25*(3), 364–377. https://doi.org/10.1080/13576275.2019.1635104

Lee, R. M. (1993). *Doing research on sensitive topics*. Sage.

Lee, Y. O., & Lee, R. M. (2012). Methodological research on "sensitive" topics. *Bulletin of Sociological Methodology*, *114*(1), 35–49. https://doi.org/10.1177/0759106312437139

Lee-Treweek, G., & Linkogle, S. (2000). *Danger in the field: Risk and ethics in social research*. Routledge.

Mallon, S. (2019). Cream cakes, hungry cats and hugs. In F. McSweeney & D. Williams (Eds.), *Designing and conducting research in social science, health and social care*. Routledge, 90–103.

Mallon, S., & Elliott, I. (2019). The emotional risks of turning stories into data: An exploration of the experiences of qualitative researchers working on sensitive topics. *Societies*, *9*(3), 62. https://doi.org/10.3390/soc9030062

Powell, M. A., McArthur, M., Chalmers, J., Graham, A., Moore, T., Spriggs, M., & Taplin, S. (2018). Sensitive topics in social research involving children. *International Journal of Social Research Methodology*, *21*(6), 647–660. https://doi.org/10.1080/13645579.2018.1462882

Richards, S., Clark, J., & Boggis, A. (2015). *Ethical research with children: Untold narratives and taboos*. Palgrave Macmillan.

Roberts, B. (2007). *Getting the most out of the research experience*. Sage Publications.

Robinson, C. (2020). Ethically important moments as data: Reflections from ethnographic fieldwork in prisons. *Research Ethics*, *16*(1), 1–15. https://doi.org/10.1177/1747016119898401

Schostak, J., & Schostak, J. (2013). *Writing research critically: Developing the power to make a difference*. Routledge.

Sieber, J. E., & Stanley, B. (1988). Ethical and professional dimensions of socially sensitive research. *American Psychologist*, *43*(1), 49–55. https://doi.org/10.1037/0003-066X.43.1.49

Vincett, J. (2018). Researcher self-care in organizational ethnography: Lessons from overcoming compassion fatigue. *Journal of Organizational Ethnography*, *7*(1), 44–58. https://doi.org/10.1108/JOE-09-2017-0041

Visser, R. (2017). "Doing death": Reflecting on the researcher's subjectivity and emotions. *Death Studies*, *41*(1), 6–13. https://doi.org/10.1080/07481187.2016.1257877

Woodthorpe, K. (2011). Researching death: Methodological reflections on the management of critical distance *International Journal of Social Research Methodology*, *14*(2), 99–109. https://doi.org/10.1080/13645579.2010.496576

Relatively normal? Navigating emergent sensitivity in generating and analysing accounts of 'normality'

Tom Witney and Peter Keogh

ABSTRACT
This article describes methodological and ethical issues associated with examining discourses of 'normality' in the context of the normalisation of HIV and relationships. It considers how sensitivity was anticipated, encountered and managed in the recruitment of participants and during research interviews, discussing the implications of these in this project. It reflects on the tensions present when generating data on topics externally deemed to be 'sensitive' but considered 'normal' by participants. In doing so, it has wider relevance for research on experiences that were once prohibited but are now considered normative in some settings, such as gay marriage. However, highlighting the importance of 'the normal' in notions of stigma, it concludes that potentially any research project that examines or questions 'normality' may give rise to sensitivity, emphasising the importance of reflexivity in assessing and managing sensitivity throughout the research process.

Sensitive research is often defined by its engagement with topics that intrude into the private sphere, or those that relate to non-normative, taboo or stigmatised subjects (Dickson-Swift et al., 2008; Lee, 1993). Despite the methodological challenges posed by research which provokes sensitivity, it has proven to be a rich seam for sociological investigation, partly because the sensitivity itself signals phenomena of social significance (Dickson-Swift et al., 2008; Lee, 1993). At the other end of the spectrum, the everyday and the ordinary have also been the focus of a significant sociological literature (Jacobsen, 2009). In contrast with a traditional sociological focus on the unusual or deviant (Lee, 1993), a sociological examination of the 'normal' has merit precisely because it is often overlooked (Scott, 2018). Researching the 'normal' is associated with methodological challenges, because its taken-for-granted nature means that it is often hidden or unseen but it is rarely associated with the challenges of sensitive research. However, as the other papers in this collection attest, problems associated with sensitivity can also arise in otherwise uncontroversial research (see Tilley et al. and Robb in this issue). Recognising the importance of context for making research sensitive (or not), Lee suggests considering the conditions in which sensitivity arose in the research process rather than seeking to define sensitivity only in terms of its subject matter (Lee, 1993). This approach shifts the focus from the subject of research towards its conduct.

Here we adopt Lee's approach to consider how sensitivity arose in relation to questions of normality drawing on interview data and reflexive journal entries from a qualitative investigation into the lived experience of thirty gay and bisexual men living in the UK who have a different HIV status to their partner (Witney, 2020). Here, reflexivity refers to an examination of both the researcher's relationship to the data (Finlay, 2011) and the influence of epistemological commitments on the research (Braun & Clarke, 2019). We explore how competing discourses of HIV stigmatisation and normalisation produced sensitivity in the research encounter and reflect on how its emergence was managed. Finally, we outline the methodological implications for other researchers working in subject areas which bridge processes of normalization and stigmatization.

Relationships where the partners have different HIV statuses (known variously as serodiscordant, sero-different or 'magnetic' relationships) have been the focus of medical and sociological study since early in the HIV epidemic (Mendelsohn et al., 2015). Serodiscordant relationships were considered sites of significant transmission risk, particularly with evidence of inconsistent condom use in sexual activity (e.g. Prestage et al., 2009). As a result, such relationships have been subject to stigma (Persson, 2013). However, recent medical research has demonstrated that effective antiretroviral therapy prevents sexual transmission ('treatment as prevention' or TasP), even in the absence of other methods of prevention (Rodger et al., 2019). While some point out the potential of this 'medical breakthrough' to make subordinate the complex social aspects of the epidemic (Nguyen et al., 2011) others have taken this as an opportunity to reframe serodiscordant intimacy, as safe and legitimate (Philpot et al., 2018) and normalise HIV in order to address stigma (Prevention Access Campaign, 2017).

Goffman (1963) highlights the importance of notions of normality in both creating and resisting stigma. Research with serodiscordant couples has shown that treatment underpins a sense of normality and sameness with other couples and thus may be key in addressing the experience of stigma (Hughes, 2017). However, normalised discourses of HIV do not go uncontested and stigmatising tropes still dominate broader social discourse (Walker, 2019). Thus people in serodiscordant relationships often remain silent about their circumstances to avoid stigma (Persson, 2008). Contemporary serodiscordant relationships occupy a space between normalising and stigmatising discourses, with partners drawing on these and their own experiences to articulate new ways of 'doing' serodiscordant intimacy (Philpot et al., 2018). In this article, we argue that in the context of an ongoing processes of normalisation and continued stigmatisation, sensitivity can emerge in unexpected and novel ways. This paper draws on reflexive journal entries generated during TW's PhD research project and is hereafter written in first person singular. However, as TW's supervisor and collaborator, PK worked closely with TW on framing the problem and developing the concepts presented in the article and inputted substantially into drafts.

Nothing to see here: an initial encounter with 'normal' sensitivity

My first encounter with sensitivity occurred before I had recruited any participants and before the study had received institutional ethical approval. Though I was in the process of preparing an ethics application that outlined the potentially sensitive nature of the interviews I was planning, this focused on 'traditionally' sensitive aspects, such as relationship intimacy and a stigmatised health condition, or the potential ethical implications of interviewing couples together and apart. There is a large body of research on HIV and relationships, with serodiscordant relationships forming a significant proportion of this literature; I was confident that this project was academically and ethically sound. However, I had not considered that the research question itself would give rise to sensitivity. Yet a chance encounter with someone who could have been eligible to participate in the research vividly brought that possibility to life, as the following research diary extract illustrates:

> I was at a friend's birthday party enthusiastically talking with some people I had met for the first time that evening about my research on serodiscordant relationships and how interesting I found the topic. As I was talking, I noticed another partygoer on the periphery of our conversation, arms folded, stern faced; a stark contrast to the others. "There's nothing interesting about our relationship, I don't know why you need to do a study. My boyfriend is positive, he's on treatment and that's it. Our relationship is normal," he said. Despite me agreeing and explaining that my motivation for doing the research was to describe the reality – and normality – of serodiscordant relationships, his hostility remained.

Reflecting on this experience, I felt sheepish. In my enthusiasm I was concerned that I had inadvertently used stigmatising language. I worried that, as someone who was not in a serodiscordant relationship myself, my interest in the subject was not legitimate. Although I reassured myself that these concerns were unfounded, I could not fully answer the potential participant's charge that by selecting serodiscordancy as something worthy of study, I was problematising the relationships I sought to examine. I had not considered that participants might object to the idea that their relationships were legitimate objects of study. In the context of a stigmatised condition such as HIV, notions of normality become entwined with discourses of stigmatisation and de-stigmatisation (Hughes, 2017). My research could potentially upset this balance and, in doing so, re-enact the social stigma potential participants were resisting. Lee (1993) also highlights how, irrespective of the topic, becoming the subject of research can itself be stigmatising. This experience began a process of reflection on, and navigation through, the normality (or otherwise) of HIV at the core of discourses of normalisation that were central to my enquiry, in dialogue with institutionalised understandings of sensitivity and research ethics.

Investigating a 'new normal'?

The first impact of the experience above was on my framing of the research and recruitment for the study. Although sampling participants from a particular population can be time consuming (Boynton, 2017), after an initial recruitment call yielded no responses at all, my concerns about potential participants' resistance towards participating in my research were compounded. Various guides and guidelines (Dickson-Swift et al., 2008; Lee, 1993; The British Psychological Society, 2014) stress the importance of respecting participants' autonomy, making research voluntary and ensuring participants understand their right not to take part in research. But while these guidelines recognize that people who could take part may choose not to, they do not provide guidance on the potential range of meanings attached to participants **not** taking part, nor how researchers should respond to non-participation. Although a lack of participation could be explained by an ineffective recruitment strategy, non-participation in an activity can also be conceived of as an act of resistance (Scott, 2018). The experience of a hostile reaction from a potential participant loomed large. In response to an imagined participant who was reluctant to become involved in a study that might be embedded in 'old' stigmatizing narratives of HIV, I focused my recruitment materials on the change and progress in HIV treatments and HIV prevention, and emphasised the need for research to reflect this new situation. However, attempting to avoid sensitivity and stigma by writing the recruitment materials this way firmly allied the study with 'normalised' discourses of HIV. The following extract from the participant information sheet shows how I constructed 'treatment as prevention' as a normalising phenomenon through its impact on transmission risk:

> A lot of research into mixed-HIV-status relationships has focused on sex and risk before the role that treatment can play in preventing transmission was fully understood. 'Treatment as prevention' provides an opportunity to look again at this subject, but also to move away from looking at risk alone and to consider the broader experience of being in a relationship.

Reflecting on these materials later in the research process, I recognised that although my motivation for communicating my research in this way was primarily a pragmatic response to a perceived distrust or suspicion in my project and an attempt to manage or mitigate sensitivity, it also led to me adopting a very visible position within a process of social change which I hoped to study through the research. While locating myself within a social constructivist ontology which eschews the concept of objective or unbiased positions, I later became concerned as to whether emphasising one position, while attempting to examine experiences from a range of alternative positions, closed down rather than opened up the focus of my enquiry: did couching my research within normalizing discourses imply an invitation for positive stories of relationships in which HIV was not an issue? Would this potentially alienate those for whom this did not ring true and make them less likely to participate in the research?

Navigating potential stigma

Whether or not it was due to the new strategies I deployed, ultimately, this recruitment approach was successful and I interviewed several participants. Bearing in mind my previous experience, even when piloting the interview schedule, I became sensitized to suggesting to participants that serodiscordancy was not normal. This led me to approach the question of its relevance in an indirect way during interviews. Although a focus on the everyday was theoretically and methodologically justified in my research, when I explained this to participants, this often served as an opportunity for me to stress that I wasn't '*just interested in HIV.*' This further reinforced to participants my focus on serodiscordancy as something part of the everyday and thus 'normal.' Consistent with this approach, I constructed the interview schedule to ask open questions about serodiscordancy in the context of a broader understanding of participants' everyday relationship experiences. However, on reviewing the recordings and transcripts from the interviews, as well as my own reflection on the experience of conducting the interviews, I noticed I departed from the question construction in the guide when it came to asking participants about their experiences of serodiscordancy, instead deploying phrasing which suggested an ambivalence towards the relevance of HIV to their relationship.

> *[Interviewer] Erm, and so we've talked about a few, kind of, factors that influence your relationship, or make it what it is. I kind of have to ask, what role does HIV play in your relationship, if anything?* Individual interview 14-01

I reflected that this phrasing helped me demonstrate to participants that I did not automatically assume that HIV was important in the everyday experience of a serodiscordant relationship. This allowed me to position myself as open to the response that it was not relevant. In order to remove potential sensitivity from the research encounter I also introduced a rhetorical distance between myself as the embodied interviewer asking the questions, and the (distant) creator of the interview schedule, '*I have to ask.*' In later interviews, I increased this distance, bringing in an additional party to the interviewer-participant dynamic, the university. In presenting the institution as not just a passive supporter of research but a powerful governor of its conduct and my employer, I foregrounded obligations often invisible during research encounters in order to minimise my agency in the conduct of the interview.

> *[Interviewer] There's some general topics, there might be some stuff that you've got to say, there might not be. [But] if we don't talk about HIV I'll probably get sacked from my studentship!* Couple interview-06

Joking with participants that I was obliged to ask about HIV in order to keep my job, signalled my ambivalence about its relevance while also retaining it as a topic of discussion in the couple interview. Despite the fact that in this instance the participants laughed with me, even in jest, I suggested that the reason we were discussing the topic was not because of its relevance to the research, but because of a need to satisfy the institutional requirements. Although the phrasing of these questions could be considered poor interview technique, or potentially deceptive, I reflected that in the context of the interview these were techniques which helped to maintain rapport with participants, many of whom had already spoken about how little HIV featured in their day-to-day relationship. These rhetorical 'fig leaves' that I adopted during the research process further helped me position myself as a sympathetic researcher who was sensitive to the idea that viewing serodiscordancy as non-normative was linked to stigmatizing discourses of HIV. Adopting the view of the interview as a social interaction and applying Goffman's analysis of the management of identity (1963) emphasises the importance of creating 'normality' through the interaction in order to manage stigma. The importance of these strategies was further emphasized when I began to analyse interview data, in which the contested nature of normality was a key factor for participants in relation to how they talked about their relationship with others (Witney, 2020). The idea of serodiscordancy being a normal, untroubled state was underpinned in participants' accounts by biomedical discourses which construct HIV as rendered unthreatening or irrelevant by antiretroviral treatment. Whether others were already familiar with these ideas was a key factor for many participants in deciding whether to discuss their serodiscordancy or not. Thus navigating the contested nature of 'normality' in the context of serodiscordancy appeared to be a crucial consideration for participants, and underscored the importance of my drawing on and emphasizing discourses of normality in presenting the research to potential participants and throughout the research process.

Discussion

I have explored how unexpected sensitivity emerged during a research project in relation to issues of 'normality.' I argued that it centres on the position of serodiscordant relationships in relation to discursive tensions generated by discourses of normalization of HIV, rather than being related to the 'sensitive' subject of HIV and relationships itself. My experience of the research, first becoming aware of an unexpected sensitivity, consciously and unconsciously managing it during the research and reflecting on it during analysis, has led to my understanding of the crucial role that ideas of normality play in creating and counteracting stigma and thus in creating or diminishing sensitivity. Beyond the specific context of this research, the issues discussed here may be relevant for researchers active in settings or subject areas where discourses of normality are deployed to claim equality for or the validity of stigmatised identities, such as Muslim identity among teenagers in Australia (Harris & Karimshah, 2019). However, in exploring my responses to the emergent and dynamic sensitivity, I am not suggesting a blueprint of techniques to manage such research. Instead, I am highlighting the importance of both personal and epistemological reflexivity (Braun & Clarke, 2019; Finlay, 2011) on the part of the researcher with regard to the way in which competing discourses of normal/not-normal are articulated during each stage of the research process.

Claims to normality are often a feature of arguments for equal treatment of minorities and have been deployed in narratives about gay and lesbian foster carers (Hicks, 2005), the validity of same-sex relationships (Heaphy, 2018) and the othering of minority ethnicities (Harris & Karimshah, 2019). Punch (1994) argues that researchers must do more than simply respect their participants or treat them with courtesy; they should actively work to elucidate imbalances of power and work towards eliminating them. I share a commitment to empowering participants (Tisdale, 2004) and recognise that enabling participants to share their stories in their own words can play an important part in shaping norms and addressing stigma (Persson et al., 2016; Plummer, 1995). Yet the experience of this project highlights the embeddedness of researchers within social power relations. Thus the benign intent of an individual researcher cannot on its own address or compensate for wider social processes of stigmatisation and normalisation. This stresses the importance of engaging with sensitivity beyond 'tick box' definition within ethics applications and highlights the need to be attuned to participants' concerns about all aspects of the research, up to and including the research question itself. Furthermore, by approaching sensitivity as an emergent phenomenon that is interpreted differently by institutional ethics committees, researchers and – importantly – participants this analysis foregrounds the power inherent in defining and 'fixing' definitions of sensitivity. It also demonstrates how formal definitions of sensitivity are navigated, negotiated and resisted in practice. This highlights how concepts of 'sensitive' and 'normal' are not mutually exclusive binaries but can co-exist as lenses through which to better understand lived experience (Hathaway et al., 2011).

In the context of normalized or normalizing phenomena, this article underlines the importance of reflection on and engagement with the discourses of normality that participants are negotiating in and, in particular, the relevance of these to issues of stigma and accompanying sensitivity. Although it is important that researchers retain their freedom to critique both stigmatising and normalising discourses, it is also important to consider the dynamics of power relations and stigma in deploying criticism of normalisation.

More broadly, the issues discussed here point to a methodological tension between the way in which researchers and ethics committees construct their research participants and the way in which participants construct themselves. As well as the stigmatising potential of being researched itself, Lee points to the role that implicit assumptions about research play in the potential for divergent interpretations to arise between the researcher and researched; a study seen as problematic by one group can be thought innocuous by another (Lee, 1993). However, drawing on Goffman (1963) and the importance of the presentation of 'normality' in avoiding stigma, illustrates how research that positions participants as outside normative bounds has the potential to generate stigma. This phenomenon is often most immediately obvious in studies engaged with 'sensitive' topics, but could arise in any study in which questions of normality are at stake. This analysis disrupts 'static' approaches to understanding sensitivity in the research process traditionally used in ethical assessment and highlights the need for a more nuanced and reflexive approach to assessing and managing sensitivity throughout the research process.

Disclosure statement

No potential conflict of interest was reported by the authors.

References

Boynton, P. M. (2017). *The research companion: A practical guide for those in social sciences, health and development*. Routledge/Taylor & Francis.
Braun, V., & Clarke, V. (2019). Reflecting on reflexive thematic analysis. *Qualitative Research in Sport, Exercise and Health*, 11(4), 589–597. https://doi.org/10.1080/2159676X.2019.1628806
The British Psychological Society. (2014). *Code of human research ethics*. https://doi.org/180/12.2014
Dickson-Swift, V., James, E. L., & Liamputtong, P. (2008). *Undertaking sensitive research in the health and social sciences*. Cambridge University Press.
Finlay, L. (2011). *Phenomenology for therapists : Researching the lived world*. Wiley-Blackwell.
Goffman, E. (1963). *Stigma; Notes on the management of spoiled identity*. Prentice-Hall.
Harris, A., & Karimshah, A. (2019). Young Muslims, stigma and the work of normality. *Sociology*, 53(4), 617–633. https://doi.org/10.1177/0038038518800632
Hathaway, A. D., Comeau, N. C., & Erickson, P. G. (2011). Cannabis normalization and stigma: Contemporary practices of moral regulation. *Criminology and Criminal Justice*, 11(5), 451–469. https://doi.org/10.1177/1748895811415345
Heaphy, B. (2018). Troubling traditional and conventional families? Formalised same-sex couples and 'the ordinary'. *Sociological Research Online*, 23(1), 160–176. https://doi.org/10.1177/1360780418754779
Hicks, S. (2005). Queer Genealogies. *Qualitative Social Work: Research and Practice*, 4(3), 293–308. https://doi.org/10.1177/1473325005055597
Hughes, S. D. (2017). HIV serodiscordant couples and the discourse of normality: Reconciling the biomedial and the social in Porto Alegre, Brazil. In A. Persson & S. D. Hughes (Eds.), *Cross-cultural perspectives on couples with mixed HIV status: Beyond positive/negative* (pp. 55–69). Springer. https://doi.org/10.1007/978-3-319-42725-6
Jacobsen, M. H. (2009). *Encountering the everyday : An introduction to the sociologies of the unnoticed*. Palgrave Macmillan.
Lee, R. M. (1993). *Doing research on sensitive topics*. Sage Publications. https://uk.sagepub.com/en-gb/eur/doing-research-on-sensitive-topics/book204085

Mendelsohn, J. B., Calzavara, L., Daftary, A., Mitra, S., Pidutti, J., Allman, D., Bourne, A., Loutfy, M., & Myers, T. (2015). A scoping review and thematic analysis of social and behavioural research among HIV-serodiscordant couples in high-income settings. *BMC Public Health*, *15*(1), 241. https://doi.org/10.1186/s12889-015-1488-9

Nguyen, V.-K., Bajos, N., Dubois-Arber, F., O'Malley, J., & Pirkle, C. M. (2011). Remedicalizing an epidemic: From HIV treatment as prevention to HIV treatment is prevention. *AIDS*, *25*(3), 291–293. https://doi.org/10.1097/QAD.0b013e3283402c3e

Persson, A. (2008). Sero-silence and sero-sharing: Managing HIV in serodiscordant heterosexual relationships. *AIDS Care*, *20*(4), 503–506. https://doi.org/10.1080/09540120701787487

Persson, A. (2013). Non/infectious corporealities: Tensions in the biomedical era of "HIV normalisation". *Sociology of Health & Illness*, *35*(7), 1065–1079. https://doi.org/10.1111/1467-9566.12023

Persson, A., Ellard, J., & Newman, C. E. (2016). Bridging the HIV divide: Stigma, stories and serodiscordant sexuality in the biomedical age. *Sexuality & Culture*, *20*(2), 197–213. https://doi.org/10.1007/s12119-015-9316-z

Philpot, S. P., Prestage, G., Ellard, J., Grulich, A. E., & Bavinton, B. R. (2018). How do gay serodiscordant couples in Sydney, Australia negotiate undetectable viral load for HIV prevention? *AIDS and Behavior*, *22*(12), 3981–3990.0123456789. https://doi.org/10.1007/s10461-018-2247-6

Plummer, K. (1995). *Telling sexual stories: Power, change and social worlds*. Routledge.

Prestage, G., Mao, L., Kippax, S., Jin, F., Hurley, M., Grulich, A., Imrie, J., Kaldor, J., & Zablotska, I. (2009). Use of viral load to negotiate condom use among gay men in Sydney, Australia. *AIDS and Behavior*, *13*(4), 645–651. https://doi.org/10.1007/s10461-009-9527-0

Prevention Access Campaign. (2017). *Risk of sexual transmission of HIV from a person living with HIV who has an undetectable viral load: Message primer and consensus statement*. https://www.preventionaccess.org/consensus

Punch, M. (1994). Politics and ethics in qualitative research. In N. K. Denzin & Y. S. Lincoln (Eds.), *Handbook of qualitative research* (pp. 83–97). Sage Publications.

Rodger, A. J., Cambiano, V., Phillips, A. N., Bruun, T., Raben, D., Lundgren, J., Vernazza, P., Collins, S., Degen, O., Corbelli, G. M., Estrada, V., Geretti, A. M., Beloukas, A., Beloukas, A., Coll, P., Antinori, A., Nwokolo, N., Rieger, A., Prins, J. M., & Janeiro, N. (2019). Risk of HIV transmission through condomless sex in serodifferent gay couples with the HIV-positive partner taking suppressive antiretroviral therapy (PARTNER): Final results of a multicentre, prospective, observational study. *The Lancet*, *393*(10189), 2428–2438. https://doi.org/10.1016/S0140-6736(19)30418-0

Scott, S. (2018). A sociology of nothing: Understanding the unmarked. *Sociology*, *52*(1), 3–19. https://doi.org/10.1177/0038038517690681

Tisdale, K. (2004). Being vulnerable and being ethical with/in research. In K. DeMarrais & S. D. Lapan (Eds.), *Foundations for research: Methods of inquiry in education and the social sciences* (pp. 31–50). Laurence Erlbaum Associates. https://doi.org/10.4324/9781410609373

Walker, L. (2019). "There's no pill to help you deal with the guilt and shame": Contemporary experiences of HIV in the United Kingdom. *Health*, *23*(1), 97–113. https://doi.org/10.1177/1363459317739436

Witney, T. (2020). *Doing serodiscordant intimacy in the era of HIV biomedicalisation: A qualitative investigation of the lived experience of gay and bisexual men in serodiscordant relationships in the UK*. The Open University.

Involving young people with life-limiting conditions in research on sex: the intersections of taboo and vulnerability

Sarah Earle and Maddie Blackburn

ABSTRACT
There is a growing literature that seeks to explore what is 'sensitive' about 'sensitive' research. In order to problematise and interrogate the concept of what may or may not be considered 'sensitive' research, this paper draws on four related projects exploring sex, intimacy and relationships for young people, over 16 years, who have life-limiting or life-threatening conditions (LLTCs). The authors focus on how, when and why these projects are regarded as 'sensitive' and consider who defines them as such. Drawing on the notion of methodological performativity, a mixture of complex phenomena that explores the relational aspects in interprofessional team practices, the authors examine aspects of the process of doing 'sensitive' research, exploring how research methods and techniques are employed because the research has already been defined (by others and the authors) as 'sensitive,' while simultaneously serving to (re)construct and (re)enforce the 'sensitive' nature of it.

Introduction

This paper outlines four projects that are at the heart of our work. We describe the perfect storm of intersecting taboos and vulnerabilities of sensitive research about sexuality and disability. Any project on sex that involves young and disabled, seriously ill people whose lives are shortened, is highly likely to be regarded as 'sensitive'. We argue that enacting this research as indisputably 'sensitive' (re)frames the potential agency for both the researcher and those being researched. We also acknowledge the inevitability of methodological performativity.

While there is no agreement among researchers on how to define 'sensitive' research, it generally encompasses a wide range of issues, undertaken across a variety of disciplines and settings, using a range of methods (Dickson-Swift et al., 2008). Sensitive topics, Lee (1993) argues are those which pose a substantial threat to those involved in the work, including the researcher.

In order to problematise and interrogate the concept of sensitive research within this special issue, this paper draws on four related projects exploring sex, intimacy and relationships for people, over 16 years, who have life-limiting or life-threatening conditions (LLTCs). In particular, we focus on how, when and why these projects were regarded as 'sensitive' and consider who defined them as such. Drawing on the notion of methodological performativity, whereby methods are seen to 'bring into being what they also discover' (Law & Urry, 2003, p. 3), we examine aspects of the process of doing 'sensitive' research. We explore how research methods and techniques are employed because the research has already been defined (by others and by us) as 'sensitive' while simultaneously serving to (re)construct and (re)enforce the 'sensitive' nature of it.

Methodologies

All four projects focus on sex, intimacy and relationships for people whose life course maybe uncertain and shortened. They were carried out by individuals or members of The Open University Sexuality Alliance; a trans-disciplinary, multi-professional and inter-sectoral consortium of individuals, co-researchers and organisations with expertise in working with, supporting, or researching people with LLTCs. The research participants were aged between 16–39 and we refer to them as 'young people' because this is how they describe themselves and how they prefer to be referred to. Nevertheless, we acknowledge it is a problematic term; it speaks to the infantilization of disabled people by society in general, and to the continued infantilization of people who live beyond original expectations.

Project One is an action-research project that engaged with young people to develop guidance and standards on sex, intimacy and relationships for professionals (see Earle & Blackburn, 2020; M. C. Blackburn et al., 2017). Previously professionals had identified the issue of sex as a problem and felt uncertain on how best to support people. Young people said that care professionals did not always appreciate how and why sex and sexuality were important for those with LLTCs. Often this was due to the professional's lack of confidence, knowledge, understanding and access to support and guidance in how to approach and talk about sex with young people (Open Learn, 2019). Via hospice organisations, four focus groups were held in England and Scotland in 2014 and 2015 with both young men and women with LLTCs, ages 16–28 years. A charity provided additional questionnaire contributions from two parents and one young person. Separately, six hospice trustees participated in a group interview. In total, 31 people participated in this project.

Project Two explored the sexuality, relationships, intimacy and reproductive choices of young people with LLTCs (Blackburn, 2018). Adopting a broadly interpretive approach, the project used guided in-depth interviews and focus group discussions (n = 13), age 16–39 years, partners (n = 2), parents (n = 10) and health care professionals (n = 10). The 35 participants, both young men and women, were recruited via two hospices in England and the fieldwork was conducted between 2014 and 2015.

Project Three was an interpretive, qualitative project involving 20 young women and men, age 16–25 years, living within LLTCs. The focus was on exploring the significance of sex, intimacy and relationships for emotional wellbeing and happiness (M. C. Blackburn et al., 2017). Recruitment was via our existing network of organisations and contacts; five focus groups were held at five separate locations in England and Scotland in 2017, with 20 people participating in total.

Project Four involves inclusive action-research to support the transition of young people, age 16–30 years, in the UK who have LLTCs, by developing their confidence in talking about sex, intimacy and relationships (see Together for Short Lives, 2018). It was developed in collaboration with AdversiTeam, a group of co-researchers whom have LLTCs, to generate open educational resources (see: https://www.open.edu/openlearn/health-sports-psychology/health/intimate-not-intimidated-its-time-talk-about-sex-and-disability).

A perfect storm: intersections of taboo and vulnerability

By exploring sex, intimacy and relationships for young people who have LLTCs, four major intersecting issues come together to be defined as 'sensitive': sex as taboo; the taboo of death; the vulnerability of youth; and, vulnerabilities of disabled people.

The first two issues relate to the issue of taboo. Taboo refers to that which is forbidden or prohibited either by law or custom or, at least, to that which should not be referred to in conversation (Walter, 1991). We argue that both sex and death can be understood as taboo. Sontag (1969) argues that in Western cultures, sex is a 'special case' in that it consistently invokes inconsistent attitudes and beliefs. On the one hand, sex is dirty and unmentionable, whereas on the other it is considered to be a core part of the modern self. In modern Western cultures death is equally taboo (Walter, 1991). Similarly, while we are indirectly bombarded by death on a daily basis – for example, in the news – it is also something that is feared and often hidden (see Fisher, 1973).

The perceived vulnerabilities of this group of research participants further intersect with the taboos of sex and death. The participants are considered vulnerable because they are young. Children are regarded as 'incomplete, irrational, unproductive and asexual whereas adults are seen to be complete, rational, productive and sexual (Liddiard & Slater, 2017). Young people are in what Lesko (2012) describes as the 'border zone' between child and adult, thus perceived as requiring special attention. The research participants are also considered vulnerable because they are disabled and seriously ill. There is a considerable body of work that has already discussed the ways in which disabled people are marginalised, infantilised and perceived as asexual (see Shakespeare et al., 1996). Disabled people, but particularly, young disabled people whose lives are limited and uncertain, are perceived as generally vulnerable in many ways. For example, young people with LLTCs were often perceived as being at greater risk of abuse and harm (Blackburn, 2018). They were also considered 'hypersexual', sometimes requiring containment (Liddiard, 2018). Participants in all four projects had been told throughout their lives that they were going to die soon and often found this deeply frustrating. In reality, they preferred to savour every moment, 'living life to the fullest' (Liddiard et al., 2018).

What makes this type of research 'sensitive' is the perfect storm of taboo and vulnerability. Below we explore how they intersect during distinct elements of the research process. We highlight the difficulties we encountered and discuss the ways we sought to manage them, successfully or not.

Project start up: managing funding, ethics and risk

Securing funding and obtaining ethical approval for projects that focus on sex is notoriously difficult; securing funding and obtaining ethical approval for projects that focus on sex with young and disabled people whose lives are shortened is even more challenging. In spite of the project team's desire to normalise sex and intimacy for young disabled people and work inclusively, it has been impossible for us to move away from narratives of 'sensitivity'. We deal with two specific issues here. Firstly, the dilemma in how we must present our work as 'sensitive' to others in order to secure funding and ethical approval. Secondly, the risk management strategies that we employed within the project team in order to address the realities of working with disabled young people who are seriously ill.

We encountered many examples of 'sex-negativity' during the research process. Sex-negativity refers to the way in which sexuality is defined as a deficiency, rather than a resource, and as something that can be regarded as dangerous and damaging from which people need to be protected (Egan & Hawkes, 2008). We encountered funders, parents, professional staff and organisations that were concerned with the notion of safeguarding and the actions that we should put into place to protect participants and disabled co-researchers. For example, in response to very robust questioning during a funder interview as to the nature of our plans for safeguarding, in Project Four, and in collaboration with the young adult co-researchers, we nominated an external 'Safeguarding Lead' responsible for safeguarding issues. In all four projects, the intersections of vulnerability and taboo raise ethical issues around the tension between protecting young people who might be considered to be vulnerable to abuse, with avoiding overprotective 'bubble wrapping' and respecting the individual's rights to take acceptable risks (De Than, 2014). As researchers we challenge the idea that young disabled people are vulnerable and in need of protection while, at the same time, want to appease funders and ethics committees that appropriate plans were in place to contain risks. Sometimes this meant that we felt the need to modify the language we used to talk about sex to avoid language that regarded as more 'explicit' (and, therefore, more sensitive), in favour of language that was less explicit and more euphemistic. When communicating with individuals and organisations which seemed more conservative, we avoided drawing on a rights-based discourse that promotes sex-positivity and sexual pleasure, in favour of a more medicalised biopsychosocial discourse which stresses the importance of sex and intimacy for health and wellbeing. So, in this sense, while not wanting to frame this area of work as de facto sensitive, we reframed the research in order to achieve success with funders and ethics committees.

All of the four projects are collaborative in nature but Project Four is the only project that is fully inclusive and led by young people themselves. Managing an inclusive research team is sensitive work and, in this instance, death and dying come to the fore. It is difficult, and awkward, to openly acknowledge that some members of your team have a higher than average probability of being very unwell or even dying during the project, while simultaneously writing this into your risk management plan. It *feels* awkward because as a society many regard death as taboo and would rather not have to raise the subject and, thus, we enact the research as sensitive. Equally, we recognise that contemporary social science literature questions for whom death is, or might be a taboo subject (Tradii & Robert, 2017; Walter, 2017)). It is often those close to the dying person who struggle in talking about death, rather than the person who is close to death (Walter, 2017)). The young people in these four projects repeatedly told us that they wanted 'to live life to the full' and that uncertainty about their life-course should not exclude them from having open and frank discussions about death.

When working with young disabled and seriously ill young people, the problems young people can encounter with travel and health can mean that face-to-face project meetings must be replaced with online meetings. This is a practical solution usually works well and has many advantage but may miss more nuanced face-to-face communication where you can sometimes gauge whether someone is well, or unwell without it being explicit. Striking the right balance between courteous enquiries about health and wellbeing which may be intrusive, and not ignoring silence, which could be detrimental to the project, is difficult. Contingencies for when co-researchers with LLTCs are unwell need to be in place at the project's outset. For example, we put into place clear protocols as to when individuals – or someone on their behalf – should advise that they were ill or in hospital and unable to work. We also introduced a system of deputies for specific project roles so that project activities could continue if someone became ill or died.

Talking about sex: asking questions about sex, intimacy and relationships

As others have noted (Liddiard, 2018; Liddiard et al., 2018), it is not easy to carry out research on sex. Indeed, not everyone wanted to participate in our projects. For example, in Projects Two and Three, a number of potential participants declined to take part in the study because they felt too uncomfortable talking about sex. However, for many of the participants, it was often the very first time that they had ever discussed it (Blackburn, 2018). We wondered whether this fact, in itself, makes our research sensitive? Plummer (1995) argues that the way in which we talk about sex is historically and culturally rooted, and that there must be 'social worlds waiting to hear' (p. 34). Our projects created an opportunity to talk about sex for this group of young people and a social world that would be interested in what they had to say.

Hollomotz (2018) argues that research about sexuality is more successful where plain language is used, and participants are consulted and can agree language in advance of the research. In Project Two, we conducted a pilot study to ascertain the preferred sexual vocabulary. Participants requested the use of plain terms and the avoidance of over-medicalised jargon. In Project Four, disabled co-researchers determined the language used.

The project team didn't always agree on how we should talk about sex but following discussions, usually reached consensus. In Project One, we developed a set of standards and guidance for those working with young people with LLTCs as part of a large multi-disciplinary, multi-professional team, recognising the different language requirements of various members. Young people with LLTCs asked for condition-specific, practical solutions, written or communicated in plain English. Practitioners argued for coherent governance and compliance measures. While academics wanted to address issues such as gender identity and sexual citizenship, and, lawyers argued for clear, jargon-free legislation. The ultimate and shared goal was developing a useful resource by (The Open University Sexuality Alliance, 2019) while challenging the taboos of sex and death.

Some members of the team believed in more direct approaches and explicit language, whereas others preferred a less direct approach. We viewed this through our own normative lens of what would make the research less 'sensitive' for participants. In Project Two, interviews began with general questions rather than questions that directly focused on sex and intimacy. We initially disagreed on this approach, but the interviewer felt that, as most of the young people had not previously discussed sex with anyone, and had been informed that they were exceptionally shy, that they would welcome initial 'rapport building discussions' before talking with strangers explicitly about sex. This raises questions as to whether 'sex' is a 'sensitive' topic for participants, or whether researchers can sometimes find it difficult to ask questions about sex too thereby enacting sensitivities where there may actually be none. There was clear evidence of methodological performativity in the data that we generated using this interviewing technique. For example, a proportion of the data generated in the project did not focus entirely on sex and intimacy, instead it focused on wider contextual and background health and social care issues related to their LLTC – a direct result of the way in which interviews were organised, what questions were asked, and in what order.

After projects end: the issue of posthumous consent

Informed consent is an essential component of responsible research practice. In our case – because many of the participants were at risk of dying either during or after the end of a project – we needed to secure posthumous consent to include their data. The literature on posthumous consent primarily relates to reproduction and the ethical and legal issues on the use of sperm and egg donation after death (Collins, 2005; Tremellen & Savulescu, 2015). There is an absence of literature addressing participants' choices about the use of their data following death, especially for young adults where family may usually feel involved in decision-making.

Securing posthumous consent in this research field is particularly important because we recognised that some participants may die during the project. This was relevant for Project Two. Because the participants were young and disabled, other people, particularly family, were likely to be intimately involved in their lives – more so than other people who are not life-limited. This, and the focus on sex, means that there can be difficulties with data use following death, if posthumous consent is not clearly secured and documented at outset or, during the project.

The practice of securing posthumous consent feels uncomfortable. Most of the participants involved were more interested in living and making the most of their lives; asking about posthumous consent meant that the issue of death needed to be brought to the fore. It may be difficult to predict how data will be used in future, particularly if a participant dies during the course of the research. During the consent process in Project Two, one young man enquired 'What will happen to my data if I die during or following your research?' to which the researcher replied, 'What would you like to happen?' The young man responded that he wanted his interview data to be used following his death to provide a 'living legacy' of his contribution about relationships, intimacy and sex. He did not set any time limits on its usage. Together, the young man and researcher included an additional sentence within his consent form, reflecting his request. The young man signed a revised consent form before his interview and died during the project.

Following his death, the young man's parents contacted us and requested that their son's data was not used in subsequent publications as they were uncomfortable about the subject matter of the project (sex). We subsequently met with the parents, explaining the purpose and intentions of the research and followed this up with a letter. The parents ultimately, although uneasily, respected their son's request to use his interview data posthumously.

Due to the intersections of taboo and vulnerability, we argue for the importance of discussing and recording the different phases of consent and assent, recognising participants nearing the end of life might die before the research is completed or published. As noted here, parents and/or care practitioners sometimes answered for and acted as gatekeepers, on behalf of the young people, both during their lives and after death. This raises issues about seeking, renewing and addressing posthumous assent or consent before death.

Concluding remarks

In this paper we have explored the sensitivities of conducting research on sex, intimacy and relationships with young people whose lives are threatened. We reflected on the learning from the process and offered suggestions as to how these might be relevant to other researchers in the future. We have focused on three elements of the process, drawing on pertinent issues that are present at project start up, our preparations for talking about sex with participants, and what we needed to consider after projects ended. There are many other issues, but we have focused on the issues that, as a project team, we either disagreed on the most or we found more challenging to address.

We have shown how we have simultaneously both rejected and embraced the definition of our research as 'sensitive' at different times during the research process, recognising that the positioning of this research as sensitive frames the process. The project team adopted a predominantly rights-based, sex-positive approach to the subject area which seeks to define sex as normal and every day, and therefore, 'not sensitive'. However, in order to secure funding, ethical approval and posthumous data rights we found ourselves drawing more on approaches that favoured safeguarding and biopsychosocial models of health, rather than a rights-based discourse. Adopting the notion of methodological performativity, we have illustrated how the defining of research as 'sensitive' by others can shape the nature of a research project, including the use of different research methods and techniques. As researchers, we have also enacted the research process as a sensitive one although we sometimes also wanted to reject this definition and didn't always agree on how to go about things. In conclusion, we agree with Sparrman (2014) who argues that research on 'sensitive' topics can be a 'messy' business and that tried and tested experiences should continue to be published.

Disclosure statement

No potential conflict of interest was reported by the author.

References

Blackburn, M. C. (2018) *Sexuality, relationships and reproductive choices in young adults over 16 years with life-limiting and/or life-threatening conditions*. [Doctoral dissertation, The Open University]. ORO http://oro.open.ac.uk/view/person/mb33645.html

Blackburn, M. C., Chambers, L., & Earle, S. (2017). Editorial: Talking about sex, relationships and intimacy: New guidance and standards for nurses and other health and social care professionals working with young people with life-limiting and life-threatening conditions. *Journal of Advanced Nursing*, 73(10), 2265–2267. https://doi.org/10.1111/jan.13089

Blackburn, M. C., Cooke, A., & Earle, S. (2017) 'The significance of sex and relationships for emotional wellbeing: The experiences of young adults with life -limiting and/or life-threatening conditions'. [Unpublished manuscript, The Open University Sexuality Alliance]. The Open University.

Collins, R. (2005). Posthumous reproduction and the presumption against consent in cases of death caused by sudden trauma. *Journal of Medicine & Philosophy*, 30(4), 431–442. https://doi.org/10.1080/03605310591008612

De Than, C. (2014). Sex, disability and human rights: Current legal and practical problems. In T. Owen & C. De Than (Eds.), *Supporting disabled people with their sexual lives: A clear guide for health and social care professionals*. Jessica Kingsley Publishers.

Dickson-Swift, V., James, E. L., & Liamputtong, P. (2008). *Undertaking sensitive research in the health and social sciences: Managing boundaries, emotions and risks*. Cambridge University Press.

Earle, S., & Blackburn, M. C. (2020). Young adults with life-limiting or life-threatening conditions; sexuality and relationships support. *BMJ Supportive & Palliative Care*, bmjspcare-2019-002070. https://doi.org/10.1136/bmjspcare-2019-002070

Egan, D., & Hawkes, G. (2008). Imperiled and perilous: Exploring the history of childhood sexuality. *Journal of Historical Sociology*, 21(4). https://doi.org/10.1111/j.1467-6443.2008.00341.x

Fisher, S. (1973). *Body Consciousness'*. Calder & Boyars.

Hollomotz, A. (2018). 'Successful interviews with people with intellectual disability. *Qualitative Research*, 18(2), 153–170. https://doi.org/org/10.1177/1468794117713810

Law, J., & Urry, J. (2003). *Enacting the social*. Published by the Department of Sociology and the Centre for Science Studies. Lancaster University. http://www.lancaster.ac.uk/fass/resources/sociology-online-papers/papers/law-urry-enacting-the-social.pdf

Lee, R. M. (1993). *Doing research on sensitive topics*. Sage Publications.

Lesko, N. (2012). *Act your age: A cultural construction of adolescence*. Routledge.

Liddiard, K. (2018). *The intimate lives of disabled people*. Routledge, Taylor Francis.

Liddiard, K., Runswick-Cole, K., Goodley, D., Whitney, S., Vogelmann, E., & Watts, L. (2018). I was excited by the idea of a project that focuses on those unasked questions': Co-producing disability research with disabled young people. *Children and Society*, 33(2), 154–167. https://doi.org/10.1111/chso.12308

Liddiard, K., & Slater, J. (2017). 'Like, pissing yourself is not a particularly attractive quality, let's be honest': Learning to contain through youth, adulthood, disabilityandsexuality. *Sexualities*, 21(3), 319333. https://doi.org/10.1177%2F1363460716688674

Open Learn (2019) 'Let's talk about sex, intimacy and relationships'. The Open University. https://www.open.edu/openlearn/talkaboutsex https://www.open.edu/openlearn/health-sports-psychology/health/intimate-not-intimidated-its-time-talk-about-sex-and-disability

Plummer, K. (1995). *'Telling sexual stories: Power, change and social worlds*. Routledge.

Shakespeare, T., Gillespie-Sells, K., & Davies, D. (1996). *The sexual politics of disability*. Cassell.

Sontag, S. (1969). *Styles of Radical Will*. Farrar, Strauss & Giroux.

Sparrman, A. (2014). Access and gatekeeping in researching children's sexuality: Mess in ethics and methods. *Sexuality & Culture*, 18(2), 291–309. https://doi.org/10.1007/s12119-013-9198-x

The Open University Sexuality Alliance (2019) *'Talking about sex, sexuality and relationships: Forthose working with young people with life-limiting or life-threatening conditions'*. The Open University. https://www.open.edu/openlearn/sites/www.open.edu.openlearn/files/tassr_very_final_web_151119.pdf

Tradii, L., & Robert, M. (2017). Do we deny death? II. Critiques of the death denial thesis. *Mortality*, 24(4), 377388. https://doi.org/10.1080/13576275.2017.1415319

Tremellen, K., & Savulescu, J. (2015). A discussion supporting presumed consent for posthumous sperm procurement and conception. *Reproductive Biomedicine Online*, 30(1), 6–13. https://doi.org/10.1016/j.rbmo.2014.10.001

Walter, T. (1991). 'Death: Taboo or not taboo'? *Sociology*, 25(2), 293–310. https://doi.org/10.1177%2F0038038591025002009

Walter, T. (2017). *What death means now: Thinking critically about grieving and dying*. Policy Press.

Part Two
'Sensitive' Ethics in action
Research encounters and 'Whose research is this anyway'?

Reflecting on asynchronous internet mediated focus groups for researching culturally sensitive issues

Noirin MacNamara, Danielle Mackle, Johanne Devlin Trew, Claire Pierson and Fiona Bloomer

ABSTRACT

Internet-mediated focus groups (FGs) have become a feature of qualitative research over the last decade; however, their use within social sciences has been adopted at a slower pace than other disciplines. This paper considers the advantages and disadvantages of internet-mediated FGs and reflects on their use for researching culturally sensitive issues. It reports on an innovative study, which utilised text-based asynchronous internet-mediated FGs to explore attitudes to abortion, and abortion as a workplace issue. The authors identify three key elements of text-based asynchronous online FGs as particularly helpful in researching culturally sensitive issues – safety, time and pace. The authors demonstrate how these elements, integral to the actual process, contributed to 'opinion change/evolution' and challenged processes of stigmatisation centred on over-simplification, misinformation as to the incidence of a culturally sensitive issue in a population, and discrimination.

Introduction

The development in information technology (IT) has heralded opportunities for researchers to adapt traditional research methods and develop new and innovative ways of engaging with research participants, especially those from 'hidden', 'hard-to-reach' or vulnerable populations (Bryman, 2015; Tates et al., 2009). Quantitative methods, such as surveys have been developed, refined and tested, and the use of IT is now commonplace. This includes face-to-face computer-assisted personal interview methods or online methods using internet-mediated technologies. In contrast, the use of such technology in qualitative methodologies has developed at a slower pace, with uptake across disciplines varying. Although the use of internet-mediated technologies in the social sciences dates back to the 1990s (Rezabek, 2000), adoption has been slower on the whole in contrast to the domains of health, engineering and computer sciences (Hesse-Biber & Griffin, 2013). This article reflects on the innovative use of an internet-mediated approach, text-based online focus groups (FGs), to conduct research on abortion.

Traditional FGs, conducted on a face-to-face basis, have long been recognised as a reliable and valid method of data collection, particularly for exploring people's views and experiences on an issue (Bryman, 2015). Online FGs operate on similar principles in relation to an emphasis on open-ended questions and discussions amongst participants, with a moderator guiding the discussion. While research may be conducted with already existing public online forums (Jamison et al., 2018), where the researcher may choose to maintain both insider/outsider positions simultaneously (Paechter, 2012), online FGs may also be created purposely for a specific time-limited study, as in the present case. Typically, online FGs are conducted in one of two ways: asynchronous groups where participants contribute at different times or synchronous groups where participants contribute at the same time. Each has its own strengths and weaknesses, for example, asynchronous groups allow participants to provide responses at a time and pace that is conducive to their own needs, but the immediacy of synchronous groups is lost (Biedermann, 2018). This article will focus on the efficacy of an asynchronous text-based online FG when researching abortion.

Abortion as a 'sensitive' issue

The way in which abortion is discursively constructed in specific settings is deeply connected to constructions of gender, the role of women, the sanctity of life and the role of the state in supposedly private matters and it is often highly stigmatised (Bloomer et al., 2017a). In Northern Ireland (NI) for example, where legislation on abortion has been extremely restrictive until recently, there is a consistent effort by anti-abortion politicians and campaigners to argue that it is necessary to balance and safeguard the 'rights' of the foetus and of pregnant people. In this discourse, women are positioned as vulnerable and incapable of making rational decisions (Pierson & Bloomer, 2017). The construction of abortion as a moral issue (rather than a healthcare issue) enables its stigmatisation and this arguably constitutes its 'sensitive' character, particularly in religious and conservative societies. The discursive positioning of the foetus as a separable being with its own 'rights' in anti-abortion discourse has no acknowledgement of its dependence on a pregnant person to reach a stage where it is 'separable' (Bloomer et al., 2018; Pierson & Bloomer, 2018).

Globally, three processes of abortion stigma have been identified. Firstly, although the decision to have an abortion is complex, and context- and individual-specific, it is over-simplified and its frequency denied through under-reporting and misclassification. Secondly, given this simplification and under-reporting, it is presented as exceptional and women who have abortions can be constructed as deviant and selfish, irresponsible, a murderer, or vulnerable and misguided. Discrimination is the final process of abortion stigma. This can include financial and emotional penalities such as high healthcare fees, loss of employment and verbal or physical abuse (Kumar et al., 2009: 630). Abortion stigma manifests and is perpetuated through media, governmental and institutional discourses and processes, and at community and individual levels.

The research objective was to explore attitudes to abortion and identify experiences of abortion as a workplace issue in NI and the Republic of Ireland (ROI) (Bloomer et al., 2017b). Due to logistical factors, we decided to conduct this research online. However, upon reflection, we concluded that the use of asynchronous text-based FGs to research culturally sensitive issues can challenge their so-called sensitivity for three key reasons. Participants are firstly relatively anonymous, and secondly they can spend considerably longer discussing the research questions. They can scroll back through previous contributions and respond to multiple participants at their convenience. This allows them to engage in a multi-layered manner. Thirdly, the relatively slow pace of a text-based online asynchronous FG arguably enables the self-reflective construction of meaning. Participants can move beyond the use of stigmatised, stereotypical perspectives, taking time to reflect and then reply, possibly challenging some of their own or others views on abortion. An unintended consequence of the study was participants acknowledging that this allowed for deeper nuance to be considered, from a range of different perspectives. This enabled, for instance, one strident anti-abortion perspective to be modified by the lived experience of those who had needed abortions.

Researching sensitive topics with 'hidden', 'hard-to-reach' or vulnerable populations

It is generally understood that research on culturally sensitive topics and with hidden, hard-to-reach or vulnerable populations requires special care in planning the methodologies used (Klein et al., 2010). Topics such as abortion, rape, HIV and drug abuse, for example, all carry high levels of stigmatisation for those affected, due to the politicisation and polarisation of views and negative portrayals in the media. Avoiding culturally sensitive research topics is not advocated, however, as it amounts to an evasion of researcher responsibility and risks disempowering populations in society whose voices might otherwise remain unheard (Dempsey et al., 2016). Researchers can both incorporate critical perspectives on the 'sensitivity' of the topic, and prioritise the welfare of the study participants. The goals of the research can be balanced with reduced risk for participants by ensuring confidentiality, enabling respectful interaction and providing supportive interventions. However, regardless of the imposition of external criteria – in this case concerning the politicisation of abortion – which could imply vulnerability on the part of the respondents to this study – the researchers did not wish to make any blanket assumptions that could suggest passivity, lack of agency or patronise individuals (Marsh et al., 2017). The research team acknowledged that respondents came to the study with a range of experiences and emotions: that some individuals assumed to be at risk may not appreciate being labelled as such and might indeed feel empowered by their participation, that others could be vulnerable but not appear so, while still others could be vulnerable due to undisclosed factors unrelated to the topic of research.

Nevertheless, researchers cannot predict in what ways individual participants might be affected, both positively and negatively, during and following research. In our study on abortion, it was evident that the process of disclosing traumatic memories could be risky for some of the participants. However, some may actually have been drawn to participate precisely because it allowed them to revisit and re-evaluate such difficult experiences (McAdams, 2006). Writing or talking about socially negative experiences is particularly associated with well-being as negative emotion from the original experience tends to be lessened in the retelling (Pasupathi et al., 2009), while socially negative experiences that remain untold may be harmful as they 'do not have the opportunity to be integrated into the self' (McLean et al., 2007:274). The opportunity to create positive meaning from a negative experience (Merrill et al., 2016) was, therefore, a potential unintended positive outcome to the participants of the current study, notwithstanding the inherent risks of such research. Whilst the stigmatisation of abortion was evident in the study, this by no means translated to a blanket negative assessment of abortion per se. As evidenced within the study, for many, abortion was regarded as a normal part of a woman/pregnant person's life and stigmatisation was often associated with criminalisation, religiosity and moral conservatism (Bloomer et al., 2017b).

In the literature more broadly, a series of advantages and disadvantages of online FGs have been identified and are reviewed in the next section.

Advantages

For the researcher the use of text-based online FGs or a discussion forum, provides a series of advantages. Administration tasks and associated costs of arranging and hosting traditional FGs are diminished. Social distancing rules observed during the Covid-19 pandemic can be adhered to. Online groups tend to be more 'geographically diverse' (Nicholas et al., 2010:110) and participants and researchers will not require travel expenses. The text-based nature negates the need for transcription, speeding up the process of analysis and also reduces human error in the transcription process (Boydell et al., 2014:208). The reduced costs of data collection are thus commonly identified as a key advantage, as well as high levels of data quality (Tates et al., 2009). However, online groups may take longer to conduct, increasing the time required for moderation (Rupert et al., 2017).

From the participant perspective, online FGs remove the need to allow travel time to the venue, anxiety about meeting new people is reduced, and with regard to asynchronous groups they can choose when to contribute and for how long (Fox et al., 2007:539; Nicholas et al., 2010). The ability to participate from a location of their choosing may be appealing, particularly if they are geographically isolated, or have restricted mobility due to other commitments, health issues or disability (Hesse-Biber & Griffin, 2013; Madge & O'Connor, 2002). Furthermore, the participant has more control over the process; they can withdraw at any stage without having to explain or make visible their withdrawal (Tates et al., 2009).

In terms of the level of content from participants, studies indicate that the level of anonymity provided via online FGs may lead to increased self-disclosure (Tates et al., 2009). In studies where visual anonymity is used, social desirability may be reduced, allowing participants to feel more comfortable voicing their viewpoints (Fox et al., 2007; Zwaanswijk & van Dulmen, 2014). Participants also have the freedom to offer their views without the risk of being interrupted (Stewart & Williams, 2005). For example, Woodyatt et al. (2016) used both traditional and online FGs to explore intimate partner violence in gay and bisexual relationships. The researchers determined that whilst there was similarity in the themes between the two types of FGs, the online format yielded one additional theme on a sensitive topic insofar as it generated more sharing of in-depth stories. The authors conclude that this format may have provided a safer space for participants; allowing participants to be more open with others and to express their disagreements more freely than face-to-face, traditional FGs. These disagreements also led to new topics of conversation and allowed the moderator to take a quiet role, with the discussion flowing more organically (Woodyatt et al., 2016:746).

The process of asynchronous written communication has the advantage of 'the absence of communication partners' (Schiek & Ullrich, 2017:593), who in face-to-face interaction, may react with surprise, shock, hostility, laughter, boredom, or appear not to listen, which can inhibit further communication. In addition, written communication encourages the self-reflective construction of meaning in relation to experiences that are only partially understood and may be fragmentary (ibid.). Online asynchronous FGs provide the opportunity for participants to reflect on what they have contributed, without immediate time pressures from the moderator or other participants and to contribute again to the issue, adding more nuance if desired (Fox et al., 2007:539; Tates et al., 2009). If group members have full access to the text from the online focus group they can assess the clarity of their statements, helping them to evaluate if their views have been sufficiently captured (Nicholas et al., 2010). The textual contributions easily lend themselves to forms of narrative analysis (including use of software) that may reveal deeper structures of thought and behaviour linked to recovery or continuing negative health impacts of emotional or traumatic experiences (Badger et al., 2011).

Asynchronous text-based online FGs therefore arguably offer participants a safer space and more time, and they progress at a slower pace. These key elements – safety, time, and pace – are well suited to critical reflection and the evolution of positions in relation to culturally sensitive topics.

Disadvantages

The primary limitations of online FGs cited in the literature are centred on IT: lack of internet access, lack of familiarity with the format; inaccessible formats for people with diverse needs; and IT problems, either with the participant's own IT system or with the platform used. In text-based online FGs, poor typing skills may hinder participation and the format also removes the possibility of assessing non-verbal behaviour and tone, although participants may use emoticons or abbreviations instead (Fox et al., 2007).

The online nature also carries the risk of security breaches (Nicholas et al., 2010). Confidentiality and anonymity cannot be guaranteed. In text-based online FGs participants could, for instance, take screenshots of conversations or copy text and share it outside of the focus group (Hesse-Biber & Griffin, 2013:45).

A particular challenge of text-based online FGs is that distress or disengagement cannot be identified using visible or audible cues. However, silence or distinct changes in tone can alert the moderator of the need to intervene and provide additional support to the participant (Hesse-Biber & Griffin, 2013). The moderator thus must be aware of such signs and take action if needed. Dominant participants also require intervention from the moderator (Young et al., 2009).

Requirements of online focus groups

The nature of interaction between moderator and participant in online FGs, whilst mediated by technology, requires many of the conditions necessary for traditional groups. Efforts to establish trust at the outset are paramount and guidelines for participation are required, emphasising confidentiality of what is discussed within the group (Boydell et al., 2014: 210).

Verifying demographic details such as age, gender and race present a particular challenge for online FGs (Boydell et al., 2014; Hesse-Biber & Griffin, 2013). The risk of participants providing false information may be minimised by the approach used to recruit participants. For instance, a mailing list of members of an organisation/staff or client users may provide access, with invitation to the online group being provided via the institution. Alternatively, the researcher may study an already existing online forum. Caution is required if an existing online forum is very open and susceptible to manipulation (e.g., through the use of bots). Not only will such interference invalidate the research results, they may also cause undue distress to other research participants. Such forums are not well suited to research on culturally sensitive topics.

Description of study

The study reported in this article explored the views of trade union members on abortion, on legal reform and on abortion as a workplace issue in NI and the ROI. Whilst there is a breadth of material on attitudes to abortion and legal reform (Altshuler et al., 2015; Francome & Savage, 2011), the consideration of abortion as a workplace issue is under-researched. Studies on attitudes to abortion and legal reform have ranged from quantitative surveys, to qualitative explorations, typically using face-to-face interviews or FGs. This study was unique in several respects. Firstly, it focused on the views of trade union members on abortion, a distinctly under-researched population. Secondly, it explored abortion as a workplace issue, on which there is a dearth of research. Thirdly and of particular relevance to this article, it made use of asynchronous text-based online FGs to discuss abortion and its associated experiences in two highly restricted legal jurisdictions, NI and ROI. Notably, following the study, both jurisdictions underwent significant legal change resulting in widening access to abortion.

The study was mixed methods in design, comprising a quantitative survey of union members and then a series of asynchronous online FGs. Participants for the survey were recruited through the membership lists of five trade unions: Unite the Union, Unison, GMB, CWU Ireland and Mandate, each of which provided funding for the study. Those participants with direct experience of abortion were asked if they wanted to take part in an online focus group. Direct experience was defined as having had, or having known of, or supported someone who had an abortion.

The research team determined an online method to be most appropriate for logistical reasons as the vast majority of potential participants had access to IT facilities, were spread out geographically and worked a range of different shift patterns (Fox et al., 2007:539; Nicholas et al., 2010). An online method was also appropriate as the topic under discussion was culturally sensitive. The group discussion format was chosen as the research team were particularly interested in how abortion was talked about from a range of perspectives in group settings (Bryman, 2015). The accuracy of demographic information collected was dependent on the honesty of participants and this is a recognised disadvantage of all survey research, including online methods, where participants are not personally known to the researchers (Boydell et al., 2014). Lastly, in terms of participation, the research team deemed it highly unlikely that multiple participations by one individual occurred as the project invitation was directly linked to an email address that participants provided once they completed the survey and no duplicate email addresses were present. Completion of the survey itself occurred via a direct link that had been issued to individual trade union members, with the link allowing only one instance of survey completion.

Ethics

Prior to commencing the study ethical approval was sought from Ulster University. This entailed producing a comprehensive project plan; consideration of the design of the study; aims and objectives; and the questions to be used in the FGs. A risk analysis was conducted, and procedures developed should participants disclose information that required an intervention. The research team moderated discussions, and any posts deemed to have used inappropriate terms were removed, their author was contacted, and they were given the opportunity to post again without offensive or inappropriate terms. Throughout the study, the research team were mindful not to make blanket assumptions that could suggest passivity, lack of agency or patronise individuals (Marsh et al., 2017). We were careful not to label particular participants as being at risk, and acknowledged too that we were not able to assess vulnerability of participants if no information on this was disclosed.

As argued by Blair (2016) regarding the labelling of the LGBT+ population as 'vulnerable', context is significant when planning research studies on abortion. Whilst the stigmatisation of abortion was evident in wider society, the immediate institutional environment in which the study was planned mediated the degree of sensitivity attributed to the study. The research team sought ethical approval within an environment which was resistant to viewing abortion in and of itself as a sensitive issue. The commissioners of the study took a similar position. This allowed the research team to approach the ethical process being mindful of the context but not being overly cautious. In addition, the institutional policy of positioning ethics as a process and not merely a procedural matter, combined with a feminist ethos in the research team provided ongoing opportunities to consider ethical issues as they arose.

Signing on

Upon completing the survey and agreeing to take part in the FG, the survey platform sent email addresses of participants to the research team. Those signing up to the FG received an email from the project team explaining its purpose, the aims and objectives and the signing on instructions for the platform to be used (https://www.discourse.org).

As the survey was separate to the FG the research team sought to gather demographic details on participants. Initial questions included age range, gender, and the jurisdiction that they lived in. Around two-thirds of participants provided this information. The demographic information was stored in a spreadsheet maintained by the research team alongside the username for each participant.

Guidelines

As part of the signing on process, a series of guidelines were provided to participants explaining the role of the moderators and how the FGs would be managed. These included the emphasis that the research team wanted to create a safe place for discussions to occur (Bryman, 2015). Participants were asked to be respectful of the multiplicity of experiences and to remain courteous and advised that if disagreements occurred participants should focus on the issue and not on an individual and use appropriate language.

In instances of inappropriate behaviour, moderators adopted the same guidelines as the platform provider, emphasising the importance of not engaging with bad behaviour and that moderators would intervene if needed. The guidance stated that possible actions following inappropriate behaviour could include removing content or a user's account.

Participants were also advised that if they were not comfortable sharing their perspective in a group setting they could contact a moderator, all of whom were members of the research team, via a private message on the forum, or by email. The overall principles of the online FGs matched those of face to face groups in terms of setting out boundaries, moderator intervention and confidentiality (Bryman, 2015).

Platform

The research team chose the platform Discourse (an open-source discussion platform) as it provided key components required for the study, specifically that:

- Its security settings are high.
- The design is user-friendly and accessible – allowing for instance, for assistive screen reader technology to 'read' the content.
- It allowed the moderating team options such as sending private messages to participants.
- It allowed users to interact with one another via their user handle (@username1), sending specific notifications via email to the person they were in conversation with.
- It allowed the moderators to address the group (@group1) who would all be notified via email of the post the moderators wished them to see.
- It had an alert system for posts that may be problematic which participants could use.
- It could be accessed on a range of devices including desktop computers, laptops, tablets, and mobile phones.

Although the platform's security settings are high, its default settings were not configured to enable self-contained groups and complete user anonymity. For this reason the researchers modified many of the default settings to ensure that groups were self-contained, that users' anonymity was maintained, and to ensure effective moderation. The platform was then tested amongst the research team over a two-week period and further settings were modified as required to ensure instructions were clear and the functionality met the study requirements.

Focus group structure

Having signed on to the focus group, participants were asked to discuss a series of open-ended questions. Participants were organised into five self-enclosed groups of 7–11 members on a staggered basis as participants signed in. In terms of frequency of participation, the moderators suggested participants could log in once a day to contribute. Participants could also return to earlier questions, expand on their thoughts and view contributions from other group members. If desired, participants could choose a 'Tracking' option to receive notifications if others replied to their comment or mentioned them in a conversation.

After posting the engagement guidelines in the common area of the forum the moderating team (MacNamara, Bloomer, Pierson) each took responsibility for leading one/two groups. To build rapport each moderator introduced themselves, provided a brief career history and personal interests. This also served to communicate that the research team were highly experienced in qualitative research methods and knowledgeable about the subject area. Again, this spoke to the practice used in face to face groups in building rapport between the research team and participants (Bryman, 2015).

To begin discussions, moderators posted a vignette related to a case of a woman in NI who had been denied an abortion on grounds of fatal foetal abnormality. The case had attracted significant attention regionally and nationally and also bore resemblance to cases in the ROI. Due to the profile of the case the research team felt this would be an appropriate way to begin the discussion. Participants were provided with a brief overview of the case and asked:

> What are your views on this case? Should individual cases be used to change the law? Was this case more welcome to politicians because it was seen as a 'deserving' case?

The first question prompted input from participants expressing a spectrum of views on abortion although two of the five groups needed a reminder post before discussion started. On occasion the moderator intervened to draw out views on comments, asking participants to expand on particular points. When discussions appeared to come to a natural conclusion, a moderator intervened to reflect back on the discussions. This served to summarise the issues raised and to assess if any further points could be added (Rupert et al., 2017).

The forum functionality meant that each group member could only see the common area and their own group's posts. The moderators could view and manage each group that they were assigned to, and the common area. Only moderators could private message participants, i.e. participants did not have the option to private message other participants.

The moderators had no indication of the views of group members on abortion before allocating them to groups. Once the initial five groups were established any further latecomers were added to one of the pre-existing five groups. This meant that they could 'catch up' on discussion by reading the previous posts. When new members were added to a pre-existing group a moderator would post a general welcome to new member(s) and a request to contribute, as and when the new members felt able. This ability to add members to pre-existing groups was a distinct advantage of the asynchronous online method. New members that joined after the initial week were added to the groups that had been established most recently to ensure that they were not joining groups whose discussions were already well developed.

Although the quantitative section of the survey had requested that only those with direct experience of abortion proceed to the online focus group section, the discussion of the initial case made clear that some participants may not have had direct experience of abortion. The moderators decided, therefore, to focus on general discussion points in the initial groups and to transfer members into subsequent experience/no experience groups once more general discussion points had been covered. The moderators also took extra care with people who discussed direct experience in the initial groups. This extra care took the form of moderator posts thanking individuals for their contribution and, if necessary, private messages to individuals thanking them for their contributions and checking in on their wellbeing.

For those in the subsequent groups without direct experience, the moderators decided to ask about their views on the role of trade unions. This included providing preliminary findings from the survey and asking for views on these. For those with direct experience, the questions were more specifically related to their own experiences, asking for instance, if they had disclosed in the workplace, the workplace response, and if it could have been handled differently.

As the study progressed it was evident that the dynamic in the direct experience group was markedly different from the five mixed initial groups. It was extremely supportive, with participants displaying real willingness to engage with the nuance of each other's experiences.

Interaction patterns

In terms of the pace of discussion and involvement of participants, the timeframe for the FGs extended over several days per question. Within each initial group the same format was followed which included the following interventions from moderators with gaps of 1–4 days depending on group dynamics:

- Posting the initial case study and asking for participants' views on same
- Posting a reminder if necessary
- Responding to initial individual posts by thanking them and asking a follow up question if necessary
- Allowing any participant interactions to evolve and run their course, only intervening if someone used inappropriate language or if the 'mood' turned from discussion of the issues to making issues personal, e.g.,, telling someone their viewpoint was 'clichéd'

- Using @username tags to thank those who had contributed and to directly ask those who had not contributed thus far if they had any thoughts
- Using the @groupname tag to address the group as a whole – for example, to summarize key issues raised during the initial stage and asking if anyone had further issues they would like to raise
- Finishing by thanking all the participants and reminding them to answer the experience/no experience question posted to the common area.

The ability to tag individual participants and to tag the group name, which generated email alerts to participants, was a key advantage. As with face to face FGs three key dynamics could be observed. Firstly, some participants did not contribute to the focus group or contributed very little whereas others dominated the discussion. Moderators could see login times, views and time spent on the forum by various users and therefore could identify and engage with those who were logging in but not posting, as well as those who were not logging in. Secondly, once participants became aware of each other's viewpoints they would either 'boost' one another or very clearly disagree with one another. Finally, as participants moved from simply addressing one another by username to tagging one another (triggering a notification), a separate interesting dynamic emerged where a user would tag a moderator and request that the discussion move on from its current direction to also consider a thus far unexplored aspect, e.g., how socioeconomic inequalities affect access to abortion and healthcare. Moderators read this as instances of when a participant perhaps felt they wanted 'out' of the current interactions without offending other participants. This was a welcome development and indicated that efforts by moderators to establish and maintain good rapport with participants were working.

As noted above, one particular concern with using online FGs to research culturally sensitive topics relates to how researchers should engage with a participant who is clearly distressed. A criticism of online methods is that it is difficult to read non-verbal cues and sufficiently gauge the mood of the group (Hesse-Biber & Griffin, 2013). This certainly has merit insofar as someone may be very distressed and decide not to post, therefore giving no indication to the moderator of their distress. Each group's moderator took care to remind participants, as appropriate, that they could be contacted via private message and also provided individual email addresses as means of contact. The moderating team assert that this was a useful function, although it may not have captured all of those in distress.

That said, contributions to the forum also clearly featured some non-verbal cues through symbols and various textual methods. Examples include the use of caps to indicate anger or importance, inverted quotation marks '' often used to indicate disbelief or a lack of faith in a term, a dotted line to indicate a pause or a degree of uncertainty, an exclamation mark used for a wide variety of reasons, and brackets to indicate a related but perhaps less relevant point. To interpret their meaning, each of these has to be read in the context of the overall post, with some remaining fairly ambiguous but others clearer. For example, one participant, who moderators named participant R, used caps in a way which clearly indicated anger and distress. Their posts were lengthy, detailing their negative direct experience of abortion, and at times they misinterpreted or did not take account of the context of the preceding discussion. This clearly confused or irritated some participants though on the whole the other participants were very considerate.

The private message function was a distinct advantage of the online method. It allowed moderators to offer support to those who needed it and to explain to other participants, who contravened the appropriate language policy of the forum, why a particular post had been removed. The private message function allowed for these difficult interactions, away from the group setting, which caused less embarrassment and thus less jeopardized the researcher–participant relationship. The moderating team posted general reminders that inappropriate posts had been removed, sending a clear signal to all participants that action had been taken to deal with such posts.

Using an online method to research a culturally sensitive topic can therefore be advantageous insofar as participants may take some time before responding to a post which irritates them and they may be more considerate as a result. On the flip side, as was the case with two participants in this study, people who hold quite strong views on culturally sensitive topics exhibited behaviour which could be interpreted as an unwillingness to listen to others or practice self-restraint.

Conclusion

To summarise, in this study we found that the advantages of using an asynchronous text-based online focus group to research culturally sensitive topics were numerous. Many of these may be relevant for the challenges presented in conducting primary research during the Covid-19 pandemic. In general terms, we identified that geographical distances are overcome; different work schedules can be accommodated; the private message function allows moderators to manage difficult interactions in a private space; and remedial strategies can be employed if the initial sample is not what is expected e.g., the subsequent divide between direct and no direct experience in this study.

In terms of the requirements for researching culturally sensitive topics, the anonymity afforded by the forum can facilitate self-disclosure in a safer space, relatively speaking. The longer time period for text-based asynchronous online FGs means that latecomers can be added to pre-existing groups and users can take the time to read previous posts and engage in a multi-layered manner. Additionally, the relatively slow pace of an asynchronous forum means that the mood can be assessed and responded to as it evolves. The slower pace encourages the self-reflective construction of meaning on the part of participants, and possible 'opinion change/evolution'. This is particularly relevant for culturally sensitive issues such as abortion whose sensitivity is a result of processes of stigmatisation such as over-simplification, misinformation as to its incidence in a population, and discrimination (Kumar et al., 2009). By participating in a forum which allowed for open discussion of what is often perceived as a culturally sensitive topic, the study participants themselves, to some extent, normalised the experiences they recounted and possibly reduced associated stigma (Marsh et al., 2017). From a research perspective, in line with the conclusions of Tates et al. (2009), we concur that the textual data obtained from an online focus group is very layered and rich in both direct and indirect meaning and the internet can be employed to provide enhanced access to sensitive topics (Jamison et al., 2018).

Of the three participants who responded to the question regarding the usefulness of the forum, all unequivocally stated that they felt it was beneficial and contributed to the further development of nuanced viewpoints, thus supporting the view that such explorations of difficult topics may allow opportunities for personal growth (Merrill et al., 2016).

In terms of disadvantages, moderating tasks, although not particularly time-consuming in and of themselves, required a longer time period than had been anticipated. The combination of being 'on-call' and the culturally sensitive nature of the subject matter meant that the moderators experienced the process as quite tiring and at times emotionally draining. As noted in other studies (Dempsey et al., 2016; Klein et al., 2010), the potential of distress amongst participants was an ongoing concern throughout the present study, with moderators being mindful of how distress could be best identified, monitored and managed. Participants who held very strong views on the topic needed to be adequately cared for and supported. This online moderation process elongates the role of the researcher, moving the role away from the time limited focus group scenario to a lengthier time frame, in the case of this study, over a three week period. Moderation extended the emotional burden on the researchers and this issue will need to be factored in if other researchers consider using similar methods. If resources allow, it would be beneficial to spread out the moderation tasks to as many of the research team as possible to minimise researcher fatigue. Additionally, dealing with 'lurkers', participants logging in but not contributing, was absent in our moderator guidelines and should be addressed in future studies.

We conclude that the method of text-based asynchronous online FGs was appropriate for both the topic of the study and for the profile of the participants. Whilst limitations were identified several of these can be mediated by revision of moderator guidelines. We adopted this methodology largely due to logistical constraints. However, on reflection, we have concluded that three key elements, integral to the process itself – namely relative safety, longer time period, and slower pace – can contribute to opinion change/evolution. These are particularly pertinent where processes of stigmatisation regarding an issue are centred on over-simplification, misinformation as to the incidence of the issue in a population, and discrimination.

Disclosure statement

No potential conflict of interest was reported by the authors.

Funding

Funded by Unite the Union, Unison, GMB, CWU Ireland and Mandate

ORCID

Noirin MacNamara http://orcid.org/0000-0002-6220-571X
Danielle Mackle http://orcid.org/0000-0001-7638-6200
Johanne Devlin Trew http://orcid.org/0000-0003-4563-1239
Claire Pierson http://orcid.org/0000-0003-0961-7157
Fiona Bloomer http://orcid.org/0000-0003-3347-6403

References

Altshuler, A. L., Storey, H. L. G., & Prager, S. W. (2015). Exploring abortion attitudes of US adolescents and young adults using social media. *Contraception*, *91*(3), 226–233. https://doi.org/10.1016/j.contraception.2014.11.009

Badger, K., Royse, D., & Moore, K. (2011). What's in a story? A text analysis of burn survivors' web-posted narratives. *Social Work in Health Care*, *50*(8), 577–594. https://doi.org/10.1080/00981389.2011.592114

Biedermann, N. (2018). The use of Facebook for virtual asynchronous focus groups in qualitative research. *Contemporary Nurse*, *54*(1), 26–34. https://doi.org/10.1080/10376178.2017.1386072

Blair, K. L. (2016). Ethical research with sexual and gender minorities. In A.E. Goldberg (Ed.), *The SAGE Encyclopedia of LGBTQ Studies*, (pp.375–380). SAGE Publications, Inc

Bloomer, F., Devlin-Trew, J., Pierson, C., MacNamara, N., & Mackle, D. (2017b). *Abortion as a workplace issue: Trade union survey - North And South Of Ireland*. UNITE the Union, Unison, Mandate Trade Union, the CWU Ireland, the GMB, Alliance for Choice, Trade Union Campaign to Repeal the 8th.

Bloomer, F., O'Dowd, K., & Macleod, C. (2017a). Breaking the silence on abortion: The role of adult community abortion education in fostering resistance to Norms. *Culture, Health & Sexuality*, 19(7), 709–722. https://doi.org/10.1080/13691058.2016.1257740

Bloomer, F., Pierson, C., & Estrada-Claudio, S. (2018). *Reimagining global abortion politics: A social justice perspective*. Policy Press.

Boydell, N., Fergie, G., McDaid, L., & Hilton, S. (2014). Avoiding pitfalls and realising opportunities. *International Journal of Qualitative Methods*, 13(1), 206–223. https://doi.org/10.1177/160940691401300109

Bryman, A. (2015). *Social research methods*. Oxford University Press.

Dempsey, L., Dowling, M., Larkin, P., & Murphy, K. (2016). Sensitive interviewing in qualitative research. *Research in Nursing and Health*, 39(6), 480–490. https://doi.org/10.1002/nur.21743

Fox, F. E., Morris, M., & Rumsey, N. (2007). Doing synchronous online focus groups with young people. *Qualitative Health Research*, 17(4), 539–547. https://doi.org/10.1177/1049732306298754

Francome, C., & Savage, W. (2011). Attitudes and practice of gynaecologists towards abortion in Northern Ireland. *Journal of Obstetrics and Gynaecology*, 31(1), 50–53. https://doi.org/10.3109/01443615.2010.522273

Hesse-Biber, S., & Griffin, A. J. (2013). Internet-mediated technologies and mixed methods research. *Journal of Mixed Methods Research*, 7(1), 43–61. https://doi.org/10.1177/1558689812451791

Jamison, J., Sutton, S., Mant, J., & De Simoni, A. (2018). Online stroke forum as source of data for qualitative research. *BMJ Open*, 8(3), e020133. https://doi.org/10.1136/bmjopen-2017-020133

Klein, H., Lambing, T. P., Moskowitz, D. A., Washington, T. A., & Gilbert, L. K. (2010). Recommendations for performing internet-based research on sensitive subject matter with 'hidden' or difficult-to-reach populations. *Journal of Gay & Lesbian Social Services*, 22(4), 371–398. https://doi.org/10.1080/10538720.2010.491742

Kumar, A., Hessini, L., & Mitchell, E. M. H. (2009). Conceptualising abortion stigma. *Culture, Health and Sexuality*, 11(6), 625–639. https://doi.org/10.1080/13691050902842741

Madge, C., & O'Connor, H. (2002). Online with e-mums. *Area*, 34(1), 92–102. https://doi.org/10.1111/1475-4762.00060

Marsh, C. A., Browne, J., Taylor, J., & Davis, D. (2017). A researcher's journey. *Women and Birth*, 30(1), 63–69. https://doi.org/10.1016/j.wombi.2016.07.003

McAdams, D. (2006). The redemptive self. *Research in Human Development*, 3(2–3), 81–100. https://doi.org/10.1080/15427609.2006.9683363

McLean, K. C., Pasupathi, M., & Pals, J. L. (2007). Selves creating stories creating selves. *Personality and Social Psychology Review*, 11(3), 262–278. https://doi.org/10.1177/1088868307301034

Merrill, N., Waters, T. E. A., & Fivush, R. (2016). Connecting the self to traumatic and positive events. *Memory*, 24(10), 1321–1328. https://doi.org/10.1080/09658211.2015.1104358

Nicholas, D. B., Lach, L., King, G., Scott, M., Boydell, K., Sawatzky, B. J., Reisman, J., Schippel, E., & Young, N. L. (2010). Contrasting internet and face-to-face focus groups for children with chronic health conditions. *International Journal of Qualitative Methods*, 9(1), 105–121. https://doi.org/10.1177/160940691000900102

Paechter, C. (2012). Researching sensitive issues online. *Qualitative Research*, 13(1), 87–106. https://doi.org/10.1177/1468794112446107

Pasupathi, M., McLean, K. C., & Weeks, T. (2009). To tell or not to tell. *Journal of Personality*, 77(1), 89–123. https://doi.org/10.1111/j.1467-6494.2008.00539.x

Pierson, C., & Bloomer, F. (2017). Macro-and micro-political vernaculizations of rights: Human rights and abortion discourses in Northern Ireland. *Health and Human Rights*, 19(1), 173–185. https://www.hhrjournal.org/2017/06/macro-and-micro-political-vernaculizations-of-rights-human-rights-and-abortion-discourses-in-northern-ireland/

Pierson, C., & Bloomer, F. (2018). Anti-abortion myths in political discourse. In C. McQuarrie, C. Pierson, F. Bloomer, & S. Shettner (Eds.), *Crossing troubled waters: Abortion in Ireland, Northern Ireland, and Prince Edward Island* (pp. 184–213). UPEI Island Studies Press.

Rezabek, R. J. (2000). Online focus groups. *Forum: Qualitative Research*, 1(1), Art.18. http://dx.doi.org/10.17169/fqs-1.1.1128

Rupert, D. J., Poehlman, J. A., Hayes, J. J., Ray, S. E., & Moultrie, R. R. (2017). Virtual versus in-person focus groups. *Journal of Medical Internet Research*, 19(3), e80. https://doi.org/10.2196/jmir.6980

Schiek, D., & Ullrich, C. (2017). Using asynchronous written online communications for qualitative inquiries. *Qualitative Research*, 17(5), 589–597. https://doi.org/10.1177/1468794117690216

Stewart, K., & Williams, M. (2005). Researching online populations. *Qualitative Research*, 5(4), 395–416. https://doi.org/10.1177/1468794105056916

Tates, K., Zwaanswijk, M., Otten, R., van Dulmen, S., Hoogerbrugge, P. M., Kamps, W. A., & Bensing, J. M. (2009). Online focus groups as a tool to collect data in hard-to-include populations. *BMC Medical Research Methodology*, 9(1), 15–24. https://doi.org/10.1186/1471-2288-9-15

Woodyatt, C. R., Finneran, C. A., & Stephenson, R. (2016). In-person versus online focus group discussions. *Qualitative Health Research, 26*(6), 741–749. https://doi.org/10.1177/1049732316631510

Young, N. L., Varni, J. W., Sinder, L., McCormick, A., Sawatzky, B., & Scott, M. (2009). The Internet is valid and reliable for child-report. *Journal of Clinical Epidemiology, 62*(3), 314–320. https://doi.org/10.1016/j.jclinepi.2008.06.011

Zwaanswijk, M., & van Dulmen, S. (2014). Advantages of asynchronous online focus groups and face-to-face focus groups as perceived by child, adolescent and adult participants. *BMC Research Notes, 7*(1), 756–763. https://doi.org/10.1186/1756-0500-7-756

'Working together is like a partnership of entangled knowledge': exploring the sensitivities of doing participatory data analysis with people with learning disabilities

Elizabeth Tilley, Iva Strnadová, Sue Ledger, Jan Walmsley, Julie Loblinzk, Paul Anthony Christian and Zara Jane Arnold

ABSTRACT
While there have been significant developments in the field of inclusive research with people with learning disabilities, there is limited knowledge about the ways inclusive research teams have conducted participatory data analysis. The authors argue this is inherently tied to the sensitivities involved in the inclusive research process. In this article, we present the experiences of two inclusive research teams (from the UK and Australia) who developed ways of working together to collaborate on data analysis. Both studies touched upon sensitive topics and crossed disciplinary boundaries. One was an evaluation of a series of history workshops with young people with learning disabilities; the other was an exploration of effective models of peer support for parents with learning disabilities. The authors explore different approaches to data analysis in inclusive research teams, and reflect on the politics of 'sensitive' research in this field, especially in relation to expectations of funders, ethics committees, and stakeholders.

Introduction

Inclusive research with people with learning disabilities, where people participate as active co-researchers (rather than as research subjects) has become a central tenet of the disability rights movement ambition 'Nothing about us, without us'. While there have been significant developments in the field of inclusive research with people with learning disabilities (see Strnadová & Walmsley, 2017 for a recent overview), there is limited knowledge about the ways inclusive research teams have tackled data analysis (Seale et al., 2015). It has been argued that a transparent data analysis process in inclusive research is important for establishing whether the presented research is both 'good science' and good inclusive research (Nind, 2011). In this paper, we argue that the lack of transparency concerning data analysis in inclusive research is inherently tied to the sensitivities involved in this aspect of the research process. Analysis is the point at which some aspects of data are emphasised and privileged over others. Interpretation occurs, drawing particular voices and perspectives to the fore, while others fade into the background. It is an active process: decisions are to be made. What is the most insightful data, and why? How might different pieces of data connect and what patterns can be observed? What data is to remain uncoded, ignored, left for another day? During data analysis we build upon or challenge existing theory; sometimes new theoretical frameworks and ways of seeing the world emerge. It is when knowledge is both produced and organised. However, in many inclusive projects, data analysis is usually the point at which academics assume greater power and control over the research process. This raises sensitive questions about the integrity of the inclusive research endeavour, the nature of relationships between different research stakeholders, how power and decision-making is shared, and who ultimately 'owns' the research (Hoggart, 2017).

This article presents the experiences of two inclusive research teams from England and Australia, who each developed ways of working together to collaborate on data analysis. Both projects adopted qualitative methods and addressed what might be described as 'sensitive topics'. This is not unique, as inclusive research often deals with research topics that can be sensitive to people with learning disabilities – such as contraception (Ledger et al., 2016), ageing (Strnadová et al., 2015) and social inclusion (García Iriarte et al., 2014). The English research was an evaluation of *MADHOUSE re: exit*, a project designed to raise awareness of the history of institutionalisation of people with learning disabilities and to reflect upon ongoing experiences of social isolation (Walmsley et al., 2018). A team that involved three University researchers and two co-researchers with learning disabilities conducted the evaluation. The Australian project explored effective models of peer support for parents with learning disabilities, with a research team comprising three University researchers and one researcher with learning disabilities (Collings et al., 2019; Strnadová et al., 2019).

Our aim in this paper is to add an original contribution to the methodological debates in inclusive research for people with learning disabilities, across different international contexts. Emboldened not only by the focus of this special issue, but also Nind's (2011) appeal for more nuanced dialogue about the tensions involved in participatory data analysis, we discuss the deep (and often unacknowledged) sensitivities involved when doing this interpretive work together. We share our reflections, struggles and achievements of participatory data analysis, including consideration of the 'sensitive approach' that may be required to support meaningful co-analysis in such projects.

In the spirit of transparency, we believe it is also important to detail the process of how we conceived and wrote this article. It was the University researchers who first considered the possibility of submitting a paper about participatory data analysis for this special issue. We then discussed the idea with our co-researchers with learning disabilities who agreed we should go ahead. The University researchers undertook a review of the literature and broadly agreed a focus and outline for the paper. Sue Ledger and Paul Christian from the history project, and Iva Strnadová and Julie Loblinzk from the parenting project, then met to discuss their experiences of doing data analysis together, basing their discussions around a set of core questions that were agreed amongst all seven authors. We decided to include extracts from the meetings within the main body of the article, so that readers can see how these conversations unfolded. In the context of community heritage exhibitions, Graham (2019) has argued that the 'radically specific' reflections of people with learning disabilities are often at risk of being hidden within the big ideas or headlines of curatorial practice. We argue that such 'interpretive hierarchies' (Serrell, 2015) are also at play in the curating of articles like this, where space must be dedicated to theoretical considerations and conceptual ideas. For this reason, direct contributions from all the researchers are identified in the main body of the article. The lead author drafted the discussion section (a further layer of analysis in the development of our argument) and the first draft of the paper was then refined by all the other named authors. This approach to co-writing mirrors and builds upon previous co-written publications we have been involved in (Brownlee-Chapman et al., 2018;

Strnadová et al., 2019). We acknowledge its imperfections, notably that it can be challenging to provide a rigorous account of the research process and findings when making space for stakeholder perspectives to be included. But we argue that we must strive towards different ways of communicating knowledge and experience, in order to challenge the boundaries of what constitutes accepted (and respected) practice within academic publications. We appreciate that this paper may be of greatest interest to those conducting inclusive research with people with learning disabilities. However, we hope the detailed explications of our data analysis processes, alongside our critical reflections, will be relevant for anyone engaged in participatory research with so-called 'marginalised' groups.

Participatory data analysis with people with learning disabilities: what we know from the literature

While the breadth and depth of inclusive research with people with learning disabilities has experienced notable expansion in recent years (Bigby et al., 2014; Nind, 2014; Strnadová & Walmsley, 2017), the process of doing data analysis together continues to be underreported. For us, participatory data analysis offers opportunities to resist the 'power takeovers' (Deleuze & Guattari, 1987: 8) of professional discourses about learning disability (including those produced through the academy), strengthening scope for what Roets et al. (2007: 325) have described as 'epistemological innovation'; a multiplicity of perspectives and truths. Data analysis offers people with learning disabilities the potential to become not just producers and users of knowledge, but also interpreters of knowledge, bringing their own wisdom, experience and judgement to bear.

But this begs the question: how best to achieve this aspiration in an ethical, rigorous and sensitive way? If we acknowledge, as many colleagues involved in inclusive projects do, that research offers pathways to disrupt marginalising discourses and unequal social structures; then the act of data interpretation is worthy of close attention. As Nind has argued 'it is through active participation in understanding the world through research that participants benefit from a transformative experience' (Nind, 2011: 354). And yet why do so few inclusive projects talk about participatory data analysis? We agree in part with Nind's (2011) suggestion that the power and status that is associated with data analysis may make it harder for academics to relinquish. But we also suspect that it is uncertainty about how to do this process well (and sensitively), combined with anxiety about how best to write about it, that explains the scant coverage in the literature.

There are some emerging accounts of participatory data analysis with people with learning disabilities. Nind and Seale (2009, as cited in Nind, 2011) undertook concurrent data collection and analysis with participants/co-researchers through a series of workshops. A different method was adopted in the Voices for Change project (Stevenson, 2014). The author describes how she collaborated with a small group of people to analyse and code the transcripts of young people with learning disabilities who had participated in a project about their life goals. Williams et al. (2009) described their use of conversation analysis to analyse the video stage of their Skills for Support study. The two researchers with learning disabilities, who had experienced interactions similar to those portrayed in the videos, participated in data analysis by identifying important parts of the videos. Frankena et al. (2019) described using Membership Categorisation Analysis (MCA) in an inclusive project that explored the roles, activities and relationships in participatory projects, enabling co-researchers to 'take the lead' (Frankena et al., 2019: 725) in analysing data. The Building Bridges Team described their visual coding process on a project exploring community inclusion (Mooney et al., 2019). Following 'discussion group' meetings, the academic supporter compiled a list of reflections that were then translated by a co-researcher into picture cards. The picture cards were subsequently used by the wider team to identify key themes in the data.

While there is now wide acceptance that people with learning disabilities can participate in research design, data collection and dissemination (Nind, 2014; Walmsley et al., 2018), Nind argues:

'we need to push on to say that people with learning disabilities can do data analysis too, not in the sense of romantic idealism or positive spin, rather of finding out what can be achieved by exploring ever-more sensitively supportive approaches to breaking down barriers, opening up possibilities and achieving access' (Nind, 2011: 355).

In the following two examples of participatory data analysis, we set out the ways in which we attempted to address the ethical and quality challenges posed by Nind, and the sensitive terrains that were navigated in the process.

Doing data analysis together: practices and reflections from two inclusive teams

Here we present the research teams' reflections about the participatory data analysis process, captured across a number of meetings based around the development of this article. What follows are the edited accounts of these conversations, based around a set of pre-agreed questions. The questions we posed to each team were:

- How did you do the data analysis together?
- What part(s) of the data analysis process felt sensitive to you?
- Why did this feel sensitive?
- How did you deal with this?
- What difference did doing the analysis together make to what you said about your research?

The accounts below were jointly compiled by the teams, but also include direct quotes from individual researchers to reflect their perspective. Direct quotes are presented in italics and are included where a member of the team felt it was important for their reflections to be captured verbatim. For more details on the two projects, please see Walmsley et al., 2018 and Strnadová et al., 2019.

Inclusive evaluation of MADHOUSE re:exit (England)

How did you do the data analysis together?

The evaluation of the *MADHOUSE re:exit* programme was conducted by a team consisting of two experienced researchers, Sue Ledger and Jan Walmsley, and two co-researchers with learning disabilities from theatre company Access all Areas, Paul Christian and Zara Jayne Arnold, with input and advice from Liz Tilley. Prior to working as an inclusive team, we had gotten to know each other quite well as Sue and Jan had led workshops on learning disability history for the theatre company. Paul and Sue had also previously worked together with Access all Areas in making a film called *No Longer Shut Up*. The co-researchers received basic training in research methods from Sue and Jan.

The main piece of collaborative data analysis we undertook related to history workshops that Access all Areas had delivered to people with learning disabilities. The data we analysed together included:

- Observation notes made in notebooks kept by evaluation team;
- Photographs from workshop sessions;
- iPhone and iPad film recordings from the workshops and evaluation session;
- Session aims from workshop leaders, who were members of Access all Areas (the 'wall of what we wanted to do');
- Interviews with the *MADHOUSE re:exit* programme leaders about the workshop aims, planning and activities;
- Data from a de-brief interview with a life history workshop leader;
- Paul's audio recording of his immediate reflections following the workshops.

We undertook a thematic analysis of our data adapted from an approach outlined by Ziebland and McPherson (2006) and also drawing on coding systems outlined by Braun and Clarke (2006). We worked systematically through the data using post-it notes to identify key segments of data. This was followed by the shared naming and clustering of codes which finally developed into thematic maps.

Prior to this coding process, we analysed the 'wall of what we wanted to do' and extracted the aims as identified by workshop leaders. A large piece of paper was used to represent the 'wall', with paper 'bricks' stuck on. These bricks were made by the Access all Areas History workshop leaders, and clarified what leaders wanted to achieve in the session. As evaluators it was important for us to understand what the leaders wanted to happen. For workshop leaders, it was important to know whether findings from the analysis showed if their original aims had been met. This data could then feed into the planning of the next workshop series. We also made a note of the aims as headings to use in our analysis, and if data related to these aims we coded the extract to these pre-determined headings. Alongside this approach, we remained open to new themes arising from the data.

When this data analysis process was underway, we developed numerous sheets of paper with different headings and placed coded extracts (with respondent identifiers) under each. Jan and Zara read out what they had seen from their notebooks and Paul shared his verbal reflections and audio recording from the session. Sue, working with Paul, then recorded the main points on sticky post-it notes and placed these on a large piece of paper. The team then discussed these together. We all decided quite easily how things should be coded and what key words to use on the post-it note along with the data extract. If a piece of information didn't fit easily with one of the headings on the paper, we made a new theme and put it in there. Some data extracts were coded to more than one theme.

Paul: *It made me feel included that I was saying the words and you were transcribing it. A research word! It helped that I could see exactly what you were doing. I felt included. If you had done something wrong I felt I could easily tell you and talk to you and Jan and Zara and then I wouldn't feel like I had been ignored. I felt my points counted this way and I could see them being written down and included. It just shows people how serious our views and thoughts are and how it means so much to us. I think being able to see the whole process was very important and it is very important that you can stop and talk openly with people like you and Jan who are helping us make sense of the data. It is important that you feel really listened to and that it is not going to cause any difficulty if you don't agree or don't understand what is being said or what is being done.*

What part(s) of the inclusive data analysis process felt 'sensitive' to you?

Sue: *One issue in data analysis that felt sensitive to me was that I took the lead in doing the writing of data extracts on the post-it notes. Paul and I were choosing the words together with Jan and Zara feeding in too, but I was doing the actual writing on the post-it notes which did, for me, feel a bit controlling at the time. Everyone was happy for this to happen – we agreed this was best as I had hadn't been evaluating at this workshop, but on reflection (and with more time available) it might have been good to share this role around.*

Paul: *Yes but it worked because we could all see what you were writing and drawing and what you were doing. I could change the words if I wanted to and I remember I did this. I never had a chance to explore this researcher side of me before and it really helped me to talk about these kind of issues with other people and for them to listen. I'll be honest it sounded a bit jargon – the term 'data analysis' – but when we started doing it I understood the concept. I think that was the best method at the time – it was done in a fashion that was cut up into small bites of information and that helped me to click on to what people were saying.*

Sue: *I would like to have had the time to try out some ways of presenting the first stage data analysis, like mind maps and flow charts and then had another team session to re-visit the coherence of our* coding, categories and themes together. When I started to think how we could do this I estimated that this would have added a further two days of work to our data analysis schedule. As there were four of us this would be more expensive for funders but in my view very worthwhile in terms of the deepening the inclusive analysis process and findings.

Why did this feel sensitive?

Paul: *Because this was analyzing data from a workshop about learning disability history and about people's lives today. In this way the actual data, it's dragging up the things that excluded us from the events in the past that somehow have still made it into our present. This has made a permanent scar on our hearts. In our team if someone in power hadn't listened when we were talking about the data it would be like a re-activator or reminder – if someone ignores us and doesn't really take careful note of what we are trying to say it can reactivate the wound which ultimately puts us back to the beginning. That didn't happen in our team, that was a very good thing. It felt we were all on a level. But I think we did need more days in our programme to give us more time to do our data analysis. I found it very interesting, the thinking and sorting out what we saw and heard in the sessions and what they meant. We would need more money to actually do more of this properly.*

Sue: *I think that you have raised for me what is the greatest tension in doing this work together. In our analysis session I think you and Zara both saw things, certainly in terms of performance, that I might have missed as I don't have a performance background. I was also very aware of the sensitive and painful issues that some participants were raising – like how people are still experiencing a lot of bullying and name-calling. This is really important data to capture and, as you say, to you and Zara it is deeply personal and it seems crucial to include your input, your reflections based on your own lived experience. Yet it feels very uncomfortable and inappropriate to be rushing the processing of this sensitive material because we have to deliver our findings on time. I also wonder if there is more pressure on us to prove ourselves as an inclusive team? In the past people have questioned whether people with learning disabilities can really do data analysis.*

How did you deal with this?

Paul: *We dealt with this by talking about it and thinking about how we would make the best use of the time we had. We also talked about how we can make a case for more time in the future – like writing this article. We are speaking about how we can make the case for people to be trained and involved in research.*

Sue: *We discussed the tensions openly. It feels risky but it needs to be said as there is a real danger of pretending to do things inclusively. When we had to cut corners we decided to explain this openly. It is much more respectful. If we as an inclusive team acknowledge the limitations of working under existing time constraints we can think together about how to work in the future in a way that can capitalize on using your time and the expertise you bring to thinking about the data and to the interpretation and analysis process.*

What difference did doing the analysis together make to what you said about your research?

Paul: *Working together is more like a partnership of entangled knowledge that helped to understand these strong issues. It helped to feedback to one another and to have debates on the issues. I think that as performers we bring our own knowledge and passion that drives it forward. It enables us to move forward and understand things that they (Sue and Jan) wouldn't have thought they would understand and so they are teaching themselves in the process. Even though it was the same goal – doing really good data analysis – we all brought different perspectives to the table. We all have different eyes and we all travel on different paths – so we all saw different things.*

Peer support for parents with learning disabilities (Australia)

How did you do the data analysis together?

The study was co-designed and co-produced by academic researchers (Iva Strnadová, Susan Collings, and Joanne Danker) and a researcher with intellectual disabilities (Julie Loblinzk). Three of us (Iva, Susan, and Julie) conducted the interviews, either in tandem (mostly Iva and Julie) or individually (Iva or Susan). We analysed the data in two different ways and teams. This was due to time constraints. We knew that we needed to submit an article to a high-quality peer-reviewed journal within 18 months of commencing the study (this was a condition of being funded). The first year was spent developing and obtaining ethical approval, recruiting participants, conducting and transcribing the interviews, and making a start on data analysis. It was these 12 months that we were funded for. Most of the data analysis was conducted after the initial 12 months of the study, and given our previous experiences of doing data analysis inclusively, 6 months was not long enough to analyse the interviews and write a high-quality article. Therefore, the data analysis was conducted by Iva, Susan, and Joanne, and in parallel by Iva and Julie. This allowed us to meet the funding conditions, and still engage in inclusive data analysis. What we describe below is based on the data analysis conducted by Iva and Julie. The actual inclusive data analysis took place in the following stages:

- We printed out all transcribed interviews (in font size 14, double-spaced).
- We listened together to each interview, while reading it in a printed version.
- We used highlighter pens to highlight main topic that each parent talked about.
- We also wrote our comments on the printed interviews.
- After listening to an interview, we discussed the main topics covered in that interview, and then summarised it. These discussions were recorded and transcribed and became a part of data.
- From each interview, we had 1–2 pages of main topics in dot points.

Julie: *We also did some of the interviews separately and I emailed the main points to you.*

In the next stage, we used highlighters to group the main headings together (e.g., purple was for parents' preferences, yellow for issues they experienced). After that, we used a butcher paper [an Australian expression for a kraft paper] to create mind-maps for each heading. We totalled the number of participants that mentioned each topic.

Julie: *Mind-mapping is the best. As we were playing to our strengths, I was happy to do the writing on the butcher paper.*

Based on the mind-maps, we created a one-page overview of the main themes. Under each theme, we listed sub-themes, in order of frequency that these were mentioned (from most to least). After that, we summarised the key findings in a narrative.

This extensive description of our data analysis process is important, as it also indicates how much time was needed for data analysis, which went beyond the funded period of the project. This was a particularly sensitive issue for **Iva**: *As an academic researcher, I am in a privileged position compared to Julie. Conducting research and writing publications is reflected in my workload, and thus I am getting paid for my research work even beyond the official funding for a research study. However, this is not the case when it comes to Julie, who conducted data analysis with me after the funding for this study ceased. I found some opportunities to pay Julie for her work, but it was not enough. Julie was happy to continue with data analysis and writing up the findings beyond what she was paid for, as she has been very passionate about the research work and the potential impact it can have, however, I felt terrible about this financial aspect of doing inclusive research.*

Despite this sensitive (and ethical) issue, the data analysis process was a new experience for Julie, and a positive experience for both Iva and Julie.

Julie: *I have just started to do data analysis. ... My previous experience with writing was with [another academic] – all we did were discussions and then [he] wrote it and I gave feedback to it before it was final. Working with you has been a lot different. It's positive, we work well together, we like our brainstorming together.*

Iva: *While I worked within inclusive research teams before, this has been a new experience for me too. Julie and I work very well together. Our collaboration developed gradually, from getting to know Julie in her work role at Self Advocacy Sydney, via Julie being a kind external help with recruitment in my studies focused on adults with learning disabilities and inviting Julie to guest lecture to my undergraduate and postgraduate students, to deciding that we would like to conduct research together on issues that are important to us. I think that this gradual getting to know each other in different aspects of our work (Julie's as a self-advocate, and mine as an academic researcher) helped to shape how we work as a team. Each and every decision is made together. Julie is a very independent and self-determined woman, so there is no feeling shy about our own opinion on either side. In my previous experience, I conducted inclusive research with co-researchers, many of whom lived in circumstances which did not allow for much self-determination or choice (like a group home). This was reflected in the way we worked together, with me and my academic colleagues shaping the approach and individual steps taken in these research studies. Julie and I work differently – we brainstorm how we want to do things together and we are not afraid to admit to each other when things don't work out. Being friends is also tremendously helpful. We know about each other's joys and sorrows, so to speak, which assists in mutual understanding and respect.*

What part(s) of the inclusive data analysis process felt 'sensitive' to you?

Iva: *The process of data analysis in terms of considerations of who has a power in this process was not sensitive for us. What we found sensitive, were the findings and what to do with them. This included issues of domestic abuse and violence, bullying, parenting rights and custody issues, and parenting skills and confidence. Some parents talked about a lack of self-confidence and accomplishments, and a few parents self-harmed as the way to deal with emotions, experiencing a lack of trust, people not caring for them, and feeling excluded. There was even a reference to feeling suicidal. These findings were – while not surprising – deeply disturbing.*

Julie: *The process wasn't sensitive; it was just what came out of it.*

Iva: *Government services are not supportive of parents with intellectual disabilities. Instead of helping parents to develop parenting skills, they tend to remove children from their custody. In cases of domestic violence, they would rather remove a child than help the mother and children.*

Julie: *Yet, all government services have to follow the National Standards for Disability Services, and Disability Services Act, which first came up in 1986.*

Iva: *How do you remember all of this?* [i.e. the year when the legislation came out].

Julie: *Because as a result of it I could speak up ... I guess we learnt that the things that came out were sensitive. What people brought up. ... People really didn't get the idea around peer support and there were a lot of issues that I thought would not come out so strongly (domestic violence and removal of children from custody). It is difficult as we can only report about it but cannot get involved. You can't go back .... It makes you want to jump right in and support, but you can't ... We could not intervene and support them with developing skills and getting support.*

Why did this feel sensitive?

Iva: *It was because of the feelings of helplessness that Julie and I had, listening to (both during the interviews and from the audio recordings when analysing the data) disturbing experiences of* domestic and family violence, as well as bullying experienced by the parents with intellectual disabilities.

Julie: *A lot of parenting and DOCS [Department of Community Services, Australia] taking away children – I don't think DOCS fully understand these parents. One mistake and a child is automatically taken away.*

Iva: *I remember how it triggered for you a memory of being in a maternity hospital with your first child and being afraid that she will be taken away from your custody, as it happened to another mother who was in the same room.*

Julie: *It gave me things to think about. It gives reflection, to look at what is happening to you ... If anybody is giving you information and it is not positive, you are going to feel towards that person. Especially if they are in a difficult situation. So, it depends what the person brings up. It can be something I can relate to as I went through it.*

Julie also brought up an important point of how having a voice, and having somebody to listen to your experiences, can have a cathartic effect.

Julie: *If you are good at interviewing and if you can bring something out, hopefully it can help them to feel better ... I have learnt how it is positive that people with intellectual disabilities can be open in interviews, because it is different in mental health.*

How did you deal with this?

Julie: *Well, we did reflections. We talked about it.*

After each interview that we listened to and made notes about, we had a discussion about the main points brought up by the parent and our thoughts about it. We recorded these reflections as part of our data. This was very helpful not only from the perspective of understanding the data, but also dealing with some distressing issues we heard about. Still, this did not lessen our feeling of limited opportunities we have as researchers to do something about the disturbing findings.

Julie: *I would love to do something about it. If it was in my role, I would take it on as part of the self-advocacy. But that is restricted by the numbers. [Self Advocacy Sydney is funded to support only up to 50 people with learning disabilities. Yet, this advocacy organisation covers the whole Sydney metropolitan area, and it is the only self-advocacy organisation in that region.]*

We agreed though, that publishing the findings and thus giving parents the voice, can assist in gradually changing their situation.

Julie: *Thanks to that there is more awareness and it gets to stakeholders so that they can use the information.*

What difference did doing the analysis together make to what you said about your research?

Julie: *We would have probably come up with same findings, but the way it was presented would be different. It was more positive doing it in teamwork than separately.*

Iva: *Each of us brought our knowledge and experiences to data analysis, and we also played on our strengths. It allowed us to understand the data on a deeper level.*

Julie: *Finally, I want to say something about the amazing positive experience of working together. Doing the research together in this way works. It demonstrates how a co-researcher and a professor can be able to achieve completing the data analysis as a team. In future, hopefully professors and* *co-researchers can be involved more to explore topics important to people with intellectual disabilities.*

Discussion

The examples detailed in this paper speak to sensitive research issues in a number of ways. While there are some differences between the two examples, there are also a number of striking similarities. First is the issue of time and resources. Despite good intentions and an awareness of what is required to de-stabilise traditional power dynamics between 'academic' and 'co-researchers', time and money place constraints on the inclusive data analysis process. Both teams identified that collaborative interpretation would have been deepened further had there been time for an additional stage of analysis. The pressures of resources and demands to publish meant this final round of review had to be abandoned. Both teams identified this as a limiting factor in terms of extending opportunities for co-researchers with learning disabilities to be more thoroughly engaged in interpretative work. Having time to consolidate and reflect is important to everyone, but particularly for co-researchers, who are not only contending with managing new skills of data analysis, but also immersing themselves in data that may be deeply personal. It is also important to acknowledge that research papers are usually written after a project's completion, when funding has ceased. It is not uncommon for co-researchers to participate in writing activities without payment; this has implications for the scope and depth of participation and raises significant ethical issues regarding unpaid labour. We need a 'slow rhythm of reflection and action' (Fals-Borda, 2013: 159) to undertake sensitive and robust participatory analysis, but the systems we work within do not always facilitate this.

The research teams both identified that participating in data analysis runs the risk of reviving past trauma. Both projects set out to address sensitive topics. But it is perhaps the immersion in that data, through the analysis process, that had a particular impact on co-researchers with learning disabilities. The data resonated with their own personal experiences, and that of people they knew. This reawakened memories of painful experiences. In Julie's case, it prompted a strong desire to reach out and help the participants with whom she had spoken. As a peer advocate, Julie provides practical and emotional support to people with learning disabilities in her 'day job'. But as a researcher, focused on revealing, understanding and interpreting experiences, she did not have the same freedoms to 'act' as she might do in her advocacy role. These are ethical dilemmas that all social researchers may face, but for those with lived experience of the issues at hand, the frustration of not being able to intervene may be especially difficult. This alerts us to the potential impact on researchers who engage in data analysis in spite of – or indeed *because* – it resonates so deeply with their own personal experiences.

The potential for reactivating trauma through the analysis process can be heightened further if academic colleagues do not listen sensitively to their co-researchers' responses. Paul said: '*In our team if someone in power hadn't listened when we were talking about the data it would be like a re-activator – a reminder – if someone ignores us and doesn't really take careful note of what we are trying to say it can reactivate the wound*'. His words remind us that the everyday practices of doing data analysis – who speaks/listens when, and how – can also have significant impacts on co-researchers; as powerful as the data itself. Power (im)balances were managed carefully on both teams, with Paul and Julie stating that that they felt listened to, respected and valued. In turn, they also engaged with diligence and attention. In this way, participatory data analysis becomes a mutual exchange in which all parties must demonstrate sensitivity and care both towards the data, and to each other.

Such sensitivity may be strengthened by the nature of the relationships within teams. In both projects reported here, the researchers were already known to one other. They had worked together previously, and had developed trust, rapport and knowledge of each other's lives. This appeared to support a context in which members of the team felt they could be open and frank about their interpretations. However, inclusive research teams will often find themselves working together for the first time. We argue that teams must therefore be prepared to invest time and energy in developing relationships, aiming to create a level of trust and psychological safety that seems to be crucial in enabling authentic collaborative sense-making to happen (Frankena et al., 2019). As Schwartz et al. (2019) have argued, this is likely to support the longer-term maintenance of inclusive research collaborations.

These two projects demonstrate that people with learning disabilities can learn to do data analysis and can benefit from the experience. In this way, we would argue that our research resists the 'incompetency discourses' (Nind, 2011) concerning people with learning disabilities that have dominated for so long. But perhaps more significantly, participatory data analysis in our projects also became a site for mutual learning. The process of acquiring skills and knowledge was a reciprocal one. The co-researchers learned how to code data; while the academic researchers learned how to view the data through a different lens. Drawing upon Gallacher and Gallagher's (2008) argument that we are all immature, developing and learning beings and researchers, Nind applies this to the inclusive data analysis process, suggesting it 'recognizes the vulnerability and potential of us all as we take risky steps forward' (Nind, 2011: 359). This mirrors our experiences, and reminds us to be sensitive to the opportunities for growth and development for all members of the inclusive team.

Both of the projects involved analysing qualitative data. While the data sets were not small (26 interview transcripts for the Australian study; a varied set of ethnographic data for the English project), our experiences do raise questions regarding how well the methods detailed in this article would support participatory data analysis when working with much larger data sets.

Finally, these projects show us that collaborative sense-making is possible. We can and should be striving towards 'entangled knowledge' (Paul). Participatory data analysis enables us to 'lean in', listen to and value different ways of understanding the world (Thrift, 2008). The two projects described in this paper show that members of the team attended to the stories, interactions, movements, pictures and words that emerged in the data in a multiplicity of ways. Participatory data analysis can help us to resist privileging those accounts that act as convenient 'tent holes and pegs' around which we can interpret the more complex and 'radically specific' accounts of people with learning disabilities (Graham, 2019). However, we acknowledge that in doing so, it might make our jobs of reporting to funders or policy-makers more difficult.

Conclusion

In this article, we argue that the pressures of being seen to do 'good science' and 'emancipatory inclusive research' can serve to silence us when it comes to describing our experiences of participatory data analysis. The desire to demonstrate rigour and efficiency in the academy can make it challenging to approach the sensitivities of collaborative interpretive work in an honest and reflective way. Anxieties of power take-overs when working within an inclusive paradigm can further constrain our confidence to approach the process of data analysis in an open way. But to engage with our colleagues on these matters is, as Sue argues above, a mark of respect. Reflecting on the difficulties together also offers the possibility of jointly constructed solutions. We are reassured and encouraged by Nind's contention that 'difficulties do not belong to people, but rather the interactive spaces between them' (Nind, 2011: 353). Our examples present two established research teams making genuine headway to negotiate the sensitivities of these interactive spaces. Both teams acknowledged imperfections in the process but their accounts demonstrate the potential for participatory data analysis to help us imagine and create new spaces for epistemological innovation.

We conclude our paper with a set of recommendations for researchers seeking to work inclusively on data analysis with people with learning disabilities or other marginalised groups:

1. Plan ahead – seek to get the additional resource that participatory data analysis will require, both in time and money;
2. Collect the data with an awareness that you will be analysing it inclusively;
3. Build trust between members of the research team – this takes time and effort and needs to be accounted for when developing research proposals;

4. Be imaginative – think of different ways to present data to support co-researchers to engage with the interpretive process;
5. Be prepared to be selective in the data you work on together;
6. Recognise, and celebrate the unique expertise everyone brings to the task;
7. Create opportunities for reflexive conversations about the process.

Disclosure statement

No potential conflict of interest was reported by the authors.

ORCID

Elizabeth Tilley http://orcid.org/0000-0003-4665-394X
Iva Strnadová http://orcid.org/0000-0002-8513-5400
Sue Ledger http://orcid.org/0000-0002-5927-6963
Julie Loblinzk http://orcid.org/0000-0003-1350-6089

References

Bigby, C., Frawley, P., & Ramcharan, P. (2014). Conceptualizing inclusive research with people with intellectual disability. *Journal of Applied Research in Intellectual Disabilities*, 27(1), 3–12. https://doi.org/10.1111/jar.12083

Braun, V., & Clarke, V. (2006). Using thematic analysis in psychology. *Qualitative Research in Psychology*, 3(2), 77–101. https://doi.org/10.1191/1478088706qp063oa

Brownlee-Chapman, C., Chapman, R., Eardley, C., Forster, S., Green, V., Graham, H., Harkness, E., Headon, K., Humphreys, P., Ingham, N., Ledger, S., May, V., Minnion, A., Richards, R., Tilley, L., & Townson, L. (2018). Between speaking out in public and being person-centred: Collaboratively designing an inclusive archive of learning disability history. *International Journal of Heritage Studies*, 24(8), 889–903. https://doi.org/10.1080/13527258.2017.1378901

Collings, S., Strnadová, I., Loblinzk, J., & Danker, J. (2019). The benefits and limits of peer support for mothers with intellectual disability experiencing domestic and family violence and child protection involvement. *Disability & Society*, 35(3), 413–434. https://doi.org/10.1080/09687599.2019.1647150

Deleuze, G., & Guattari, F. (1987). *A thousand plateaus. Capitalism and schizophrenia*. Continuum.

Fals-Borda, O. (2013). Action research in the convergence of disciplines. *International Journal of Action Research*, 9(2), 155–167.

Frankena, T., Naaldenberg, J., Tobi, H., van der Cruijsen, A., Jansen, H., Lantman, V. S., de Valk, H., Leusink, G., & Cardol, M. (2019). A membership categorization analysis of roles, activities and relationships in inclusive research conducted by co-researchers with intellectual disabilities. *Journal of Applied Research in Intellectual Disabilities*, 32(3), 719–729. https://doi.org/10.1111/jar.12567

Gallacher, L, Gallagher, M. (2008). Methodological immaturity in childhood research? Thinking through 'participatory methods'. *Childhood* 15(4): 499–516.

García Iriarte, E., O'Brien, P., McConkey, R., Wolfe, M., & O'Doherty, S. (2014). Identifying the key concerns of Irish persons with intellectual disability. *Journal of Applied Research in Intellectual Disabilities*, 27(6), 564–575. https://doi.org/10.1111/jar.12099

Graham, H. (2019). How the exhibition became co-produced: Attunement and participatory ontologies for museums. In P. Bjerregaard (Ed.), *Exhibitions as research: Experimental methods in museums* (pp. 181–194). Routledge.

Hoggart, L. (2017). Collaboration or collusion? Involving research users in applied social research. *Women's Studies International Forum*, 61, 100–107. https://doi.org/10.1016/j.wsif.2016.08.005

Ledger, S., Earle, S., Tilley, E., & Walmsley, J. (2016). Contraceptive decision- making and women with learning disabilities. *Sexualities*, 19(5–6), 698–724. https://doi.org/10.1177/1363460715620576

Mooney, F., Rafique, N., & Tilly, L. (2019). Getting involved in the community—What stops us? Findings from an inclusive research project. *British Journal of Learning Disabilities*, 47(4), 241–246. https://doi.org/10.1111/bld.12283

Nind, M, Seale, J (2009) Concepts of access for people with learning difficulties: towards a shared understanding. *Disability & Society* 24(3), 273–287.

Nind, M. (2011). Participatory data analysis: A step too far? *Qualitative Research*, 11(4), 349–363. https://doi.org/10.1177/1468794111404310

Nind, M. (2014). *What is inclusive research?* Bloomsbury.

Roets, G., Goodley, D., & Van Hove, G. (2007). Narratives in a nutshell: Sharing hopes, fears, and dreams with self-advocates. *Intellectual and Developmental Disabilities*, 45(5), 323–334. https://doi.org/10.1352/0047-6765(2007)45[323:NIANSH]2.0.CO;2

Schwartz, A., Kramer, J., Cohn, E., & McDonald, K. (2019). "That felt like real engagement": Fostering and maintain inclusive research collaborations with individuals with intellectual disability. *Qualitative Health Research*, 30(2), 236–249. https://doi.org/10.1177/1049732319869620

Seale, J., Nind, M., Tilley, E., & Chapman, R. (2015). Negotiating a third space for participatory research with people with learning disabilities: An examination of boundaries and spatial practices. *The European Journal of Social Science Research*, 28(4), 483–497. https://doi.org/10.1080/13511610.2015.1081558

Serrell, B. (2015) Exhibit Labels: An Interpretive Approach, 2nd edn. Lanham, MD: Rowman & Littlefield

Stevenson, M. (2014). Participatory data analysis alongside co-researchers who have Down Syndrome. *Journal of Applied Research in Intellectual Disabilities*, 27(1), 23–33. https://doi.org/10.1111/jar.12080

Strnadová, I., Collings, S., Loblinzk, J., & Danker, J. (2019). Parents with intellectual disabilities and their perspective of peer support: "It depends on how they give it". *Journal of Applied Research in Intellectual Disabilities*, 32(4), 879–889. https://doi.org/10.1111/jar.12579

Strnadová, I., Cumming, T. M., Knox, M., Parmenter, T. R., & Lee, H. M. (2015). Perspectives on life, wellbeing, and ageing by older women with intellectual disability. *Journal of Intellectual and Developmental Disability*, 40(3), 275–285. https://doi.org/10.3109/13668250.2015.1043873

Strnadová, I., & Walmsley, J. (2017). Peer-reviewed articles on inclusive research: Do co-researchers with intellectual disabilities have a voice? *Journal of Applied Research in Intellectual Disabilities* 31(1), 132–141. https://doi.org/10.1111/jar.12378

Thrift, N. (2008). *Non-representational theory*. Routledge.

Walmsley, J., Ledger, S., Z J, A., Christian, P., & Tilley, L. (2018). *MADHOUSE re: Exit:Evaluation summary*. Access all Areas.

Walmsley, J., Strnadová, I., & Johnson, K. (2018). The added value of inclusive research. *Journal of Applied Research in Intellectual Disabilities*, 31(5), 751–759. https://doi.org/10.1111/jar.12431

Williams, V., Ponting, L., Ford, K., & Rudge, P. (2009). Skills for support: Personal assistants and people with learning disabilities. *British Journal of Learning Disabilities*, 38(1), 59–67. https://doi.org/10.1111/j.1468-3156.2009.00570.x

Ziebland, S., & McPherson, A. (2006). Making sense of qualitative data analysis: An introduction with illustrations from DIPEx (personal experiences of health and illness). *Medical Education*, 40(5), 405–414. https://doi.org/10.1111/j.1365-2929.2006.02467.x

Difficult data: reflections on making knowledge claims in a turmoil of competing subjectivities, sensibilities and sensitivities

Lesley Hoggart

ABSTRACT
Much care has been paid to reflexivity, including considering emotional sensitivities in relation to face-to-face interviews. However, less attention has been paid to the impact of sensitivities on the process of data analysis and the presentation of research findings. This paper focuses on what constitutes 'the data' to be analysed, who analyses and interprets the data, what is silenced and what is made public, and what this might mean for feminist research practice in areas considered to be 'sensitive'. It examines these issues by focusing on research on abortion decision-making in which the views and emotions of the researcher were profoundly challenged by women's constructions of narratives containing a theme of abortion regret. The paper demonstrates how theoretical perspectives – in this case, feminist standpoint theory – can be used in sensitive research, to allow the researcher to resolve such tensions by providing a means through which greater attention can be paid to the context of participants' narratives.

Introduction

This research paper adds nuance to understandings of sensitive research through an exploration of the emotion of distress when conducting research on abortion. The distress was experienced by both the participant and the interviewer (myself), but in very different ways. The participant's distress was visibly shown through sorrow and verbally expressed through guilt. I experienced empathy with her sorrow, but my distress was dominated by anger, an emotion rarely discussed in research literature, and an emotion concealed in the research encounter.

At the heart of this paper is a reflexive exercise about a researcher–participant interaction that occurred during a qualitative interview for a research project on young women and unintended pregnancy and involved a participant – a young mother – discussing her experiences of an abortion, during which she repeatedly talked about 'killing my baby'. Whilst I was upset at her expressions of distress and guilt, I was also distressed and angry that she should feel this way. Maybe rather naively, I had not anticipated such a virulent reaction to her recent abortion. Upon considerable reflection, I understood that I had not challenged my own assumptions adequately and that I experienced intersecting tensions that related to three identities brought into the research. As a feminist pro-choice activist, I had spent many years campaigning for abortion rights and was also aware that 'killing my baby' is a core element of anti-abortion discourse and rhetoric. As an applied social researcher, I was seeking to maintain a professional distance and minimise subjectivity. And, as a feminist researcher committed to grounding knowledge in women's experiences and voices, the dilemma that I knew would come later was how to interpret and represent these unwelcome data.

I begin by outlining relevant methodological issues: in particular, sensitivity and reflexivity; emotions and empathy; and subjectivities. I then describe the research encounter, and the consequent data analysis dilemma. Finally, methodological implications of these issues are discussed, focusing on the possibility for multiple interpretations of the data, for competing subjectivities and for the potential of feminist standpoint to resolve these dilemmas.

Sensitivity, reflexivity and emotions

Researcher reflexivity is mostly concerned with how researcher–participant interactions unfold, and the implications of this for knowledge generation (Mao & Feldman, 2019). Whilst establishing rapport and encouraging open dialogue is seen as critical in qualitative interviews (Charmaz, 2014; Rapley, 2004), it is widely acknowledged that the researcher does not remain neutral in this process. Qualitative researchers actively shape the whole of the research process, constructing the collection, selection and interpretation of data (Finlay & Gough, 2008; Finlay, 2008). Reflexivity is arguably particularly relevant in areas viewed as sensitive research, for sensitive research may invoke researcher emotions that can affect knowledge generation.

Reflexivity can thus take different forms, one of which Finlay (2008) describes as 'intersubjective reflection' which captures the emotional investment that researchers have in the research. This involves recognising qualitative interviews as inter-subjective emotional encounters, as well as allowing researchers to ensure that they act in accordance with those values (Rodríguez-Dorans, 2018).

Feminist research in practice: embracing subjectivities

The 'myth' of value-free research has long been challenged by feminist researchers' values with interpretations being acknowledged as central to the research process (Roberts, 1981). Similarly, feminist research has long advocated reflexivity as an essential practice that may facilitate greater understanding of research encounters as social encounters (Ramazanoglu & Holland, 2002).

It has also been argued that feminist researchers should do more than simply reveal themselves, through reflexive research, but openly reflect on the significance of their own identities for their research, indicating how this may have influenced their behaviour in the field (Ryan-flood & Gill, 2010). This can be extended to data analysis and dissemination, for the researcher is an active interpreter of what is heard and then reported from the interview (Johnson & Rowlands, 2012). All interpretations and voices are thus subject to conflict and dispute (Denzin, 1997).

Feminist research that invokes an open acknowledgement of subjectivity has been subject to considerable scholarship (Ramazanoglu & Holland, 2002). The feminist critique of positivism has involved developing a critical awareness of research processes, with a particular focus on researcher/researched relationships. This entails a challenge to the positivist perception of an objective, neutral observer who leaves the field without influencing the data. This has been characterised as a myth (see for example, Miller et al., 2012; Ribbens & Edwards, 1998). An interesting alternative approach is presented by Rolls and Reif (2006) who argue that if researchers increase their own reflexive capacity this can increase their understanding of the phenomena and thus improve objectivity.

Undertaking applied social research invariably involves encounters with positivism, as evidence-based policy and practice does not easily accommodate competing subjectivities. It is a particularly hazardous activity for feminist academics who wish to remain true to feminist principles whilst simultaneously seeking to influence policy and practice (Gillies & Alldred, 2012). Bringing together feminist political struggle and research has long been a significant strand in feminist work (Henwood et al., 1998), but the various sensitivities involved in doing this have rarely been acknowledged. This paper focuses on political sensitivity and clashing value frameworks.

Standpoint feminism rejects the view of objectivity as 'value-free' yet makes the claim that feminist research may be more objective than androcentric traditional research because it produces less distorted knowledge (Harding, 1987). Standpoint feminism further makes the case that, because women's lives and roles in almost all societies are significantly different from men's, women hold a different type of knowledge. Harding (1987) argued that knowledge grounded in women's experience of struggles against male domination can produce a more complete knowledge of gendered social lives than that based only on men's experiences. Feminist standpoint theory therefore sought to develop new feminist knowledge of gendered social lives through women speaking their truth (Hartsock, 1997).

Feminist standpoint theory does make knowledge claims, albeit partial, and yet political, and thus remains an attractive methodological approach for feminist political activists who are also engaged in applied social research. This was the methodology adopted in the research project I am reflecting upon now. In that project the original research team attempted to ground the knowledge produced in women's experiences, and produce research that would be politically useful, as well as policy-relevant. As I show in the account below, this approach was to prove extremely challenging.

The research encounter

In subjective accounts of fieldwork, qualitative researchers are concerned to explore how their biographies interact with their interpretations (Finlay, 2008), and this is what I will do here. The relevant biographical information concerns my political activism from the 1980s onwards, to defend and improve abortion policy and provision in response to anti-choice campaigns that had sought to limit abortion. An important self-motivation for undertaking research on abortion was to understand what could help improve women's experience of abortion in the UK.

The research encounter presented here occurred during a research project on teenage pregnancy (Hoggart, 2012; Hoggart and Phillips 2011). In one of the early interviews, I interviewed Cara (pseudonym). Cara had experienced what she described as three unintended pregnancies: the first at 16 ended in miscarriage. The second time she was pregnant, 2 months after her miscarriage, she had considered the option of having an abortion but decided to proceed with the pregnancy, a decision she explained by drawing on the concept of responsibility: *'in my mind I was like, if I'm a big enough girl to lie down with a man, then I'm big enough to take the responsibility'*. When I interviewed Cara, 3 years after becoming a mother, she had recently had an abortion. When we talked about her decision-making for her most recent pregnancy, her narrative, whilst making it clear that it had been a difficult decision, was initially focused on her own social and economic circumstances, incorporating those of her daughter and current partner (not her daughter's father):

> *I'm still going college, he's working, there's not really enough space for a baby, that's the only reason why I had the abortion, because it wasn't right and I didn't want to bring another baby in the world not working and not being settled, not knowing what I was going to do with my own life. I thought it would be unfair*

This complex mixture of influencing factors (considerations of child(ren), partner, own education, living conditions, own future life) is a common theme in abortion research (Rowlands, 2008). What is not so common, but this may be because it is not reported, is what Cara told me a little later in the interview when she was talking about her abortion experience:

> *I'm not ever going to do it again, it's a horrible experience, like gonna be hanging over my head for a long, long time, that I killed a baby, the baby didn't ask to be here but the baby's here, I should have kept the baby and then I'm thinking I couldn't think like that because I'm just going to bring myself down and I'm going to hurt even more, I'm gonna regret it, I'm regretting it and I just lost my mind for a while.*

Within this quote there is a narrative theme of regret, a theme that is central to anti-abortion propaganda; and pro-choice political activists are wary of the concept of post-abortion regret. I was simultaneously empathising with and upset for Cara, but also angry and upset that she could feel this way; as well as immediately dismayed by the dilemma I knew the research team on this project would face: what would we do with these data? It was a theme that was repeated, though not so intensely, in a few other interviews.

My subjective response of shock and anger was repressed. Two people in any kind of conversation affect each other, in ways that may not be fully understood (Bourne and Robson 2015; Bondi, 2014). My practice had always been to seek to minimise the extent to which my own views may affect participants' responses. Maybe this was why I had also failed to prepare for the possibility of such a clash of subjectivities through a critical consideration of the potential for conflicting views, a consideration that should have been a key element of feminist research practice. Unfortunately, I was not only a feminist researcher in this project. Indeed, as an applied social researcher under pressure to conform to what is seen as professional practice (Gillies & Alldred, 2012), I had striven to appear neutral as was my usual practice and did not disclose my pro-choice sympathies or activism in any overt way. It is possible that my efforts to appear neutral and non-judgemental and not disclose my own values on abortion enabled Cara to be honest, but equally she may have felt that this was an expected response. The recruitment process may also have played a role, as participants had been recruited (in the first instance) by abortion providers using materials that simply stated that we wanted to learn about their experiences and hear their voices, in order to improve services in the future. Whatever uncertainties remain about factors influencing Cara's narrative, and it is important to acknowledge there are invariably such uncertainties, what is clear is that the data were unwelcome to the researchers.

Researchers have a role as interpreters and co-constructors (with the research participants) of knowledge (Hesse-Biber & Leavy, 2007). Even whilst accepting that researchers construct research narratives (Gill, 1998), and that multiple readings of the same data are entirely possible (Seu, 1998), the dilemma remained: how to represent the data? We had given participants the opportunity to relate their experiences and express their views, but how should we validate those views? Whilst researchers may acknowledge subjectivity and the role of interpretation what does this mean, and how far do you take it? To draw on interpretive 'freedom' and ignore what was a significant theme would surely be an abuse of interpretive privilege only made possible by the power position of the researcher.

Discussion

For this particular project, this research moment encapsulated a theme that appeared to challenge an assumption of our feminist standpoint methodology: that grounding knowledge in women's abortion experiences could produce research that may be politically useful, in this case for pro-choice activism. This research might instead be politically useful to anti-abortion activists.

An immediate issue concerned interpretation and representation in the research report. This is not an uncommon issue for feminists undertaking applied social research, where policy-makers are expecting 'objective' evidence. (Willot, 1998). As reflexivity acknowledges viewing reality as a matter of competing interpretations, it is inevitably problematic for applied social researchers because the subjective knowledge may be seen to undermine the value of social research. This is confounded by the overriding tension between being a researcher and being a feminist. As a feminist, you want to listen and value women's voices, but what if – as shown in this research – you fundamentally disagree with the direction of travel that those voices may be pushing the research. Additionally, as a feminist activist, it is not really enough to give voice; you would seek that voice to guide your political action. The issue that we faced as a research team was how to represent this participant's experience and views in a situation in which the narrative could be co-opted by anti-choice activists.

Ultimately, we sought to retain our initial objective of staying close to the 'reality' of our participants and therefore began to explore the emergent theme of immorality ('killing my baby') in our analysis (Hoggart, 2012). We did not want to repress Cara's views and feelings – her subjectivity – in favour of our own, and we were also aware that though this was not a dominant theme, neither was it an outlier. Our analysis recognised the importance of moral decision-making for the research participants, but we also acknowledged that this focus can be problematic for some women who do not feel comfortable about their abortion, as indeed it had been for Cara. This led to recommendations around challenging abortion stigma (a sense of abortion as morally wrong), and reframing abortion as a sexual health issue in Sex and Relationships Education (SRE) rather than an opportunity to discuss moral dilemmas in Religious Education (RE) (Hoggart, Phillips, Birch, Koffman, 2010)[2].

Some time later, following the completion of the project, and further reflection which was enabled by a shift in career away from working for an applied research institute, I was able to return to the data to explore this clash of emotions further. I had retained an anxiety that we had privileged our 'truth', and not really engaged with the emotions of the research participants. The value of analysing emotions in research has been increasingly acknowledged: 'When strong emotional reactions emerge during the research process, these can be used to understand the researched phenomenon' (Rodríguez-Dorans, 2018, p. 748). I was curious to explore how this might be done utilising feminist standpoint methodology.

Historically, a fundamental critique of the Standpoint claim that feminist research may be more objective than androcentric traditional research because it produces less distorted knowledge (Harding, 1987), was that this is misguided; and that feminists should privilege subjectivity over objectivity; emotionality over rationality; and experience over experiments (Stanley & Wise, 1983, 1993).[1] Feminist standpoint theory continues to challenge positivist claims to neutrality and objectivity in research, whilst continuing to privilege the idea of research subjects as 'knowers' (Intemann, 2010). It has, however, become more grounded. Whilst arguing that research involving marginalised groups should begin with the experiences of marginalised groups (Harding, 2008), feminist standpoint also increasingly foregrounds the influence of social and cultural contexts (Harding, 2004; Intemann, 2010). There is thus a close connection to understanding that qualitative research is embedded in complex historical and cultural contexts (Denzin, 2010), and that narratives are socially and historically situated (Jackson, 1998; Squire, 1998). Finally, feminist standpoint acknowledges that politics are intimately involved in research (Harding, 2004). Indeed, Hartsock (2004) argued that because feminists are involved in political activity, it is in their interests to strive towards truth in their research projects, as flawed research may precipitate ineffective political activity.

These insights have been crucial to my own work on abortion over the last few years. I have consciously developed an analytical approach based on an exploration of abortion-related stigma that is socially located and, crucially, includes analysis of the negative emotions – including distress and regret – that might accompany abortion experiences. Examples include theorising the ways in which young women's moral anxieties about abortion may negatively affect their pregnancy decision-making (Hoggart, 2012); and arguing that academic research on abortion should engage with the issue of emotions, particularly post-abortion emotions (Hoggart, 2018). This shift in direction would most likely not have been achieved without dwelling on that emotional moment and engaging with feminist standpoint theory in a curious and flexible manner. Continuing with the reflexivity at the heart of this paper, however, leads me to think again about whose truth is being represented. For whilst Cara's voice has been represented, and that the reflexive approach has affected the knowledge created, it is difficult to deny that the interpretation remains that of the researcher.

Note

1. Feminist standpoint has also been criticised for its reification of a single, universal feminist standpoint, which allows for the continued marginalisation of a range of perspectives (including for example, black, lesbian, post-colonial, or working-class perspectives) (hooks, 1990; Stanley & Wise, 1993). Recently, such different perspectives have been brought together through the development of intersectionality theory which recognises

the multiple intersections in people's lives, including race, gender, skin tone, accent, education level, migration status, language and other life situations (Crenshaw, 2001), and feminist standpoint too has developed. Patricia Hill Collins first introduced the idea of Black feminist epistemology to standpoint feminism, arguing that it derives from the personal experience of Black women dealing with both racism and sexism. Collins (1990) went on to utilize the concept of intersectionality originally developed by Crenshaw (2001) to theorise simultaneous overlapping of multiple forms of oppression, such as race, class, gender, sexuality and nation as intersecting, mutually constructing systems of power.

2. This report repeated the title from the research commissioned. Since publishing the report we have understood that the term 'repeat abortion' is stigmatising of people who have more than one abortion, and we regret the use of it.

Disclosure statement

No potential conflict of interest, beyond that discussed in the paper, was reported by the author.

ORCID

Lesley Hoggart http://orcid.org/0000-0002-4786-7950

References

Bondi, L. (2014). Understanding feelings: Engaging with unconscious communication and embodied knowledge. *Emotion, Space and Society*, 2014,*10*, 44–54. https://doi.org/10.1016/j.emospa.2013.03.009

Bourne, A., & Robson, M. (2015). Participants' reflections on being interviewed about risk and sexual behaviour: Implications for collection of qualitative data on sensitive topics. *International Journal of Social Research Methodology*, *18*(1), 1056–1116. https://doi.org/10.1080/13645579.2013.860747

Charmaz, K. (2014). *Constructing grounded theory*. Sage.

Collins, P. H. (1990). *Black feminist thought: Knowledge, consciousness and the politics of empowerment*. Routledge.

Crenshaw, K. W. (2001). Mapping the margins: Intersectionality, identity politics and violence against women of colour. *Sanford Law Review*, *43*(6), 1241–1299. https://doi.org/10.2307/1229039

Denzin, N. K. (1997). *Interpretive ethnography: Ethnographic practices for the 21st century*. Sage.

Denzin, N. K. (2010). *The qualitative mandate*. Left Coast Press.

Finlay, L. (2008). The reflexive journey: Mapping multiple routes. In L. Finlay & B. Gough (Eds.), *Reflexivity: A practical guide for researchers in health and social sciences* (pp. 3–20). Blackwell.

Finlay, L., & Gough, B. (eds). (2008). *Reflexivity: A practical guide for researchers in health and social sciences*. Blackwell Science.

Gill, R. (1998). Dialogues and differences: Writing, reflexivity and the crisis of representation. In Henwood, K., Griffin, C. & Phoenix, A. (Eds.), *Standpoints and differences: Essays in the practice of feminist psychology* (pp. 18–44). Sage Publications.

Gillies, V., & Alldred, P. (2012). The ethics of intention: Research as a political tool. In T. Miller, M. Birch, M. Mauthner, & J. Jessop (Eds.), *Ethics in qualitative research* (2nd ed.) (pp. 43–60). Sage Publications.

Harding, S. (ed). (1987). *Feminism and methodology*. Open University Press.

Harding, S. (2004). A socially relevant philosophy of science? Resources from standpoint theory's controversiality. *Hypatia*, *19*(1), 25–47. https://doi.org/10.1111/j.1527-2001.2004.tb01267.x

Harding, S. (2008). *Sciences from below: Feminisms, postcolonialities, and modernities*. Duke University Press.

Hartsock, N. (1997). Comment on Hekman's 'truth and method: Feminist standpoint theory revisited': Truth or justice?'. *Signs*, *22*(21), 367–374. DOI:10.1086/495161

Hartsock, N. (2004). The Feminist Standpoint: Developing the ground for a specifically feminist historical materialism. In S. Harding (Ed.), *The feminist standpoint theory reader: Intellectual and political controversies* (pp. 35–54). Routledge.

Henwood, K., Griffin, C., & Phoenix, A. (eds). (1998). *Standpoints and Differences: Essays in the practice of feminist psychology*. Sage Publications.

Hesse-Biber, & Leavy. (2007). *Feminist research practice: A primer*. Sage.

Hoggart, L. (2012). "I'm pregnant ... what am I going to do?" An examination of value judgements and moral frameworks in teenage pregnancy decision making. *Health, Risk & Society*, *14*(6), 533–549. https://doi.org/10.1080/13698575.2012.706263

Hoggart, L. (2018). Moral dilemmas and abortion decision-making: Lessons learnt from abortion research in England and Wales. *Global Pubic Health.14*(1), 1–8.https://doi.org/10.1080/17441692.2018.1474482

Hoggart, Lesley; Phillips, Joan; Birch, Angela and Koffman, Ofra (2010). Young people in London: abortion and repeat abortion. Government Office For London, London.

hooks, B. (1990). *Yearning: Race, gender and cultural politics*. South End Press.

Intemann, K. (2010). 25 years of feminist empiricism and standpoint theory: Where are we now? *Hypatia*, *25*(4), 778–795. https://doi.org/10.1111/j.1527-2001.2010.01138.x

Jackson, S. (1998). Telling stories: Memory, narrative and experience in feminist research and theory. In Henwood, K., Griffin, C. & Phoenix, A. (Eds.), *Standpoints and differences: Essays in the practice of feminist psychology* (pp. 45–64). Sage Publications.

Johnson, J. M., & Rowlands, T. (2012). The interpersonal dynamics of in-depth interviewing. InGubrium, J. F., Holstein, J. A., Marvasti, A. B., & McKinney, K. D.(Eds.), *The SAGE handbook of interview research*. (pp. 99–114). Sage.

Mao, J., & Feldman, E. (2019). Class matters: Interviewing across social class boundaries. *International Journal of Social Research Methodology*, *22*(2), 125–137. https://doi.org/10.1080/13645579.2018.1535879

Miller, T., Birch, M., Mauthner, M., & Jessop, J. (eds). (2012). *Ethics in qualitative research* (2nd ed.). Sage.

Ramazanoglu, C., & Holland, J. (2002). *Feminist methodology: Challenges and choice*. Sage Publications.

Rapley, T. (2004). 'Interviews'. In C. Seale, G. Giampietro, J. F. Gubrium, & D. Silverman (Eds.), *Qualitative research practice* (pp. 15–33). Sage Publications.

Ribbens, J., & Edwards, R. (1998). *Feminist dilemmas in qualitative research*. Sage Publications.

Roberts, H. (ed). (1981). *Doing feminist research*. Routledge.

Rodríguez-Dorans, E. (2018). Reflexivity and ethical research practice while interviewing on sexual topics. *International Journal of Social Research Methodology*, *21*(6), 747–760. https://doi.org/10.1080/13645579.2018.1490980

Rolls, L. and Relf, M. (2006) Bracketing interviews: addressing methodological challenges in qualitative interviewing in palliative care and bereavement. Mortality, *11*(3), 286–305.

Rowlands, S. (2008). The decision to opt for abortion. *Journal of Family Planning and Reproductive Health Care, 34* (3), 175–180. https://doi.org/10.1783/147118908784734765

Ryan-flood, R., & Gill, R. (2010). *Secrecy and silence in the research process: Feminist reflection*. Routledge.

Seu, I. B. (1998). Shameful women: Accounts of withdrawal and silence. In Henwood, K., Griffin, C. & Phoenix, A. (Eds.), *Standpoints and differences: Essays in the practice of feminist psychology* (pp. 135–155). Sage Publications.

Squire, C. (1998). Women and Men talk about aggression: An analysis of narrative genre. In Henwood, K., Griffin, C. & Phoenix, A. (Eds.), *Standpoints and Differences: Essays in the practice of feminist psychology* (pp. 65–90). Sage Publications.

Stanley, L., & Wise, S. (1983). *Breaking out: Feminist consciousness and feminist research*. Routledge.

Stanley, L., & Wise, S. (1993). *Breaking out again: Feminist epistemology and ontology*. Routledge.

Willot, S. (1998). An outsider within: A feminist doing research with men. In Henwood, K., Griffin, C. & Phoenix, A. (Eds.), *Standpoints and differences: Essays in the practice of feminist psychology* (pp. 174–190). Sage Publications.

Part Three

'The ideal sensitive researcher'

Reflexivity, internalisation
and the cost to self?

Internalising 'sensitivity': vulnerability, reflexivity and death research(ers)

Erica Borgstrom and Julie Ellis

ABSTRACT
Research about dying is viewed as inherently sensitive because of how death is perceived in many societies. Such framing assumes participants are 'vulnerable' and at risk of 'harm' from research. Simultaneously, with increasing recognition of the importance of reflexivity, researchers can become (deeply) preoccupied with their actions and experiences in the field. Whilst reflexivity is often described as a helpful process, in this paper we consider when introspection becomes problematic and even harmful for death researchers, in both a professional and personal sense. Identifying a process we call 'internalising sensitivity' the paper describes our own experiences of working *and* living with the pervasive ethical notions of sensitivity, vulnerability, risk and harm. We argue that these discourses can get 'under the skin' of researchers in that they impact researchers intellectually, emotionally, and physically, and this in turns affects their relationship with the research process and their place within, and beyond it.

Introduction

'Much has been said on what the researchers must do to avoid harming participants ... but less is written of the potential risk of harms for the researcher who studies sensitive topics and uses sensitive methods' (De Laine, 2000, p. 75).

The starting point for this paper is that, whilst much has been written about conducting 'sensitive research' with some explicit focus on the topics of death and dying (Goodrum & Keys, 2007; Mckenzie et al., 2017), there is still limited discussion about the impact this has on the researcher (Burles, 2017; Visser, 2017; Woodthorpe, 2007). Here we unpack how framing death research as *inherently sensitive*, and therefore involving *vulnerable* participants and requiring the use of reflexive approaches, can lead to experiences of uncertainty, vulnerability, and harm for the researcher. By sharing our own experiences, we seek to expand theorisations of researcher vulnerability, beyond the primary discussions about personal safety and emotionality, to examine how the ethical discourses we operate within, and our reflexive attempts to navigate these, might contribute to our own vulnerability as researchers.

As scholars working in death-related contexts we recognise that our research is framed by other researchers, ethics committees and funders as inherently 'sensitive' (Addington-Hall, 2002). This very idea is deeply pervasive in encounters we have about our work. For instance, when we identify ourselves as death researchers, when we notice how similar research is discussed in academic spaces, and in particular when we have to navigate through the various concerns of ethics committees. Because of these assumptions, the participants in our research are considered de facto 'vulnerable' and at risk of potential harm. Whilst this is not uncommon in projects deemed to be 'sensitive' (Lee, 1993), it does not adequately represent how we view our research and its participants: these are not the ontological assumptions that we make about studying the end of life.

As social scientists, we appreciate how discourses are constructed and shape the realities in which we can operate (Hacking, 1999). Indeed, scholars have begun to challenge assumptions about 'sensitive research' arguing these can be reifying and stigmatising for participants, and (to a limited extent) researchers (Lee, 1993; Liamputtong, 2007). In this paper, we extend these critical discussions in a novel direction by examining how the discursive construction of sensitivity, which draws extensively on ethical notions of risk, vulnerability and harm, can affect the researcher, and in turn, the research they produce. The first section of the paper discusses this discursive context. Then, through reflexive analysis of personal examples, we show how these ideas are internalised by researchers and can feel weighty in intellectual, emotional, and embodied ways. We refer to these feelings as 'internalising sensitivity' and our examples explore the effects of this on academic and personal life. The final section problematises the assumption that reflexivity is inherently and always good. The wider salience of our observations for researchers doing 'sensitive' work and 'practicing' reflexivity both within and beyond death studies is also considered.

Background

'Sensitive' death studies and its 'vulnerable' participants

There are some topics that are presumed intrinsically 'sensitive' to study (Lee, 1993; Sieber & Stanely, 1988). Death in England (and in many other countries) is an obvious example. Although researchers have critiqued the label of 'sensitive research' for several decades now (Dickson-Swift et al., 2007; Lee, 1993), work related to death, dying, and end-of-life care is frequently categorised as sensitive in funding proposals, ethics applications, publications, and presentations. We suggest these generalised ideas about sensitivity derive in part from a negative, problems-based view of death and dying (Kellehear, 2009). Often when people talk about death research as sensitive, they do so in general terms rather than stating explicitly *what* makes it so. As Lee and Renzetti (1990) note, the term 'sensitive topic' is frequently used in a common-sense way without being defined. When concerns are articulated they tend to centre upon death's emotionality (Cain, 2012; Cook & Bosley, 2007), or the fact that dying participants have limited, 'precious' time (Barnett, 2001) and reduced capacity to consent due to illness (Gysels et al., 2013). Death (and talking about it) is also considered 'taboo' in many countries (Lee, 2008). Even if sociological literature has problematized this idea (Kellehear, 1984), the label 'sensitive' may reflect generalised anxiety about a perceived social stigma associated with death. It points to an academic narrative about doing death research, which draws on societal discourses and expectations about what studying death 'is like', even if existing research literature speaks to a more nuanced way of understanding the field.

Moreover, it is not uncommon for the terms 'sensitive' and 'vulnerable' to be used interchangeably to describe death research, or other topics deemed to be 'sensitive' (Liamputtong, 2007). Since it is presumed this research is 'sensitive', there is a logical extension that its (human) subjects are essentially 'vulnerable'. For example, ethics committees are frequently concerned about how researchers will manage and respond to participants' emotions during interviews (Borgstrom, 2018). The most common presumption is that talking about death will upset participants; and whilst not unreasonable to have this concern, informal discussions with members of ethics committees indicate that similar fears may not always be extended with quite such apprehension to other kinds of 'sensitive' research topics. This vulnerability – or potential to cause 'harm' by initialising 'upsetting' conversations – is framed as a 'risk' inherent in this kind of research and something that *responsible* researchers are expected to mitigate and manage.

Vulnerability as problematic for research

Following the 'reflexive turn' in the social sciences, researcher emotions have, to some extent, become a focus of analysis (Parvez, 2018). Less attention has been paid to researcher *vulnerability* specifically and its methodological implications. This is despite those who research 'sensitive topics' feeling personally stigmatised by the 'taint' of their area of study (Hockey, 2007). Researchers can also be exposed to risks presented by their research methods (Blackman, 2007) and a burgeoning literature testifies that they experience a range of challenging emotions engendered by their work (Fincham et al., 2008; Hubbard et al., 2001; Woodby et al., 2011; Woodthorpe, 2007). It is now recognised that feelings can shape the data researchers generate, the course of their analysis (Mauthner & Doucet, 2003) and any subsequent conclusions they make (DeLuca & Maddox, 2016). Yet, often researchers are expected to conceal, deny, or demonstrate how they will minimise their vulnerability. Since consciousness of vulnerability can permeate the researcher's interactions with their participants, one's own vulnerability is considered an impediment to access and data collection (De Laine, 2000). Vulnerability of both participants and of researchers is therefore often framed in the research literature as problematic for the wider research endeavour as well as for individuals. Even in disciplines which seek to foreground human experience, acknowledging and exposing the vulnerability of the researcher can be difficult and problematic for the research process, and one's career (Behar, 1996; Visser, 2017).

In procedural ethics (Guillemin & Gillam, 2004), the vulnerability of participants and the *safety* (rarely 'vulnerability') of researchers is also deemed problematic by committees. The committees and their documentary processes are essentially concerned with identifying risk – the likelihood and extremity of which is considered greater in 'sensitive' contexts where participants are understood to be more vulnerable. Thus, the underpinning rationale for ethical governance is the procedural avoidance of harm caused by research studies and indeed, by extension, the people carrying out this work. Its association with harm and also exploitation means that vulnerability is largely considered as a negative thing and something to be avoided, mitigated and managed.

By means of its processes of formalisation, procedural ethics also gives the impression that issues like 'sensitivity' and 'vulnerability' can be rendered 'knowable'. It implies that many potential risks, harms and uncertainties can be managed in linear, foreseeable ways via the spelling out of protocol, delineation of categories and rarefication of the research process (Van den Hoonaard & Hamilton, 2016). Although some researchers have been critical of the excessive and inappropriate application of notions of 'harm' from biomedical science to research in the social sciences (Burr & Reynolds, 2010; Dingwall, 2006; Haggerty, 2004), these ideas have been exponentially pervasive and have significantly shifted attitudes towards the regulation of all research involving human participants. This places a weight of responsibility on researchers to be able to *operationalise* discourses such as sensitivity – to turn these ideas into knowable quantities, situations and scenarios in the context of their proposed work. They are required to make (convincing) plans for how they will eliminate or at least significantly reduce the likelihood that 'bad', unethical things will happen. By extension, this process can feel like a personal measure of the robustness of one's own moral sensibilities. Frequently within death studies, reflexivity is cited as a methodological tool that can be deployed for negotiating these issues (Visser, 2017). And whilst this has led to a useful recognition of the possibilities for disjuncture between procedural ethics and situated 'ethics in practice', it has also expanded the meaning of reflexivity from a largely methodological concern to one that also carries important ethical responsibilities (Guillemin & Gillam, 2004).

Reflexivity as personal responsibility

In the social sciences, reflexivity – an explicit self-analysis of one's own role in research – has become an expected element of qualitative research. This is particularly the case in contemporary ethnographic work where the researcher can forge prolonged and close relationships with participants. It is now generally understood that through careful reflection we can start to unpick the tangled subjectivities of researcher and researched and to recognise how one's power, positionality and biography shape the research process and the knowledge we produce (Dean, 2017). Thus, the fundamental relationship involved in the pursuit of reflexivity is one between thought (reflection) and action (reflexive practice) and this has its origins in the philosophy of individualism (May & Perry, 2017). In the case of 'sensitive' research, reflexivity is often presented as a responsible means of negotiating issues such as vulnerability and exploitation, which essentially involves the self-management of *individual* researchers and their potential to 'do harm' via diligent introspection.

Denzin (1997) has suggested that the 'ideal' researcher is ' ... a morally involved, self-aware, self-reflexive and interacting individual who holds the self personally responsible for the political and ethical consequences of their actions' (Denzin, 1997, p. 277). Whilst important, contemporary researchers are striving to attain this ideal and to meet their ethical responsibilities within a complicated regulatory context proliferating with guidelines, policies and procedures, which direct and delineate what 'good' (correct) research looks like. In our experience, this can feel overwhelming for 'junior' researchers in particular. And so whilst we agree with the many accounts which argue that reflexivity is important – that it is methodologically helpful and constitutes ethical practice (Guillemin & Gillam, 2004) – we acknowledge its problematic elements (Riley et al., 2003) and highlight the neglected issue of the various 'costs' of introspection for researchers.

In the following section we 'trouble' our own reflexive experiences. Through writing about our challenges, we raise the possibility that cycles of introspection about the 'sensitivity' of one's work and what this assumes about a potential to act unethically, exploit vulnerability and cause harm, may ironically engender vulnerabilities in us as researchers.

About the research

Our 'sensitive' research projects

Over the last 10 years, we have both conducted ethnographic fieldwork in England about care and relationships towards the end of life. This section describes the projects that gave us the specific experiences we draw on within this paper. Whilst we focus here on two studies carried out at the start of our careers as death researchers, our subsequent research experiences looking at multi-disciplinary team working in healthcare settings, online forums for individuals with life-threatening illness, and baby loss and post-mortem, also inform what we have come to describe as 'internalising sensitivity'. Like Smart (2014), we consider sustained involvement in qualitative research as biographically significant for the researcher and our research careers to date foster an understanding of the 'fuzziness' of research beginning and endings. In this sense we value Smart's (2014) description of data as research fragments that accumulate over time, acquiring the potential to reveal, affect and haunt us in different ways.

'Constructing' end-of-life care

Erica's research has focused on how the 'end of life' is constructed, practiced and experienced, from the perspective of policy(-makers), those providing professional and informal care, and those who are supposed to be the subject of end of life care. Her largest fieldwork to date on this subject involved observing 50 hours of policy-related events, 250 hours of participant-observation in clinical settings, care homes, and disease-related support groups, and 100 interviews with policy-makers, health and social care professionals, and people living with life-limiting illness and/or their partners/family/carers. She also spent up to 14 months regularly visiting people living with life-limiting conditions near the end of life (and their families and health or social care professionals were possible) in their homes and other locations related to their everyday life and care (Borgstrom, 2014). These visits included anything from informal chats, to sharing family meals, to accompanying people on their clinic appointments or visiting them when in the hospital and ranged in the spectrum of participant-observation depending on the context and arrangement with participants. Encounters included witnessing emotional and/or physical distress, sensing family tension, and in some cases, being present shortly before the death of the person. As part of the research design process and ethics committee approval, these kinds of scenarios and 'appropriate' responses were explored, including how to ensure participant consent, provide for researcher safety, and account for the potentially emotionally charged nature of the research. Throughout the research, parallel field notes and field diaries were maintained, and combined with regular academic and peer-support supervisions. A reflexive approach was inherent within the project's methodology and was actively used to frame the study's findings. This is evident in the doctoral thesis, where extracts from the field diary were used to introduce each analytical topic.

Family practices and the end of life
The experiences Julie describes in this paper relate to her ethnographic work exploring how everyday family life is pursued when someone in the family has a life-threatening or terminal illness (Ellis, 2010). This study used the concept of family practices (Morgan, 1996) to theorise the mundane and everyday aspects of living as a family nearing the end of life both at home and when staying on a hospice inpatient ward. Julie completed 175 hours of participant-observation at the ward where she took-up the role of hospice volunteer, chatting with patients and relatives, making drinks, tidying around and assisting at mealtimes. To record her reflections, Julie kept fieldnotes which integrated observational details, analytical thoughts and emotional and personal responses to spending time with severely ill people and their family members. She also conducted 39 in-depth interviews with relatives from nine different families where one member was living with a life-threatening illness. These were very informal and involved repeat interviews with some family members where circumstances and illness trajectories allowed. Interview participants were recruited via the hospice's day care service which is based in the North of England. Fieldnotes were completed following each interview encounter, recording important contextual information and the researcher's personal feelings, which were reflected upon during analysis. Both interview transcripts and fieldnotes were coded and analysed using a narrative approach to thematic analysis. Like Erica, a reflexive methodological approach was adopted throughout the research process. It featured regularly during formal supervision with Julie's doctoral supervisor. At the time, the personal toll of completing the work was discussed and vulnerabilities, which feature in the example below, could be evoked, although they never felt fully articulated.

Our experiences of internalising sensitivity

We have chosen the following examples after careful consideration and discussion about how the discourses of 'sensitivity' have impacted upon how we experience our research and how they continue to affect and haunt us in different ways (Smart, 2014). We have shared similar examples previously in conference presentations (with varying receptions), in discussions with colleagues, and in our PhD theses and subsequent publications (Borgstrom & Ellis, 2017). However, some of the specific instances we discuss here are making a tentative and somewhat nervous first appearance in print for a wider audience. Tentative because we do not want to suggest that the examples offer comprehensive coverage of the issues we explore, nor do we expect they are particular to us. We offer them here as an invitation to others to share their experiences of living with 'sensitivity' in the various contexts of their work. We are also very aware of how we may have selected certain examples rather than others in an effort to 'protect' ourselves as 'vulnerable researchers' from the risky and exposing nature of reflexive publication (Blackman, 2007; Dean, 2017). With these issues duly acknowledged, the purpose of us offering these examples is to enliven methodological discussion. In doing so, we hope to expand theorisations of researcher vulnerability that extend beyond issues of personal safety and emotionality. This enables us to examine how the ethical discourses we operate within might contribute to our own vulnerability as researchers.

We have selected three examples:

- Experience of family bereavement immediately after fieldwork involving end-of-life care
- Being alone with a dying person during fieldwork
- Writing about 'the mundane' towards the end of life

In each of these sections, we write in first-person about our accounts and experiences, sometimes drawing on adapted extracts from our field diaries to demonstrate the visceral and emotional sense of vulnerability as it 'got under our skin'.

Can I just feel it? Family deaths filtered

Here we describe how discourses around death studies shape how we view ourselves and our personal responses to death outside periods of formal fieldwork. As ethnographers, we are trained to think about our own everyday experiences as on a continuum with fieldwork, a continual quest to make the familiar strange. This has enabled us to note and seek to make sense of these occurrences within a framework of 'doing' research. It has also, perhaps, desensitised us to how strange it may be that the discourses that surround the type of work we do have affected our 'non-professional' lives. To illustrate this, Erica reflects on caring for her paternal grandmother, an experience which highlighted the impact of her exposure to the idea that participants in death research are inherently vulnerable.

> Weeks after finishing my fieldwork about end-of-life care in England, I was back in the USA visiting family. Whilst I was there, it was revealed that my grandmother had recently been diagnosed with cancer. She was in the midst of deciding to decline further investigations and treatment. Soon I would visit again and effectively become her 'carer'.
>
> During this time, I had a desire to separate work from personal life, and an inability to do so. Months later, my mother remarked that my grandmother was excited that I could be 'studying her', something I resisted in practice. I wanted to just experience the moments for what they were, not to be making mental fieldnotes. I wanted to have memories that were not categorised or tainted with anthropological theories, analysis, or attempts to generalise from the particular.
>
> Yet, it was when I was caring for her, doing the gardening one afternoon that I really connected with my previous fieldwork experiences. As I picked up sticks from the grass, something reverberated through me that made me recall a conversation I had with a man who knew he was dying, a side remark about how much waiting there is in the process of dying. I could begin to understand aspects of what my participants told me that seemed trivial before.
>
> It was only later that I realised that my desire to separate my personal experience from my fieldwork mode was because I thought I needed to protect something, and someone – me and my experiences of personal deaths. I had, through the way research is framed in death studies and in healthcare research, seen myself, as a soon-to-be-bereaved grand-daughter, as someone who needed to be protected around the time of death. Someone for whom intrusion – from research – had to be limited. I had projected myself as a 'vulnerable person' because that is how the participants of my research are often portrayed; and I was now in similar circumstance. But without this notion of vulnerability, I did not necessarily feel I was particularly emotionally vulnerable because of being a carer to a dying grandmother. It was because I thought *I should be vulnerable* that caused me to become unsettled.
>
> Moreover, I began to see myself as 'uniquely vulnerable'. Vulnerable both because of the situation (caring for a dying grandmother), but also because of the heightened knowledge I had about death due to my research. I had gained knowledge about death and dying that most people don't have until they experience it first-hand.

And I became angered because there was no one to protect me (the grand-daughter) from me (the researcher with knowledge), and I blamed reflexivity for my ability to be critically aware of this dual positionality. Those who knew both my research and personal situations did not view me as 'vulnerable'. In fact, the opposite was often presumed: that if I could 'handle it' professionally, then personal encounters with death would not be particularly difficult.

Reflexivity, although considered a prerequisite of contemporary social science research, can be quite unpredictable (Kress & Frazier-Booth, 2018), and this series of realisations felt unpredictable. This example highlights how the discourses of vulnerability and sensitive research that permeate death studies can impact our own personal experiences of death. It also illustrates how being reflexive can heighten this awareness, without necessarily providing an outlet for the emotionality that it engenders. In other contexts, this dual positionality is viewed as potentially productive; for example, in creating more compassionate doctors when the doctor self-identifies as a patient-practitioner (Rowland & Kuper, 2018). Whilst the dual positionality here may have furthered aspects of Erica's analysis, it also had unintended consequences of disturbing the experiences of familial death.

Should I be here? What to do when observing

A common experience in our fieldwork in end-of-life contexts is asking ourselves: should I be here? Should I be witnessing this? On and off throughout our careers we have been fearful of the charge of voyeurism (Hockey, 2007) and what our desire to observe 'vulnerability' in this rather 'extreme' sensitive context might suggest about us as 'moral' individuals. Here we provide a particular example from Erica's research where her internal dialogue about whether this was the 'right' thing to do manifested in deeply embodied ways in the field (Okley, 2007). What Erica notes echoes experiences that Julie had during her fieldwork when she agonised over if and when it was OK to enter a patient's room on the ward. This was experienced in embodied terms in her discomfort at hanging conspicuously and awkwardly around door frames.

> I found Mable in the care home. She had been discharged after her rather lengthy, unexpected hospital stay. A care worker showed me to her dowdy room, where she promptly left me. As I peered around the doorframe, I saw Mable in the bed. I softly announced my arrival and made my way to the room's only chair. Sitting down, I explained to Mable what I was doing whilst simultaneously unsure of myself. Mable had previously said I could visit, even if I found her asleep, but this being the first time, and her body restless, it felt odd to be there. I wasn't quite sure how she was doing or what this sleep 'meant' – could she be in her last days of life?
>
> I took out my notebook, like I felt a dutiful anthropologist should, and jotted a few lines about the layout of the room and what was going on. The chair I was sat on was at the foot of her bed. I realised I couldn't just sit and observe her. I was reminded how the university research office joked about how tabloid papers might report on my project: 'researcher watched my mother die'. They were worried not just about the ethics of the project, but the social and moral response to such a 'sensitive topic'. But, at the same time, I was constrained by 'ethical procedures' to 'not doing anything' – according to the ethics committee and university research office, I was to observe, not to intervene. Yet, what would 'intervening' in this situation look like?
>
> At some point during my visit, I sat on Mable's bed near her legs. I continued to speak softly to her, talking about the flowers and saying things like 'it is okay'. I did not want to wake her. Thinking back, I do not know where those words came from. I lightly touched her, and I recoiled. Not because I did not want to offer the compassion that I associated with the action, but because I questioned it in light of the 'ethics' of doing death research. What right did I have to touch her? What obligation did I have not to? When I visited Mable in the hospital, she often wanted to hold my hand as I listened to her stories. At the time of writing this article, I can still feel the folds of her paper-thin skin in between my fingers as I type.

Recalling such scenarios serves to illustrate how discourses around the sensitive and vulnerable nature of doing research about the end of life makes us question these actions in the field. The actual details of *what it is like* to be alone in the presence of someone who, as it turned out, was in their last few hours of life was not something that was discussed in all the research design and ethical approval processes. Procedural measures covered consent, not how it would feel. The other times Erica had such 'exposures' was in the company of nurses or doctors, serving both a potential model for behaviour but also an additional site of research focus. Being alone with Mable, Erica was left to wonder what she should do whilst in the room and even if it was appropriate for her to be there at all. Was Mable 'too vulnerable' for Erica to be witnessing her toss and turn? And this, in turn, clashed with the rhetoric about 'not being alone' towards the end of life as being an integral part of a good death (Seale, 2004). Without Erica present, Mable would have been alone, and yet at the same time, Erica felt internally as if she herself was deserted. Left without a guide in how to be. It is an example of how even with detailed ideas about how fieldwork will be conducted, it is not always possible to foresee all encounters (Cohen, 2000). This lack was apparent to Erica in how uncomfortable she was in her body whilst in that room. The seat was not quite right – she could not settle for long, as if she was unconsciously mimicking how Mable tossed in the bed. Sitting on her bed felt simultaneously wrong and right.

What this experience also highlights is the concern that researchers – and those who supervise or fund their research – have about the stigma attached to conducting 'sensitive research' and how their methods may be interpreted (Lee, 1993). Reflexivity has enabled us to acknowledge that this fear of stigma influenced the research office's remarks about the project, and in turn affected how Erica made sense of her own actions on the day. Nonetheless, reflexivity cannot mitigate the feelings of stigma, discomfort, and shame which persist long after the fieldwork has ended and continue to make writing about such experiences feel risky (Dean, 2017).

Can I publish this? Data and revealing

In this final example, Julie shares her thoughts about 'the analytical aftermath' of doing research, acknowledging that the post-study period is not readily discussed in terms of how it affects the researcher and the emotional labour involved. Here we focus on an example of 'chilling'. Chilling is when researchers defer or deliberate about dissemination of research on a particular topic because they await possible hostile reactions (Lee, 1993). The following are notes from Julie's fieldwork diary taken at the time of the study.

> In the car driving home, I felt strange - subdued and numb, but also a little tearful. It made me sad to think about what Malcolm and Tracey[1] are facing and I began to feel troubled about putting the thesis together. I get mixed feelings - sometimes feeling bad for having a numb and detached feeling and not being overwhelmingly burdened by the circumstances I find people facing. Perhaps their ability to just get on and do makes me able to be saddened but not paralysed by distress. But then, I do feel compelled lately to reflect on my own life and the time I have and how I use it ... time is passing quickly and studying dying is magnifying the importance of maximising it. I feel so guilty because I imagine I ought to be more committed to the thesis and not have to struggle to sit down and work on it. I'm aware that the sheer enormity of the task is overwhelming - I feel lost for ideas - not sure of what I want to say about any of this. Could this explain the numbness and detachment - the lack of motivation? Of course, feeling indebted to the families who have spoken with me is an added burden - I feel like I'm struggling with getting themes to emerge - I'm 'feeling' the 'ordinary' yet specific life worlds of individual families and I am starting to wonder if illness experiences within families are just different and what more can I say than that? If I simply re-tell their stories how am I doing anything they couldn't? Ultimately the work seems trivial ... imagining Malcolm's isolation [due to deafness] makes the thesis feel small, like nothing - like it couldn't do anything to touch the magnitude of what that experience must be like - yet the mundane comes in as the everyday world keeps on ticking over. What can I say about this?

As this extract shows, Julie was troubled by any 'mundanity' in her own approach to, and reflections about, the research. Whilst this suggests a sense of ambivalence about generally being able to get on and not feel emotionally overwhelmed, it also points to difficulties in analytically working out how to make sense of the 'everydayness' in the data. In the process of considering her own emotions, she began to see how she was struggling to formulate an analytical perspective on how the everyday and the mundane intersected with the more extraordinary and emotional experiences associated with dying. Assumptions regarding the intensity and drama of death meant that constructing an account that gave voice to the mundane and everyday present in family stories was challenging. This was both analytically and emotionally challenging as Julie felt in danger of trivialising such a 'momentous' issue.

Against a background of discursive framing which tends to conceptualise dying as fearful, denied and ontologically troubling, it has felt quite challenging and exposing to talk about interpretations of data which foreground the 'everydayness' of dying people's feelings and the ordinariness in their accounts. Whilst it has not been Julie's intention to suggest that living with life-threatening illness is not an extraordinary, emotional and difficult experience, there is a worry that in making a case for the explanatory relevance of the mundane, it might be seen this way by others. Whilst even the most robust researchers might feel anxious about whether the patterns they see in their data and the interpretations they present as 'findings' are accurate, fair and make sense, these worries and crises of confidence feel especially difficult to shake when researching 'emotive' subjects like dying. In other words, discourses around participant vulnerability have heightened our own vulnerability – induced by an ever-present but unhelpfully nebulous awareness of our potential to cause 'harm' – something we carried throughout fieldwork and which persists into the dissemination. Being reflexive has helped us to be attuned to this potential to cause harm but it has also, particularly in Julie's case, encouraged a level of critical introspection that at times felt almost destructive (personally and professionally). For her it has not always been possible to retain perspective on the limits of what one can feasibly control – particularly at the point of dissemination when control must be given up to the scrutiny of others. And so, with this last example we illustrated how researcher vulnerabilities can become entangled with and fuelled by a concern to always act 'sensitively' and this can have a direct impact on managing aspects of the research process.

Discussion

In this paper we have drawn on reflexive examples from our own research to illustrate how discourses of vulnerability, due to our research being 'sensitive', have been internalised and 'gotten under our skin'. These examples illustrate how this internalisation has influenced the way we feel and think about our research and personal experiences. Our discussion of reflexivity illustrates how 'fragments' of research often extend beyond the boundaries and time limits of individual projects, and can continue to 'haunt' us (Smart, 2014). In attending to our own vulnerability, we see the possible limits of current ethical framings of 'sensitive research', and of reflexivity as a methodological tool, where our points are aligned with discussions about the need to do ethics-in-practice rather than be procedural (Pollock, 2012; Sikic Micanovic et al., 2019). Beyond acknowledging this, sharing these examples generates a space where the limits of reflexivity within sensitive research can be explored.

Firstly, we are not suggesting that reflexivity is not useful – it is often very helpful. We both continue to work reflexively; this paper is an example of that. Reflexivity has enabled us to make analytical connections through introspection. For example, Julie was able to wrestle with what appeared to be the paradox of the mundane in the extraordinary. And Erica began to understand what participants had told her after going through similar experiences herself, a phenomenon familiar to other anthropologists who have experienced a personal bereavement (Behar, 1996). Reflexivity also enabled us to question our positionality in the field and when collecting data, as illustrated in the second example. This is often the reason cited for why reflexivity is utilised within the social sciences and related disciplines (Abdullah, 2019; Kleinsasser, 2010). However, as evident in ethical discourses about protecting 'vulnerable participants' of 'sensitive research', reflexivity tends to be associated with the idea of protecting participants from harm (Kumar and Cavallaro, 2018).

Reflexivity is used within social research to mitigate (primarily) participant vulnerability and/or harm caused to participants through their engagement with research. The individual researcher is expected to use a reflexive approach to consider power dynamics, biases, and subjectivities (Pillow, 2003). Therefore the researcher – as a person – is an instrument in the process (Geertz, 1973), and the site for mitigating vulnerability and harm. One 'solution' offered for managing sensitive research, therefore, is to manage the individual researcher via introspection and reflexivity. What has been less explored is how for the individual researcher, this responsibility may be challenging and potentially harmful.

By drawing on examples that highlighted our own vulnerability, we raise awareness about the limitations of reflexivity in terms of protecting researchers from 'harm'. We have done this by sharing how reflexive practices have amplified our own sense of vulnerability at different times in our lives. While as a research community we are getting better about discussing the emotional implications for the researcher of doing sensitive research, attention is generally on the period when researchers are in the field engaging with participants (Dickson-Swift et al., 2007; Woodthorpe, 2011). Other aspects of the research process – such as producing notes and transcripts, performing detailed analysis, recounting stories for dissemination, or even listening to other researchers as part of peer-support – are also emotionally tiring and pose moral dilemmas (e.g. Evans et al., 2017). It is important to note that often these experiences can be highly individualised, personal and lonely, even in team environments because whilst research teams may sometimes write ethics applications collaboratively, the responsibility for translating these linear narratives into actions (or inactions) in the field lies with individual researchers. At times, as this paper demonstrates, doing research and living with its consequences has felt as if it could be 'harmful' to us as people. That we have begun to consider that *we could be harmed* through the research and reflexive process further indicates the internalising of the vulnerability discourse.

This sense of our own vulnerability resonates with Smart's (2014) suggestion that social researchers can be 'haunted' by living with the fragments of other people's lives. For us, experiencing aspects of our research as 'haunting' is rather apt, given that data analysis actually involves 'working with the ghosts' of dead participants (Komaromy, 2005), which have accumulated through our various projects generating a cumulative effect over time. Hearing their voices in recorded material or recalling time spent with them, makes the responsibility of producing an account of their experiences even more overwhelming. Smart (2009) suggests these feelings of responsibility are central to developing a 'sociological conscience': the intersection of a researcher's personal life with the practice of doing research. This haunting collides then with an ethical and moral imperative for us to not only produce 'good data' (Kleinsasser, 2010) but to be also ultimately 'good researchers' (Macfarlane, 2010). However, to-date, there appears to be little space within the academic community to comfortably share these experiences.

When writing this paper, we have reflected on the practices that have helped and hindered our experiences of vulnerability. Individually and collectively we have spent a considerable amount of time thinking, writing, and talking about our experiences, benefiting from doing this together and with other colleagues and friends. What has helped us beyond the reflexivity, and we understand may not work for all other researchers, are several things around the structures of conducting sensitive research. Firstly, pacing data collection (e.g. only conducting one interview in a day or only three in a week) and analysis can provide time to emotionally process the encounters as well as manage the energy required to be present during sensitive research. Whilst we experienced more control over timings during our doctoral studies, we are aware that due to time and/or monetary constraints of some funded research projects these can have periods of intense data collection and/or analysis. We recommend, where possible, those responsible for designing projects purposefully and carefully consider the timing and pacing of the various aspects of work in terms of the impact it has on those in the team primarily responsible for carrying out data collection and analysis. In doing so, it becomes less of an individual responsibility to manage the emotional and temporal intensities of the project, whilst at the same time, this can create an ethos within the project team where emotional labour can be recognised and discussed.

Secondly, the way project proposals (and grant applications) may be written can presume that research assistants/fellows are hired in to conduct sensitive research and focus solely on a particular project. However, such approaches can formally minimise the recognition that these are individuals with research (and personal) biographies that will influence their experiences on any one project.

Whilst this is sometimes addressed when researchers openly acknowledge their positionality and/or discuss how their analysis was informed by previous work, we have found it helpful being able to engage with and think across our past projects and other entanglements in sensitive research. Whilst we have managed this informally, and sometimes with non-academics working in related fields who can provide different perspectives or through therapy, we would welcome research cultures that engage with the legacy of one's research in terms other than 'research impact' and career progression.

This relates to our last point, which is about the expectations of 'timely' writing and dissemination. We have found that sometimes waiting to write about a project or particular elements of it can provide us with new perspectives because of the distance it provides. Or, as in this paper, more confidence to reveal aspects that at times feel very raw and emotionally revealing that is counter to most of our professional cultures. Yet such delays can cause problems with meeting institutional and project objectives or activities such as the Research Excellence Framework. More could be done within institutional and funding structures to accommodate publishing patterns that account for researchers' experiences, wellbeing and reflexive practices.

We are therefore adding a note of caution to the idea that reflexivity can always function to alleviate vulnerability in sensitive research, particularly when experienced by researchers. Specifically, what reflexivity does not always provide is a solution to the 'living with' of our research and the effects of the vulnerability it can engender. By introducing the idea of 'internalising' discourses such as sensitivity and vulnerability we hope to offer a conceptual means for researchers to talk and write about similar difficult feelings in a way that avoids moral judication of the research or the researcher. Whilst our experiences stem from our work in death studies, what we describe has broader implications. It is particularly useful for the growing field of sensitive research, and thinking about the longer-term impacts of conducting research that is 'sensitive'. Being able to discuss how research experiences can indicate internalised sensitivity is useful in enabling us to think critically about research methods, training of researchers, and communities of practice.

Note

1. Malcolm and Tracey participated in a series of interviews for Julie's research. They were married and both in their 50s. Malcolm was living with a terminal cancer diagnosis.

Acknowledgments

The authors would like to thank the people who have all been part of their studies and those that have supported them along the way. Additionally, the authors would like to thank the editors and reviewers for their feedback on earlier drafts.

Disclosure statement

No potential conflict of interest was reported by the authors.

Funding

Ellis' doctoral research was funded by an Economic and Social Research Council Studentship; grant reference PTA-030-2005-00154. Borgstrom's doctoral research was funded through a National Institute of Health Research (NIHR) Collaborations for Leadership in Applied Health Research and Care (CLAHRC) for Cambridgeshire and Peterborourgh doctoral scholarship held at the University of Cambridge.

References

Abdullah, N. (2019). *Vulnerability in the field: Emotions, experiences, and encounters with ghosts and spirits*. Springer. https://doi.org/10.1007/978-3-030-20831-8_25

Addington-Hall, J. Research sensitivities to palliative care patients. (2002). *European Journal of Cancer Care*, *11*(3), 220–224. Blackwell Science Ltd. https://doi.org/10.1046/j.1365-2354.2002.00343.x

Barnett, M. Interviewing terminally ill people: Is it fair to take their time? (2001). *Palliative Medicine*, *15*(2), 157–158. Sage PublicationsSage CA: Thousand Oaks, CA. https://doi.org/10.1191/026921601666846232

Behar, R. (1996). *The vulnerable observer: Anthropology that breaks your heart*. Beacon Press.

Blackman, S. J. (2007). 'Hidden ethnography': Crossing emotional borders in qualitative accounts of young people's lives. *Sociology*, *41*(4), 699–716. https://doi.org/10.1177/0038038507078925

Borgstrom, E. (2014). *Planning for death? An ethnographic study of english end-of-life care*. University of Cambridge. https://www.repository.cam.ac.uk/handle/1810/245560

Borgstrom, E. (2018). Using an ethnographic approach to study end-of-life care: Reflections from research encounters in England. In Emma Garnett, Joanna Reynolds and Sarah Milton (Eds.), *Ethnographies and health* (pp. 67–83). Springer International Publishing.

Borgstrom, E., & Ellis, J. Introduction: Researching death, dying and bereavement. (2017). *Mortality*, *22*(2), 93–104. Routledge. https://doi.org/10.1080/13576275.2017.1291600

Burles, M. C. (2017). Negotiating post-research encounters: Reflections on learning of participant deaths following a qualitative study. *Mortality*, *22*(2), 170–180. https://doi.org/10.1080/13576275.2017.1291605

Burr, J., & Reynolds, P. (2010). The wrong paradigm? Social research and the predicates of ethical scrutiny. *Research Ethics*, *6*(4), 128–133. https://doi.org/10.1177/174701611000600404

Cain, C. L. (2012). Emotions and the research interview: What hospice workers can teach us. *Health Sociology Review*, *21*(4), 396–405. https://doi.org/10.5172/hesr.2012.21.4.396

Cohen, J. H. (2000). Problems in the field: Participant observation and the assumption of neutrality. *Field Methods*, *12*(4), 316–333. https://doi.org/10.1177/1525822X0001200404

Cook, A. S., & Bosley, G. (2007). The experience of participating in bereavement research: Stressful or therapeutic? *Death Studies*, *19*(2), 157–170. https://doi.org/10.1080/07481189508252722

de Laine, M. (2000). *Fieldwork, participation and practice: Ethics and dilemmas in qualitative research*. Sage.

Dean, J. (2017). *Doing reflexivity: An introduction*. Policy Press.

DeLuca, J. R., & Maddox, C. B. (2016). Tales from the ethnographic field. *Field Methods*, *28*(3), 284–299. https://doi.org/10.1177/1525822X15611375

Denzin, N. K. (1997). *Interpretive ethnography: Ethnographic practices for the 21st century*. Sage Publications.

Dickson-Swift, V., James, E. L., Kippen, S., & Liamputtong, P. (2007). Doing sensitive research: What challenges do qualitative researchers face? *Qualitative Research*, *7*(3), 327–353. https://doi.org/10.1177/1468794107078515

Dingwall, R. (2006). Confronting the anti-democrats: The unethical nature of ethical regulation in social science. *Medical Sociology Online*, *1*(1): 59–60. Retrieved March 29, 2019, from http://irep.ntu.ac.uk/id/eprint/13739/.

Ellis, J. (2010). *Family practices during life-threatening illness: Exploring the everyday*. University of Sheffield.

Evans, R., Ribbens McCarthy, J., Bowlby, S., Wouango, J., Kébé, F. (2017). Producing emotionally sensed knowledge? Reflexivity and emotions in researching responses to death. *International Journal of Social Research Methodology*, *20*(6), 585–598 1–14.https://doi.org/10.1080/13645579.2016.1257679

Fincham, B., Scourfield, J., & Langer, S. (2008). The impact of working with disturbing secondary data: Reading suicide files in a Coroner's office. *Qualitative Health Research*, *18*(6), 853–862. https://doi.org/10.1177/1049732307308945

Geertz, C. (1973). *The Interpretation of Cultures*. Basic Books.

Goodrum, S., & Keys, J. L. (2007). Reflections on two studies of emotionally sensitive topics: Bereavement from murder and abortion. *International Journal of Social Research Methodology*, *10*(4), 249–258. https://doi.org/10.1080/13645570701400976

Guillemin, M., & Gillam, L. (2004). Ethics, reflexivity, and "ethically important moments" in research. *Qualitative Inquiry*, *10*(2), 261–280. https://doi.org/10.1177/1077800403262360

Gysels, M., Evans, C. J., Lewis, P., Speck, P., Benalia, H., Preston, N. J., Grande, G. E., Short, V., Owen-Jones, E., Todd, C. J., & Higginson, I. J. (2013). MORECare research methods guidance development: Recommendations for ethical issues in palliative and end-of-life care research. *Palliative Medicine*, *27*(10), 908–917. https://doi.org/10.1177/0269216313488018

Hacking, I. (1999). *The social construction of what?* Harvard University Press.
Haggerty, K. D. (2004). Ethics creep: Governing social science research in the name of ethics. *Qualitative Sociology, 27*(4), 391–414. https://doi.org/10.1023/B:QUAS.0000049239.15922.a3
Hockey, J. (2007). Closing in on death? Reflections on research and researchers in the field of death and dying. *Health Sociology Review, 16*(5), 436–446. https://doi.org/10.5172/hesr.2007.16.5.436
Hubbard, G., Backett-Milburn, K., & Kemmer, D. (2001). Working with emotion: Issues for the researcher in fieldwork and teamwork. *International Journal of Social Research Methodology, 4*(2), 119–137. https://doi.org/10.1080/13645570116992
Kellehear, A. (1984). Are we a `death-denying' society? A sociological review. *Social Science & Medicine, 18*(9), 713–721. https://doi.org/10.1016/0277-9536(84)90094-7
Kellehear, A. (2009). What the social and behavioural studies say about dying.. In Allan Kellehear (Ed.), *The study of dying: From autonomy to transformation* (pp. 1–26). Cambridge University Press.
Kleinsasser, A. M. (2010). Theory into practice researchers, reflexivity, and good data: Writing to unlearn. *Theory Into Practice, 39*(3), 155–162. https://doi.org/10.1207/s15430421tip3903_6
Komaromy, C. (2005). *The production of death and dying in care homes for older people: An ethnographic account.* The Open University.
Kress, T. M., & Frazier-Booth, K. J. (2018). The luxury of vulnerability: Reflexive inquiry as privileged praxis. *Decentering the Researcher in Intimate Scholarship (Advances in Research and Teaching), 31*, 105–121. https://doi.org/10.1108/S1479-368720180000031009
Kumar, S., & Cavallaro, L. (2018). Researcher Self-Care in Emotionally Demanding Research: A Proposed Conceptual Framework. *Qualitative Health Research, 28*(4), 648–658. https://doi.org/10.1177/1049732317746377
Lee, R. L. M. (1993). *Doing research on sensitive topics*. Sage.
Lee, R. L. M. (2008). Modernity, mortality and re-enchantment: The death taboo revisited. *Sociology, 42*(4), 745–759. https://doi.org/10.1177/0038038508091626
Lee, R. M., & Renzetti, C. M. (1990). The problems of researching sensitive topics: An overview and introduction. *American Behavior Scientist, 33*(5), 510–528. https://doi.org/10.1177/0002764290033005002
Liamputtong, P. (2007). *Researching the vulnerable*. Sage.
Macfarlane, B. (2010). *The virtuous researcher*. The Chronicle of Higher Education.Retrieved March 29, 2019, from http://chronicle.com/article/The-Virtuous-Researcher/64931/.
Mauthner, N. S., & Doucet, A. (2003). Reflexive accounts and accounts of reflexivity in qualitative data analysis. *Sociology, 37*(3), 413–431. https://doi.org/10.1177/00380385030373002
May, T., & Perry, B. (2017). *Reflexivity: The essential guide*. Sage.
Mckenzie, S. K., Li, C., Jenkin, G., & Collings, S. (2017). Ethical considerations in sensitive suicide research reliant on non-clinical researchers. *Research Ethics, 13*(3–4), 173–183. https://doi.org/10.1177/1747016116649996
Morgan, D. H. J. (1996). *Family connections: An introduction to family studies*. Polity Press.
Okley, J. (2007). Fieldwork embodied. In C. Shilling (Ed.), *Embodying sociology: Retrospect, progress and prospects* (pp. 65–79). Blackwell.
Parvez, Z. F. (2018). The sorrow of parting: Ethnographic depth and the role of emotions. *Journal of Contemporary Ethnography, 47*(4), 454–483. https://doi.org/10.1177/0891241617702195
Pillow, W. (2003). Confession, catharsis, or cure? Rethinking the uses of reflexivity as methodological power in qualitative research. *International Journal of Qualitative Studies in Education, 16*(2), 175–196. https://doi.org/10.1080/0951839032000060635
Pollock, K. (2012). Procedure versus process: Ethical paradigms and the conduct of qualitative research. *BMC Medical Ethics, 13*(1), 25. https://doi.org/10.1186/1472-6939-13-25
Riley, S., Schouten, W., & Cahill, S. (2003). Exploring the dynamics of subjectivity and power between researcher and researched. *Forum Qualitative Sozialforschung/Forum: Qualitative Social Research, 4*(2), 2. http://dx.doi.org/10.17169/fqs-4.2.713
Rowland, P., & Kuper, A. (2018). Beyond vulnerability: How the dual role of patient-health care provider can inform health professions education. *Advances in Health Sciences Education, 23*(1), 115–131. https://doi.org/10.1007/s10459-017-9777-y
Seale, C. (2004). Media constructions of dying alone: A form of "bad death". *Social Science & Medicine, 58*(5), 967–974. https://doi.org/10.1016/j.socscimed.2003.10.038
Sieber, J. E., & Stanely, B. (1988). Ethical and professional dimensions of socially sensitive research. *American Psychologist, 43*(1), 49–55. https://doi.org/10.1037/0003-066X.43.1.49
Sikic Micanovic, L., Stelko, S., & Sakic, S. (2019). Who else needs protection? Reflecting on researcher vulnerability in sensitive research. *Societies, 10*(1), 3. https://doi.org/10.3390/soc10010003
Smart, C. (2009). Hauntings: Living with other people's lives. Turning personal: an interdisciplinary conference, University of Manchester.
Smart, C. (2014). Fragments: Living with other people's lives as analytic practice. In C. Smart, J. Hockey, & A. James (Eds.), *The craft of knowledge: Experiences of living with data* (pp. 131–148). Macmillan.

Van den Hoonaard, W. C., & Hamilton, A. (2016). The ethics rupture: Exploring alternatives to formal research ethics review. In *The ethics rupture*. University of Toronto Press.

Visser, R. C. (2017). "Doing death": Reflecting on the researcher's subjectivity and emotions. *Death Studies, 41*(1), 6–13. https://doi.org/10.1080/07481187.2016.1257877

Woodby, L. L., Williams, B. R., Wittich, A. R., & Burgio, K. L. (2011). Expanding the notion of researcher distress: The cumulative effects of coding. *Qualitative Health Research, 21*(6), 830–838. https://doi.org/10.1177/1049732311402095

Woodthorpe, K. (2007). My life after death: Connecting the field, the findings and the feelings. *Anthropology Matters, 9*(1), 1. https://doi.org/10.22582/am.v9i1.54

Woodthorpe, K. (2011). Researching death: Methodological reflections on the management of critical distance. *International Journal of Social Research Methodology, 14*(2), 99–109. https://doi.org/10.1080/13645579.2010.496576

Researching perinatal death: managing the myriad of emotions in the field

Kerry Jones and Sam Murphy

ABSTRACT
This paper addresses the role of 'emotional labour' in conducting sensitive research. As such it begins to unpick the emotional and embodied consequences of working with data which covers sensitive subjects, in this case perinatal death, and considers how such responses are likely to impact on the analysis of data. We draw upon two doctoral studies which explored parental experiences of perinatal bereavement. We argue that researchers need to understand and consider carefully how emotions experienced during the research may impact upon the findings. By exposing the authors' own positionality in this research based on their own experience of perinatal loss, we acknowledge that we are actors in research which has an impact on the process and final product of the studies.

Introduction

The introduction to this special issue has outlined the background to the sensitivities involved in researching particular subjects, for example, sexual behaviours, drug abuse and deviance (Lee, 1993). One difficulty in researching such subjects lies in the management of emotions during the research process. Originally, this area of the methodological literature focused on the emotions of the research participants (Corden et al., 2005), however, there is now considerable interest in the emotions of the researcher and how they might impact upon the research process. As Evans et al. (2017) note, a '[r]ecognition of the emotional labour of the research process is of vital importance in research on "sensitive topics"' (p. 595).

It is this recognition that we focus on as well as how the emotions of the researcher might impact upon the findings. We explore these issues through the lens of perinatal death, that is, the death of a baby following 24 weeks' completed gestation and up until 28 days of life (Perinatal Institute, 2011). As researching death requires participants to re-rehearse episodes which are particularly painful to them, it is widely acknowledged to be a sensitive subject to research (Lee, 1993; Liamputtong, 2007). Indeed, Lee (1993) points out that, alongside death, the topics of sex and reproduction have traditionally been seen as taboo in western-industrialised societies. Perinatal loss is an experience that encompasses all three of these taboo areas and so we consider it to be one of the most sensitive of subjects to research in our cultural context.

Through researching reproductive loss, we consider the role of emotions in producing knowledge. We do this through a joint auto-ethnographical account of our two doctoral studies where we were researching perinatal death from an 'insider' perspective. Both of us had experienced the death of a baby: Jones through neonatal death and Murphy by stillbirth. In so doing, we acknowledge Cotterill and Letherby (1993) assertions that all research contains elements of autoethnographic accounts both 'intellectually and personally that document not just one life, but many. As such, they are relevant to academic social empirical research be it a survey, interviews or ethnographic research (Cotterill & Letherby, 1993, p. 14).

In order to set the context, we begin by briefly exploring some of the literature on qualitative interviewing and the emotions associated with this activity before going on to give a brief overview of the methods each project used. Following that, we collate the emotions experienced by both authors when interviewing parents and subsequently analyse these accounts to outline the various ways in which our emotions overlapped. In doing so, we trace the highs and lows of our emotions which were not restricted merely to sadness, anger and pain, as might be expected, but that also included humour, gratefulness and disbelief. We suggest that it is important that researchers understand that the emotions experienced in the field have some bearing upon how the data is interpreted and used, for example, whether one account is privileged over another. We use the concept of 'emotionally sensed knowledge' to account for this. Moreover, we also feel that it is important to note that research into death is not all doom and gloom. The moments of humour, for example, which novice researchers may not expect and may find difficult to manage, are not only to be expected but also shine a light over the ways in which people come to terms with the death of a baby. In outlining and being reflexive about the emotions the two of us experienced, we also highlight how two different researchers might experience different emotions when researching the same subject.

Qualitative interviewing, emotions and sensitive research

Later in this article we outline the detail of the research projects but, at this point, it is suffice to say that both Jones and Murphy were undertaking exploratory research where they were interested in the lived experiences of bereaved parents (Jones, 2014, 2013; Jones et al., 2019). Consequently, we both used qualitative research methods with Jones (2010) taking a narrative inquiry (Etherington, 2004) using the voice relational method framework (Mauthner & Doucet, 1998), while Murphy (2009) took a symbolic interactionist perspective using in-depth interviews and deployed grounded theory as a tool for analysis (Strauss & Corbin, 1998). Both studies received favourable ethical approval by their respective universities; Murphy also had ethical approval from her local NHS Ethics Committee.

Qualitative interviewing has been accepted to involve a significant amount of emotional labour. This concept, put forward by Hochschild (1998), suggests that workers will manage their emotions to conform to workplace norms. As such, this has been a helpful concept for researchers in terms of managing emotions while interviewing. At first, this attention was mostly with regard to the interviewee rather than the interviewer (Cylwik, 2001) and so the focus had been on ensuring that participants in research were not overly upset or traumatised by an interview. Cylwik has suggested, however, that this focus meant that, in some research, there was a tendency to fail '... to acknowledge the researcher as influential on the research process' (p. 243). She has argued though that the researcher:

> ... should occupy a central position in the research process ... emotions that are produced contextually and relationally can be used as a tool to reveal some of the researcher's own beliefs and assumptions (pp. 249-50).

Writing that same year, Hubbard et al. (2001) outlined three emotional dimensions of the research process. First, the emotional labour of a researcher; second, 'emotionally-sensed knowledge' – '... where emotion contributes towards understanding and knowledge' (p. 121); and third, the sociology of emotions which is the description of emotions that a participant exhibits. They pointed out that '[t]he emotions of the respondent, and also those of the researcher are likely to influence and inform our understandings of the topic under investigation' (p. 121). This was an important acknowledgement – the feelings brought to the research process are ones which influence how the data is collected, interpreted and analysed. We agree but also suggest that there is a potential for these emotions to influence the importance attached to one participant's experience over another's. As Komaromy (2020) has more recently pointed out:

> [n]o representation is unproblematic and ethnographic writing reflexively involves both a conscious attempt to reveal the writer's assumptions as well as recognizing the likelihood of an unconscious contribution made by the author of the text which can present itself through things such as focusing on data that connects with past experiences or an individualised style of writing up. (p. 5)

Of interest for this paper is the notion of 'emotionally-sensed knowledge'. While they contrast this type of understanding with objective approaches, Hubbard et al. (2001) suggested that, while researching, it is '... appropriate to perceive ... emotional and cognitive functioning as inseparable' (p. 126). So, while Strauss and Corbin (1998) might suggest that using grounded theory enables the researcher to

> ... achieve a certain degree of distance from the research materials and to represent them fairly; the ability to listen to the words of respondents and to give them a voice independent of that of the researcher (p. 35)

we would argue that this is very difficult to do particularly with subjects which are highly emotive. However, as researchers, we are required, while feeling emotions, to not necessarily display them or, at the very least, to keep them in check as much as we can (Hochschild, 1998; Komaromy, 2020). This is an example of the emotional labour of the researcher – emotional management to improve the experience of the participant in much the same way as Hochschild's flight attendants kept their feelings in check to enhance the experience of the passengers. However, when hearing people's stories of grief and bereavement, it is hard for the researcher to keep in check the feelings of sympathy and empathy which may emerge – the researcher is, after all, only human. Having said that, Goodrum and Keys (2007) maintained that, following some initial difficult emotions in their studies on murder and abortion, respectively, they were able to develop a detachment during interviews that allowed them '... to continue with the data collection and preserve [their] mental health, while remaining compassionate to participants needs' (p. 256). Goodrum and Keys (2007) were, however, referring to the interviews themselves, but as others such as Ratnam (2019) have discovered that emotions aren't switched off at the same time as the recording device. There is the journey home, the possibly sleepless night mulling over the interview, the transcription and then the data analysis which might involve multiple re-readings. The constant re-rehearsing of the interview, in whatever form it takes, has the potential to repeatedly take the researchers back to the heightened emotions of the interview – perhaps even many years after the event. Here we argue that it is possible that such reliving of emotions might impact deleteriously on researchers over time but that also the experiencing of the emotions during the process might dictate which accounts are privileged over others. Moreover, for the researcher hearing stories which may be akin to their own experiences, these feelings may be even harder to keep in check. As the 'personal is political', often it has been the case that researchers who investigate pregnancy loss of any kind have experience of it themselves (see, for example, Layne, 2000; Letherby, 1993).

If we consider the concept of 'emotionally-sensed knowledge', at its heart is the idea that it is our emotions, as much as our other senses, that contribute to our understanding of the social world. Hubbard et al. (2001) documented emotions such as being upset, anger or an over-empathising with the participants as ones which are likely to contribute to particular interpretations of data. They advocated that qualitative researchers need to be mindful of emotions and discuss with their teams how they are feeling during the research but also the suggested that there was a need for researchers to interrogate their own emotional responses to data. For example, if one asks oneself why a particular experience of a participant makes one angry, important insights into the complexity of social life or the concept under exploration may be garnered. They acknowledge the difficulty this can bring, however, for researchers who operate within the confines of ' ... an academic environment that, on the whole, trains researchers to be objective and "extract out" emotion' (p.

135). This is despite the reflexive turn in the social sciences which allows for reflection an acknowledgment of the positionality of the researcher in the research process (Brewer, 2000).

Researchers such as Evans et al. (2017), who researched experiences of death in Senegal have also considered the idea of 'emotionally-sensed knowledge' using reflexivity. The research team was comprised of members from the United Kingdom and from Senegal – interviews were conducted in the local language and then translated into French and then into English. Noting the sensitive nature of the subject, the researchers adopted a 'contextual feminist ethics of care' which recognised that emotional labour would be used by both interviewee and interviewer. In opposition to Goodrum and Keys (2007) emotional detachment, they found that listening repeatedly to stories of death had the capacity to ' ... have a significant emotional impact on researchers' (p. 590). Moreover, one team member ' ... found it more emotionally demanding to read and make sense of the written transcripts once back in the more comfortable surroundings of her home in the UK' (p. 591).

They have, therefore, recognised that emotions have 'epistemological significance' and that their emotional reactions to the data were bound up with individual biographies, that is, the points at which they were either 'insider' or 'outsider'. Indeed, when thinking about the impact of being an insider researching a sensitive topic, Hubbard et al. (2001) have suggested that there is a danger inherent in over-emphasising where,

> either the particular topic or the emotions it evokes in a respondent can result in a sharing of experiences which are so close to those of the researcher that the maintenance of any kind of professional detachment becomes extremely compromised. (p. 129)

When it comes to death, we can possibly argue that everyone is an 'insider'. In documenting her experience of participant observation in cemeteries, Woodthorpe (2011) noted how she was often moved to tears and when she reached the analysis stage which she expected to be a time of 'remote scrutiny', she then revisited those feelings. Indeed, she questions whether any researcher would even *want* to detach themselves fully when researching death:

> ... the expectation that the researcher can disengage from their research topic may not only idealistic, but also unworkable. When doing research associated with death, arguably a complete scholarly detachment or a sense of critical distance is never fully feasible. (p. 107)

Hubbard et al. (2001) suggested that a way forward to help deal with emotions during research is for the research team to be open with each other about the emotions experienced during the process and this is a suggestion taken up by Evans et al. (2017). However, one wonders where this might leave the doctoral student who might feel unable to open up to a supervisor due to issues of hierarchy and possibly a perceived need to retain the cloak of 'objectivity': a situation which both of us were in. Or, indeed, any research dynamic where power permeates the relationship, such as with early career researchers and those on fixed-term contracts. This could also especially be the case where researchers are also 'insiders' – again, the position of both authors of this paper. So, in common with Evans et al. (2017), we acknowledge the importance of 'emotionally-sensed knowledge' throughout the research project and recognise the importance of the researcher's biography in the production of these emotions. Later we document the emotions experienced during the two studies but before this, we outline the methods used in both projects and how this paper came about.

Emotions and research into perinatal grief

The genesis of this article can be traced back to 2005 when we were put in contact with each other by one of Murphy's PhD supervisors. We were researching similar subjects at roughly the same time. We had separately realised that there was little research at the time on reproductive loss from a sociological perspective and both of us were keen to redress this. This came from an acknowledgement that bereavement does not happen in a social vacuum: the experience is entirely social, with family, friends and healthcare professionals involved as well as societal discourses around pregnancy, motherhood, fatherhood and death that come to bear upon it. Both of us had also realised that also there had been little research on male experiences of loss – whether psychological or sociological – and this was a gap we were also both keen to partially fill throughout doctoral studies.

Study one by Jones

The study on *Parental Perspectives on Grief and Loss Following Stillbirth and Neonatal Death* analysed 27 bereaved parents' experiences by utilising a voice relational method framework (Mauthner & Doucet, 1998). This method represented a transfer of relational ontology into the methodology by considering parents' narratives in light of the relationships to people (friends, family and health professionals) and to the broader social, structural and cultural contexts (medicine, employment and discourse around pregnancy and birth) within which they live (Brown & Gilligan, 1993; Mauthner & Doucet, 1998). The research collected accounts of loss from parents who attended a monthly support group following the death of their baby, of which Jones was a member/facilitator. While the parents' focus was on memorialisation and being able to talk about their baby without fear of censure or judgement by others, parents expressed their sense of powerlessness about an event in which their grief was neither acknowledged nor recognised (Doka, 1989). Few parents had prior awareness that perinatal death was something that occurred, at that time, to other families (SANDS, 2010) and there was little available literature on other parents' experiences, particularly men's. Within the therapeutic literature, a psychological understanding of loss dominated and framed bereaved people's experiences, with scant attention given to any social or cultural context. Yet, bereaved parents in the support group commented that they felt deeply impacted by the responses of family, friends, employers, health professionals, and the health system in which the death of their baby took place. It was critical to analyse these experiences further and within a sociological framework as developed by Brown and Gilligan (1993) and later by Mauthner and Doucet (1998).

Interviews were conducted in couple pairs and individually to capture social accounts of loss and four focus groups were conducted to further develop the research schedule and interview. While I was keen to enlist as many men as possible to the study, the sample of men recruited in the end was not as many as I had anticipated but this is not unusual for researchers in this area (Armentrout, 2005). Ultimately, the sample consisted of twenty women and seven men and, of these men and women, 13 had experienced a loss as a result of stillbirth, and 14 parents had experienced a neo-natal death.

Study two: Murphy

The *Parenting the Stillborn* study was a grounded theory analysis of the experiences of the parents of 29 babies who were either stillborn or who died neo-natally in the United Kingdom (Murphy, 2009). While ostensibly the focus of the research was on stillbirth, the inclusion of parents bereaved by neonatal death was useful in terms of providing a small comparison group. The aim was to interview couples – both together and then separately – in order to understand the social aspects of bereavement by perinatal death. As such, I was asking parents to tell me their stories and I would then explore particular areas of their experience which focused on the social and cultural aspects of their bereavement. As with many research projects, doctorates or not, the planned empirical research did not match the eventual research sample and so, in the event, I interviewed some couples but had more interviews with mothers whose partners were not interested in taking part. Like Jones I, too, had difficulty in recruiting men to the project so, when interviewing women, I included a line of enquiry that explored their partner's experiences. While this was secondary data, it was useful to collect as the mothers' perception of the fathers' feelings and behaviours would impact upon their own experiences.

It was interesting to note that, while I was undertaking the research and since, many people (academic as well as non-academic) told me that it was not a piece of research that they would be able to undertake themselves. I assumed it must be because that they would find it too emotionally upsetting and therefore too traumatic for them to even contemplate – a sensitive research project for one researcher is possibly too sensitive to others.

In writing this paper, we have drawn on the extensive discussions we have had for the past decade or more. Each of us documented the emotions we encountered and, once we compared notes, found many similarities but were also surprised by some of the differences we found. The next section goes on to outline the emotions that saturated the process of researching perinatal loss for both researchers.

The emotions of perinatal bereavement research

When we consider sensitive research and the emotional impact it can have on both researcher and participants, the literature focuses on upsetting emotions such as sadness and depression but the range of emotions we experienced went beyond these. Since interviews were discussing loss, we anticipated that some interview questions would trigger painful emotions for the participants and we were both prepared for our own emotions to be affected by what we would hear. For example, some men and women became upset when describing their loss and how shocked and dismayed they were that their baby had died in the womb when everything had seemed fine; parents on the neo-natal ward who related saying goodbye to their baby; and occasions where some men got visibly upset when talking of designing a headstone for their baby. All the narratives we heard were incredibly moving and throughout our data collection, our attempts to regulate our own emotions and remain a 'professional distance' was an on-going challenge because our overriding ethic was of compassion: the need to be empathic and supportive towards a participant's distress. The remainder of this section begins by highlighting the areas of commonality which includes 'anxiety around interviewing', 'guilt', 'sadness', 'disbelief' and 'anger' before going on to note where there was divergence.

Anxiety around interviewing

Anxiety was an emotion that affected both of us and which was partly engendered by being novice researchers (as doctoral students) in addition to the sensitive nature of the subject. However, while the emotion was the same, often it appeared to have different root causes. For example, Jones would be concerned prior to interviews that parents would refuse to be interviewed concerned that she had put off a parent in initial discussions. While she had one parent who did refuse because they felt it was not the right time to share their experience, she did question whether or not it was her enthusiasm about giving parents a voice (albeit one that would be published anonymously) that had contributed to this parent withdrawing from the research. She was reassured by other parents that they wanted their story imparted to others through literature to raise awareness of the impact of their loss. Her second source of anxiety surfaced prior to interviews with couples. She feared that there would be disagreement between parents about how events unfolded or that there would be discord about how a story should be narrated. Murphy's anxiety was focused more on whether or not participant(s) would open up to her; whether her follow-up questions would be reasonable ones or would she miss obvious areas to explore which she would later regret. There was also anxiety around the impact that the interview(s) might have on the participants – would they become so emotionally upset that she had made a traumatic situation worse?

Guilt

For Jones, concern around making participants upset surfaced as guilt. She had experienced considerable concern about asking parents to share a story that would be traumatic to tell. Indeed, most parents did cry, and felt guilty about being an observer of their emotional pain –

a very intimate emotion to display to a stranger. Similarly, Murphy would feel guilt when parents became upset and both, at this point, would sit awkwardly, not sure of what to say or to do. Similarly following the interview both of us would continue to wonder whether parents had felt supported during and after the interview, and whether or not we had said the right thing at the right time or whether we should have said nothing at all. For both of us what we were asking parents to do was to tell us a story which could end with significant gain for ourselves – an academic qualification of some standing and thus enhance our career prospects. While ostensibly we could tell ourselves that our aim was to allow parents to be heard we were also aware that not everyone would consider the research as being entirely altruistic.

Sadness

We both felt sadness as each story was its own unique tragedy and being 'insiders' we both experienced a high level of identification with our interviewees' experiences during the interviews. Following interviews, Jones felt it important to turn to her reflexive journal to record not only the impact of the interviews but also thoughts about disclosing an aspect of one's own experience when invited to do so. She found that she carefully selected information to avoid becoming re-immersed in grief by not recalling upon in any great depth, some painful emotions associated with her own experience. This sadness continued on into the transcription of interviews and during data analysis due to the repeated reading of interviews, a method which was necessitated by employing the 'voice-centred relational method' which meant reading and coding data at least four times to capture the way a parent narrates a story (Mauthner & Doucet, 1998). Reflexivity through use of the journal and in clinical supervision helped to 'unpack' her feelings associated with personal experience with those that belonged to participants' narratives.

Murphy, however, while concerned about its potential impact on her emotional wellbeing, in the end seemed to be distant enough from her stillbirth (more than 10 years prior to the research) that she was not personally traumatised by the perpetual hearing of stories of loss, although she would not consider herself as achieving the level of remoteness that Goodrum and Keys (2007) described. That was not to say that she did not feel sad while interviewing – on more than one occasion during the interviews she was moved to tears. However, it was during the data analysis that feelings of sadness seemed to be stronger. There were two potential reasons for this: as with Jones, it could have been the close analysis that prompted these feelings but, equally it could have been that, in the space of her own home the full import of the experiences was brought home to her. This was in common to the team member referred to earlier in the literature review where the emotion engendered from the interview was greater during analysis in the UK than during the interview in Senegal (Evans et al., 2017). During the interviews, it seemed to Murphy that her brain worked on two levels: one part listening to the interviewee(s), the other formulating the next question. While she is far from being a psychologist, she would suggest that the brain working in this way can protect the researcher to some extent, at least during the interview itself. When analysing the data, full attention is paid to the data so this might be why the process of analysis can be more upsetting than the interview itself.

Disbelief

Perhaps surprisingly, both Jones and Murphy experienced feelings of disbelief towards their participants at times. Murphy occasionally doubted the veracity of parental accounts and wondered whether she was the victim of an elaborate hoax only to be relieved when parents would supply her the evidence of the loss in the form of photographs or mementoes of the baby. Quite where these suspicions came from she finds it difficult to ascertain although one or two parents did mention that people posed as bereaved parents on the internet to garner attention – would posing as bereaved for a research project be the next step for some people? Or the feelings of disbelief may have come from a childhood where the author was bullied and teased mercilessly at school – experiences that gave rise to general feelings of mistrust in the world around her.

Disbelief for Jones was in a different form where she felt incredulity while listening to parents' narrations. One concerned an interview with a parent who was dismissive of another bereaved mother who belonged to the same support group. She had assumed that the loss of a baby and shared membership of a group would bring about support and compassion for another bereaved parent: as a bereaved parent herself this was how she viewed membership of the group.

This posed a dilemma for Jones as she had interviewed this other bereaved mother yet was not able to disclose this during the interview due to ethics. Further reflection through clinical supervision, meant Jones then recognised that participant responses could be a form of projection that possibly came from feelings of guilt or inadequacy.

In another interview, a parent told Jones about a mother who had experienced a miscarriage at 17 weeks and who shared photographs of her baby soon after delivery. This parent had felt disgust at the images. Jones found this bewildering as such images validate parental experiences but she also had the sense of disbelief that a bereaved parent could be insensitive to the needs of another bereaved mother, especially knowing herself how insensitive responses can impact. While this was not something Murphy experienced particularly, she had heard anecdotal reports of factions within support groups – often divisions would be between those parents who had conceived through IVF and those who had fallen pregnant naturally.

Anger

Both of us experienced anger during our studies; hus we had to work hard to contain an outward emotional display of how we felt – a very real and conscious exertion of emotional labour. We heard accounts of comments and responses from others (friends, family, health professionals, and colleagues) which were deemed by our participants as insensitive and even callous. We both felt angered that parents had to endure not only the emotional pain of their loss but did not receive acknowledgement of the impact of the death on their lives and that their grief had been 'disenfranchised grief' (Doka, 1989). This triggered for Jones a memory of her own personal losses where she had had empathic interlocutors and how this had enraged her.

For Murphy, there was a point where her anger was directed against a couple she interviewed who used forums in the wake of their loss. They mentioned a contributor to a babyloss forum that they followed. On here was an account from a women who had a particular experience of loss that marked her out from other people. However, the particular nature of the loss meant that at times the details she posted were inconsistent. The couple interviewed were angry about this, feeling that this inconsistency meant that this particular mother was lying. Murphy's anger was for two reasons. First, she was convinced she had also interviewed the forum contributor that they were referring to and knew that the account would be true. Second, she was angry at the ethics committee as, under their constraints, she felt unable to reveal that it was entirely possible that the account was true. Ethics then got in the way of being able to challenge some accounts and defend other participants from spurious claims.

Black humour

As noted earlier, there were some emotions experienced by one author but not the other. Murphy, for example, found participants had found a lot of black humour in their experiences which they shared with her: tears of sadness intermingled with tears of laughter during many of the interviews. It was interesting to see how, despite the tragic nature of their experience, a dark humour was drawn upon by parents who could still see the funny side to some aspects of what happened to them. Laughter, of course is well known to be a coping strategy and, while emotions ran high at points during the research, humour was also a way of deflecting it. For example, in one interview that

Murphy conducted a participant revealed the joke name she had given to her son and giggled uncontrollably. Moreover, another couple were keen to recall the humour a midwife brought to their experience where he (sic) compared the mother's reproductive organs to a car engine. This serves to remind the researcher that, while ethical considerations might be paramount in researching sensitive subjects, individuals have the capability and the agency to utilise techniques that will dissipate difficult emotions, whether it is through changing the subject; the use of gallows humour or irony. As one participant put it:

> You know you have to trust these people with your lives and the lives of your prospective children and they didn't deliver ... literally.

Shame

Due to her work as a counsellor, Jones felt a sense of shame. She heard many accounts from parents who had sought counselling for their grief. While most who did so benefitted from it, one parent felt that she had not done so. When she recounted to the counsellor her relationship difficulties, the mother felt resentment when she was informed by the counsellor that she just had to accept things. Jones felt a sense of professional shame: as a trained therapist herself, she had supported many bereaved parents, and felt strongly the counsellor could have better supported this participant.

Other feelings: relief, responsibility, gratitude and happiness

Other feelings referred to by Jones included *relief, responsibility* and *gratitude*. Stories were at times difficult to listen to and to tell. For this reason, she offered parents the opportunity to have a copy of the transcript and some parents took up this offer. Her sense of relief was apparent when parents encouraged her to publish these stories. This relief was felt alongside her sense of gratitude that despite their loss, they shared their stories willingly. She felt a responsibility to get these stories out and was duty bound to ensure that professionals and others heard about the impact on bereaved parents (Jones, 2014, 2013; Jones et al., 2019). This was also the case for Murphy (Murphy, 2019, 2013a, 2013b, 2012; Murphy & Thomas, 2013).

Finally, it is worth noting the *happiness* that Murphy felt during the research as some of the women she spoke to were expecting a subsequent child and, without exception, she would later be emailed with news and photos of a new arrival. She always welcomed those emails which counterbalanced the negativity of the interviews.

Emotions after the interviews

For both Jones and Murphy the range of emotions did not just start and finish with the interview process but were experienced during the transcribing and analysing of the data too: emotions came back to haunt both of us. They were also present in what we term 'the spaces between'. These are the times before the interview and afterwards as we would travel home (for Murphy this was often by car which made her wonder now how safe she might have been driving home). Going to sleep that same night and waking up the next morning were also points at which the emotions might return. Discussion of the interviews with supervisors or during conference presentations would also spark emotions too – in particular anger. For example, Murphy relates mentioning to someone that she knew (anecdotally) of some parents who took their stillborn baby out for a walk in its pram. Rather than an expression of interest, she encountered anger from the person who said 'God, some people just take it too bloody far!' This example also highlights how it is unpredictable to know when these different emotions will come to the fore.

When analysing data both Murphy and Jones continued to experience similar emotions to those experienced during the fieldwork. Jones, for example, would rankle every time she read the comment from the couple describing another participant as a liar; she would continue to feel guilty at the very personal nature of the information parents were giving her and to feel anger at the insensitive words of a health professional or friend; and with some of the interviews, both of us would continue to look for signs she was being hoaxed. Some interviews would distress Jones more since the accounts were expressed with a great deal of emotion and again a sense of guilt would pervade her thoughts. Even at writing this article, as she engages with the data many year later, her sense of disbelief at the lack of compassion expressed by one bereaved parent for another and the anger she had felt towards insensitive comments remains as present now as it was at the time.

As mentioned earlier, Murphy used grounded theory which meant that when an interview had been transcribed, she would revisit it – more than once – to break the data up into codes and categories. While she had no concerns that the research distressed her or had a negative impact, there is one thing worth mentioning which is relevant. Following the interviews, and up to this day, Murohy can read one of the interviews or recall a comment that was said to her, and she can see herself straight back in that participant's home. She can hear their voice and see the room clearly. She can remember the visceral feel of the sofa or chair that she sat on, the bodily reactions to the account of their experiences. As she sits and writes this now, a decade later, such flashbacks almost feel like she has at least one symptom of post-traumatic stress disorder (PTSD) (NHS, online, undated).

Emotions, objectivity and research

For these studies, our research encounters were an embodied experience that required emotional labour of which one aspect was the management of emotions. What do we mean by this? For Hochschild (1998:9) emotional management is ' ... an effort by any means, conscious or not, to change one's feeling or emotion.'

Part of the emotion work that we engaged in while undertaking our qualitative research was to manage our own internal feelings with outward displays of emotion. This meant that we had to consciously manage and reflect upon our embodied experience. During some interviews we found ourselves displaying emotions that were at odds with how we felt: while this might be the professional way to behave, is it an honest one? But when respondents discussed other bereaved parents in a hostile or derogatory way which evoked anger or disbelief in each of us as researchers, we had to contain it to stay within the ethical requirements of our research. Instead, we found ourselves merely nodding as if in understanding, rather than showing our horror or disgust at a point when we really wanted to challenge a respondent's account. In writing up experiences we then needed to be careful that some participants who had made us angry (or who we might have disbelieved) were not overlooked in the presentation of our data. Was it more likely that we favoured the quotes of some participants over others? For both of us, undoubtedly. Moreover, some participants were incredibly articulate and explained their experiences and feelings so well that it was too easy to rely on them. But it is probable too, that the emotions engendered by some parents, made them more likely to be drawn upon when writing up. The greater levels of empathy with some parents may also have resulted in their accounts being over-emphasised at the cost of others.

If we appeared detached in some research encounters, this was both to retain a professional distancing as well as to protect ourselves. Indeed, some of the difficulties we encountered in conducting research with bereaved parents was attributable to us constantly having to manage emotions in the field. As Schaffir et al. (1980: iv) note:

> [t]he intensity of the field work process typically accompanied by a psychological anxiety result[s] in a continuous presentation and management of self when in the process of those being studied.

Indeed, the constant management of self in our research was prevalent during interviews where there was a high degree of emotion expressed by participants.

However, the emotional impact of conducting the interviews did not simply stop when it ended. The sense of sadness which prevailed felt overwhelming at times, triggering as it did, for Jones, her own sense of hopelessness and bereavement responses following her own previous loss. We would agree with Visser (2017) that researchers need to be warned of the emotional impact of interviewing but it strikes us that it should be highlighted that this warning should be extended to every stage of the research project and that the management of emotions should be built into the study design whether this is to use a research journal or the use of clinical supervision. While it might be that colleagues on research teams have colleagues happy to talk over the emotionality of interviewing as a support mechanism, the lone researcher – such as a doctoral student – is more isolated and this needs to be acknowledged with measures being available to support lone researchers where necessary.

Data analysis and emotionally-sensed knowledge

So what of emotionally-sensed knowledge? That we were impacted to some degree by these encounters is in no doubt, but what of the data? When presenting qualitative research findings we are, by necessity, partial in the sense that we have to make choices about which data we use to demonstrate a point and what is left in the transcripts. This is not merely an intellectual decision but might also be an emotional one. To take the example of anger, where we are presented with data from participants which makes us react emotionally more than others we are more likely to use those ones than others in order to inspire anger and empathy in our readers. This is especially the case when our research is disseminated to health professionals as we are hoping to inspire action for change. We are then at risk of privileging some accounts over others. At the other extreme, what are we likely to do when presented with an account which means we are angry at the participants themselves? It may mean that we are less likely to use such an account and therefore that participant's experience is discounted. Certainly in terms of empathizing with the woman who lost two babies in one pregnancy, Murphy was at risk of not valuing so much the account of the couple who thought that that women was lying. For Jones perhaps her anger at the woman who was unsympathetic to someone who had had a similar loss might mean she would discount other things the woman was saying. In both scenarios, there is the danger that in under-valuing accounts due to our emotions we may miss valuable research data. Indeed, while Hubbard et al. (2001) suggest that there is a danger in over-empathising with participants, perhaps we can be at risk of under-emphasizing with them too – a concern that is not often raised when considering issues of empathy in qualitative research.

To that end, our experience highlights the importance that, as qualitative researchers, we need to pay full attention to the emotions our data gives rise to, not only to be aware of our subjectivities but also to counter the risk of bias against individual participants whose stories might not fit what we would expect or, indeed, would like to hear.

Conclusion

We have outlined in this article the emotions that we both experienced while undertaking research with parents around perinatal death. As documented these emotions were not limited to sadness but ranged from humour and happiness through to anger and guilt. When researching such subjects it is important for researchers to exercise reflexivity and be aware of their emotions throughout the process – from study design through to data analysis and preparing the final report. To that end drawing on concepts such as 'emotionally-sensed knowledge' can give useful insights around how decisions are made about data analysis and to avoid privileging some accounts over others. Indeed, it can be useful to see how emotions can lead us to under-empathise with participants where, very often, we are at pains not to over-empathise with them.

Disclosure statement

No potential conflict of interest was reported by the authors.

References

Armentrout, D. C. (2005) *Holding a place: A grounded theory of parents bringing their infant in their daily lives following the removal of life support and subsequent infant death* [Unpublished PhD thesis]. The University of Texas Graduate School of Biomedical Sciences at Galveston.
Brewer. (2000). *Ethnography*. Open University Press.
Brown, L. M., & Gilligan, C. (1993). Meeting at the crossroads: Girl's psychology and development. Harvard University Press
Corden, A., Sainsbury, R., Sloper, R., & Ward, B. (2005). Using a model of group psychotherapy to support social research on sensitive topics. *Western Journal of Nursing Research*, *10*(2), 163–175. DOI:10.1080/13645570320001195711
Cotterill, P., & Letherby, G. (1993). Weaving stories: Personal auto/biographies in feminist research. *Sociology*, *27*(1), 67–80. https://doi.org/10.1177/003803859302700107
Cylwik, H. (2001). Notes from the field: Emotions of place in the production and interpretation of text. *Social Research Methodology*, *4*(3), 243–250. https://doi.org/10.1080/13645570110057924
Doka, K. J. (ed.). (1989). *Disenfranchised grief*. Lexington Books.
Etherington, K. (2004). *Becoming a reflexive researcher: Using our selves in research*. Jessica Kingsley.
Evans, R., Ribbens McCarthy, J., Bowlby, S., Wouango, J., & Kebe, F. (2017). Producing emotionally sensed knowledge? Reflexivity and emotions in researching responses to death. *International Journal of Social Research Methodology*, *20*(6), 585–598. https://doi.org/10.1080/13645579.2016.1257679
Goodrum, S., & Keys, J. L. (2007). Reflections on two studies of emotionally sensitive topics: bereavement from murder and abortion. *International Journal of Social Research Methodology*, *10:4*(4), p249–258. https://doi.org/10.1080/13645570701400976
Hochschild, A. (1998). *The managed heart: Commercialisation of human feeling*. University of California Press.
Hubbard, G., Backett-Milburn, K., & Kemmer, D. (2001). Working with emotion: Issues for the researcher in fieldwork and teamwork. *International Journal of Social Research Methodology*, *4*(2), 119–137. https://doi.org/10.1080/13645570116992
Jones, K. (2010) *Parental perspectives on grief and loss following stillbirth and neonatal death* [University of Bristol PhD thesis]. https://ethos.bl.uk/OrderDetails.do?uin=uk.bl.ethos.529861
Jones, K. (2013). Researching Sensitive Subjects Among a Vulnerable Population. *Methodological Innovations Online*, *8*(1), 113–127. https://doi.org/10.4256/mio.2013.008
Jones, K. (2014). Parental identity in narratives of grief following perinatal death. *Grief Matters: The Australian Journal of Grief and Bereavement*, *17*(2), 38–42.
Jones, K., Robb, M., Murphy, S., & Davies, A. (2019). New understandings of fathers' experiences of grief and loss following stillbirth and neonatal death: A scoping review. *Midwifery (Early Access)*, *79*, 102531. https://doi.org/10.1016/j.midw.2019.102531
Komaromy, C. (2020). The performance of researching sensitive issues. *Mortality.24*(3), 364–372. https://doi.org/10.1080/13576275.2019.1635104
Layne, L. L. (2000). He was a real baby with real things: A material culture analysis of personhood, parenthood and pregnancy loss. *Journal of Material Culture*, *5*(3), 321–345. https://doi.org/10.1177/135918350000500304
Lee, R. M. (1993). *Doing research on sensitive topics*. Sage.
Letherby, G. (1993). The meanings of miscarriage. *Women's Studies International Forum*, *16*(2), 165–180. https://doi.org/10.1016/0277-5395(93)90006-U
Liamputtong, P. (2007). *Researching the vulnerable: A guide to sensitive research methods*. Sage.
Mauthner, N., & Doucet, A. (1998). Reflections on a voice centred relational method. In J. Ribbens & R. Edwards (Eds.), *Feminist dilemmas in qualitative research: Public knowledge and private lives*. (pp. 119–144). Sage.
Murphy, S. (2009) *Parenting the stillborn': Gender, identity and bereavement* [Unpublished PhD thesis]. University of Surrey.
Murphy, S. (2012). Reclaiming a moral identity: Stillbirth, stigma and 'moral mothers'. *Midwifery*, *28*(4), 476–480. https://doi.org/10.1016/j.midw.2011.06.005

Murphy, S. (2013a). Finding the positive in loss: Stillbirth and its potential for parental empowerment. *Bereavement Care*, *31*(3), 98–103. https://doi.org/10.1080/02682621.2012.740277

Murphy, S. (2013b). Bereaved parents: A contradiction in terms? In S. Earle, C. Komaromy, & L. Layne (Eds.), *Understanding reproductive loss: Perspectives on life, death and fertility* (pp. 117–128). Ashgate.

Murphy, S. (2019). "I'd failed to produce a baby and I'd failed to notice when the baby was in distress": The social construction of bereaved motherhood. *Women's Studies International Forum*, *74*(May-June), 35–41. https://doi.org/10.1016/j.wsif.2019.02.009

Murphy, S., & Thomas, H. (2013). Stillbirth and loss: Family practices and display. *Sociological Research Online*, *18*(1), 27–37. https://doi.org/10.5153/sro.2889

National Health Service. (undated). *Post traumatic stress disorder – Symptoms*. Retrieved November 12, 2018, from https://www.nhs.uk/conditions/post-traumatic-stress-disorder-ptsd/.

Perinatal Institute (2011). *Perinatal mortality definitions*. Online. Retrieved March 29, 2019, from http://www.pi.nhs.uk/pnm/definitions.htm.

Ratnam. (2019). Listening to difficult stories: Listening as a research methodology. *Emotion, Space and Society*, *31*, 18–25. https://doi.org/10.1016/j.emospa.2019.03.003

SANDS. (2010). *Bereavement care report*.

Schaffir, W. B., Stebbins, A. A., & Torowetz, A. (eds). (1980). *Fieldwork experience: Qualitative approaches to social research*. St Martin's Press.

Strauss, A., & Corbin, J. (1998). *Basics of qualitative research*. Sage.

Visser, R. (2017). Doing death: Reflecting on the researcher's subjectivity and emotions. *Death Studies*, *41*(1), 6–13. https://doi.org/10.1080/07481187.2016.1257877

Woodthorpe, K. (2011). Researching death: Methodological reflections on the management of critical distance. *International Journal of Social Research Methodology*, *14*(2), 99–109. https://doi.org/10.1080/13645579.2010.496576

'Men, we just deal with it differently': researching sensitive issues with young men

Martin Robb

ABSTRACT
This article discusses the sensitivities that come into play when researching issues of gender identity and relationships with young men, particularly when the researcher is male. The article argues that the nature of hegemonic masculinity, and the way that masculinity 'works' in the research process, means that research with young men on these issues is inherently sensitive and brings with it considerable challenges for researchers. Adopting a psychosocial approach to issues of gender identity, and to conceptualising the research process, the article also argues that it is important to understand the research encounter as an intersubjective process in which the identities of both researcher and researched influence each other in dynamic though often hidden ways. The article discusses these challenges in detail and suggests ways in which researchers might respond to them.

Introduction

This article discusses the sensitivities that come into play when researching issues of gender identity and relationships with young men, particularly when the researcher is male. It argues that the nature of hegemonic masculinity, and the way that masculinity 'works' in the research process, means that research with young men on these issues is inherently sensitive. Adopting a psychosocial approach to issues of gender identity, the article also argues that it is important to understand the research encounter as an intersubjective process in which the identities of both researcher and researched influence each other in dynamic though often hidden ways. The article discusses these challenges and suggests ways in which researchers might respond to them.

The research studies

This paper draws on the author's experiences of researching men and masculinity, which have included studies of men working in early years childcare (Robb, 2001) and fathers involved in the care of their young children (Robb, 2004a, 2004b). However, the article will draw principally on two studies with socially disadvantaged young men, undertaken between 2013 and 2017. In the first, I acted as Principal Investigator for the ESRC-funded study (Grant No. ES/K005863) 'Beyond male role models: gender identities and practices in work with young men', which explored the role of gender in work with young men using social care services (Featherstone et al., 2017; Robb, Featherstone et al., 2017; Ruxton et al., 2018; Ward et al., 2017). In the second, I was Principal Investigator for 'Young men, masculinity and wellbeing', exploring the links between social expectations surrounding masculinity and young men's emotional wellbeing (Robb & Ruxton, 2018; Robb et al, 2017).

Psychosocial research studies the ways in which subjective experience is interwoven with social life, maintaining that subjective experiences 'cannot be abstracted from societal, cultural and historical contexts, but nor can they be deterministically reduced to the social'. Instead, social and cultural worlds are 'shaped by psychological process and intersubjective relations' (Association for Psychosocial Studies, undated).

A psychosocial perspective on research with men

This approach assumes that research data are produced dynamically in the interactions between researcher and researched. On the one hand, it acknowledges that this is a socially constructed process, in which the social identities of those involved and the wider social context will, influence the data that is produced. However, a psychosocial perspective maintains that the research process is also influenced by unconscious and intersubjective factors. Common to all psychoanalytic schools is 'the idea of a dynamic unconscious which defends against anxiety and significantly influences people's actions, lives and relations' (Hollway & Jefferson, 2000, p. 19). More specifically, the same authors argue, a psychosocial approach construes 'both the researcher and researched as anxious defended subjects, whose mental boundaries are porous where unconscious material is concerned.'

Much writing about the research process focuses on the impact of the process on participants, paying less attention to the impact on the researcher. However, a psychosocial approach cannot overlook the fact that the researcher is also a person with a constantly evolving identity, which includes their gender identity, and with unconscious motivations that inevitably come into play in the research encounter. While there is a substantial literature on the impact of researcher identity, including his or her gender or ethnic identity (for example, see Gough, 2003; Gunaratnam, 2003), analysis tends to focus on one direction of influence, being interested primarily in the impact of the researcher's identity on participants. However, in this article I want to suggest that the influence is two-way, and that researcher and researched are bound together in a dynamic loop of intersubjective influence. There is a need to encourage a critical reflexivity on the part of researchers about how their own identities and interactions both shape and are shaped by the research encounter. This is particularly the case when the topic being researched is of a sensitive nature, such as research focusing on issues of gender identity, since it may generate sensitivities for researchers as well as for participants.

The identities that come into play in the research process, and dynamically influence it, include the gender identities of both researchers and participants. A psychosocial approach to gender shares, with writers from a sociological perspective such as Connell (1995), the notion that masculinities and femininities are plural, socially situated and constantly formed and reformed in social interactions, rather than being static or biologically predetermined. However, a psychosocial perspective also includes a keen awareness that, to quote Redman (2005, p. 535), 'the various practices through which boys and young men "do" masculinity are saturated with unconscious fantasy, intersubjective communication, and inextricably blurred boundaries between self and other.'

One of the specific contributions that a psychosocial approach can make to understanding the way masculinity 'works' in sensitive research with men and boys, derives from the work of psychoanalytic feminist writers, such as Benjamin (1998), who argue that masculinity, particularly in the contemporary western context, is a defensive structure achieved via distancing from the feminine and a 'repudiation of femininity' (Benjamin, 1998, p. 136). Redman (2005, p. 535) argues that phenomena such as 'homophobia, misogyny … and the disparagement of that which is perceived to be "effeminate", suggest profound levels of unconscious anxiety and confusion and, in consequence, a desperate attempt to split off and locate inside others that which feels too painful to tolerate.' This defensiveness may be particularly evident when an individual's masculinity is felt to be under threat: for example, in a research interview or focus group when sensitive issues relating to gender identity are being explored. Male participants may respond to the invitation to explore such sensitive areas by employing defensive strategies, including avoiding directly answers to questions, or diverting the conversation on to less threatening topics.

A psychosocial view shares with sociological accounts of gender construction a view that gender identities, are constantly in process and need to be continuously 'performed' (Butler, 1990). Given the defended nature of masculine identity, this sense of performance will be intensified in the presence of other men: for example, in an all-male focus group, or where the researcher is male. This article will suggest that a psychosocial perspective not only deepens understanding of researching sensitive subjects with men, but can also help to provide strategies for dealing with some of the challenging issues that arise from that process.

'Bottle it up and get on with it': young men talking about emotions

One of the ways in which the masculine identities of participants can shape research with young men on sensitive issues, is the social expectation that men and boys will be unwilling, and to some extent unable, to share their feelings openly in a public setting. Research on the sociology of the emotions, and work on emotional labour, has analysed the gendered social construction of emotional life (Hochschild, 1983). It could be argued that 'common sense' assumptions about gender differences of this kind have been given academic credibility by the work of researchers such as Gilligan (1982), who argued that women and men have different 'moral voices', with the former focused on relationships and care and the latter more concerned with questions of rights and justice. Out of the work of Gilligan and other 'difference feminists' has grown the burgeoning field of feminist care ethics (Held, 2005; Kittay, 1999). At the same time, developments in neuroscience have lent credence to conventional assumptions that women 'are better able to connect feelings to words and use language to express interior experiences and memories' which 'helps them to communicate verbally with others, which builds relationships' (Bottaro, 2018).

It might be countered that, even if differences in emotional expressivity have traditionally existed between men and women, they have largely been eroded, as notions of what constitutes acceptable masculinity have changed, and as younger generations of men grow up with different masculine gender norms, including greater encouragement to share their feelings (for example, see Anderson, 2009). More men are now involved in the direct care of their children (Dermott, 2008), more fluid ideas of gender identity have come to the fore, and the image of the ideal man as 'buttoned up' and inexpressive has been supplemented in popular culture by alternative images of men as caring, expressive individuals (Robb, 2020).

However, one of the persistent findings from research with boys and young men, is that many still find the articulation of feelings difficult, and that this difficulty is in part the result of persistent expectations about how 'real' men should behave (Robb & Ruxton, 2017). Researchers on young masculinity have consistently reported a lack of emotional openness in the groups they encountered. Holland and colleagues described the 'unsupportive' nature of talk in boys' peer groups, with their 'collective pressure to express and define themselves in a particular way in order to prove their manhood' (Holland, J., Ramazonoglu, C., Sharpe, S. and Thomson, R, 1998, pp. 12–13; see also Mac an Ghaill, 1994). Conversely, Frosh and colleagues found that while the boys they interviewed were reluctant to talk openly about personal issues in group settings, they were prepared to do so in one-to-one encounters (Frosh et al., 2002). Thus, young men's lack of confidence in sharing feelings in the research encounter may be partly contextual, and therefore dependent on creating an environment in which there is less need to 'perform' masculinity in front of peers. At the same time, it should be remembered that masculine identities are diverse and, at least in part, socially constructed, so that the identities of young men will shaped by varying social expectations around gender. Particular issues will be more or less 'sensitive' for different groups of young men, depending to some extent on their background and experience.

The stereotype of the inexpressive young male certainly found some support in our second study with young men from a range of social, ethnic and cultural backgrounds (Robb, Ruxton et al., 2017). When dealing with emotional problems, some participants said that they would find specifically 'masculine' ways of dealing with them, rather than sharing their feelings with others or seeking professional help. As one participant said: 'Men, we just deal with it differently ... we've got other channels for expressing our feelings'. Some suggested that if they were experiencing problems they would simply 'bottle it up and get on with it' or 'work it out'. While it would be easy to dismiss this kind of talk as a way of evading emotional engagement, recent research on men's 'banter' has suggested that it can be better viewed as a creative way of dealing with difficult feelings (Nichols, 2018).

Humour was certainly one of the ways in which this reluctance to talk openly about emotional issues manifested itself. Other strategies included giving brief or superficial responses, or simply avoiding the question and passing on to other issues. This was the case in our attempts in this study to raise the issue of sexuality and particularly of same-sex relationships. However, perhaps the most significant strategies for not engaging with sensitive emotional issues involved active diversion away from these issues, confirming what was said earlier about the defended nature of masculine identities.

'It's weakness ... it's an excuse': defensive masculinities on display in the discussion of sensitive issues

Anderson (2005) suggests that defensive masculinity is particularly evident in contexts where masculine identity is threatened, including what are perceived to be 'feminised terrains'. It can be argued that a research study on sensitive issues such as gender identity and relationships would certainly be perceived by some young men as a 'feminised' setting. This is because, despite the changes in gender relations described earlier, there continue to be few social spaces where it is legitimate for men to discuss issues of this kind with each other (Robb, 2004a).

This masculine defensiveness can have an impact on the research process. In a focus group with black and ethnic minority young men, one participant consistently deflected any discussion of his own feelings about relationships by directing blame towards young women:

The government gives all the benefits to the female, all the parental responsibilities to the female ... If I see another single mum walking down the street, yeah, I'm going to explode in my mind ....It's gone from men being sexist to men having all the power to now really and truly women have got all the power.

This young man had been through some painful experiences in his intimate relationships, but all of his emotional energy was directed outwards, towards women and girls. In attempting to understand reactions of this kind, it is important to see them in the context of the anti-feminist backlash and rise of men's rights movements in recent years. Young men will have been exposed to these insurgent discourses, as well as to 'official' discourses of gender equality (Flood, 2004). Other defensive strategies may include attempts to deny that a problem exists, or in discussing a painful issue to direct attention away from the personal to the societal level. In the same group discussion with young men, this dynamic was evident in the forceful refusal by some participants to allow that men might experience problems with depression:

P1: *If anyone who says they have depression, for me, I think there's weakness in them.*
P2: *Exactly.*
Interviewer: *You think it's weakness?*
P1: *Yeah, yeah it's weak, it's an excuse.*
Interviewer: *Right, why do you think that?*
P1: *Because ...*
P2: *It's an excuse.*

P1: Well I was going to say, obviously from my background, my parents are from Nigeria, so I know people who struggle – you get what I'm saying to you?

Despite this attempt to shut down the discussion, a third participant eventually managed to give voice to his own experience of mental health problems. However, he did this in in a way that could itself be seen as defensive and evasive:

P3: Yeah, but what you've got to remember is that a lot of teachers, not the teachers, a lot of doctors, like once they find out that that kid's bad, they'll just slap it on him, 'Oh, he's got ADHD' [Attention Deficit Hyperactivity Disorder] ... They slap it on him, oh he's got ADHD, oh he's got autism. Like from when I've grown up, yeah, my family has a history of mental illness ranging from my nan to her mum, and every boy in the family has something wrong with them, put it like that.

Interviewer: Every boy in the family?

P3: Yeah, every boy in the family, but the girls are calm. I don't know how that works, but that's just how it goes. But at the same time, when I was younger they diagnosed me like with ADHD and autism when I was five. I've been to like five different schools. ... But as you get older it's like raw. It's still there, but it's not, you know how to control it more, if you know what I mean. But nowadays it's just like everyone's just getting slapped with it. Oh he's a bad – you, ADHD, he's a bad – you, ADHD.

In this example, a young man who had experienced mental health problems couches that admission within a general complaint about how boys are labelled, which to some extent undermines and diverts attention away from what he is saying about his own suffering. Within the hostile context established by the other participants in the group, perhaps that is the closest it was possible for him to come to an admission of something as unmasculine as emotional pain.

A psychosocial approach to research tends to support the use of an open-ended, narrative method for exploring sensitive issues with participants. For example, the 'free association narrative interview' technique advocates allowing participants' ideas and views emerge in their own words and following participants' own 'ordering and phrasing' of their story (Hollway & Jefferson, 2000, p. 53). However, in the focus group examples here, this approach allowed participants to *avoid* open discussion of sensitive issues, and at the same time to obstruct other participants' emotional honesty. On reflection, a more interventionist approach by the interviewer might have resulted in a more productive exchange. The strengths and weaknesses of narrative methods for researching sensitive issues will be discussed in more detail below.

Being a man: the experience of a male researcher

As stated earlier, the research encounter is a two-way, intersubjective process, in which the identity of the *researcher* also plays a part. Since gender identities are not simply inherent in the individual, but continually produced in interactions and relationships, it is important to take into account the impact of the researcher's identity on the process.

From a psychosocial perspective, the discussion of sensitive issues will inevitably have an impact on the researcher as well as those he is researching. Given that the male researcher has a masculine identity of his own, this means that the discussion of topics that are sensitive for men will have an impact on him emotionally. In turn, this will have an impact on his behaviour as a researcher. But it should also be borne in mind that the researcher will also be 'performing' masculinity, and the ways in which he does this, like the participants' performance, will be partly dependent on how he, at both a conscious and unconscious level, positions the 'other', the participant.

At the same time, participants' performance of masculinity in the research encounter will to some extent be *in response to* the researcher: and thus the ways in which the participant perceives the researcher's gender identity will have an impact on their own performance of masculinity. Elsewhere I have argued that this is made up of a complex web of identifications and disidentifications, most of them hidden from view (Robb, 2004a).

It is also important to add that these issues cannot be considered in isolation from other social identities, such as social class, ethnicity and age. In our second study, we were keenly aware of our identities as older, white male academics, facilitating focus groups with much younger, ethnically diverse and mostly socially disadvantaged men. The ways in which participants positioned us, reflected in the questions they asked about our backgrounds (for example, whether we were married or were fathers ourselves), arguably had an impact on the ways in which they performed their masculinity, and how they responded to our questions on sensitive topics.

These researcher-participant relationships inevitably have an unconscious component that evokes associations with previous relationships. For example, a younger man might possibly see in an older male researcher traces of his own father, or of other authority figures in his life, and position the researcher accordingly. There will then be identifications and disidentifications based on these positionings and the ways in which these play out are not necessarily predictable or easy to disentangle (Robb, 2004a). As argued below, there is a need for researchers both to reflect critically on these processes, as part of their analysis, and to enlist the support of others to enable them to do so.

Identifications can arise from an unconscious desire to be like, or be liked by, the other party. This can be true for the researcher as much as the person being researched, and can lead to either party adjusting aspects of their identity, or framing their questions or responses in a way designed to gain affirmation from the other party. After all, being 'liked' by participants can be conducive to the production of useful data. Disidentifications can lead to defensiveness or hostility, and a desire to emphasise differences from the other person. As a consequence, in exploring a sensitive issue such as gender identity, a participant may opt to emphasise ways in which his identity and experience do, or alternatively do not, align with those of the researcher.

Some of this may be conscious or strategic: a researcher may consciously decide to 'play up' similarities in order to gain the trust and engagement of the research participant. But I would argue that particular issues of identification and its opposite arise when both researcher and researched are male. Something about the performative, defensive nature of masculinity means that gender identity will always be 'in play' in the encounter, influencing it in particular ways. When the focus of the discussion is a sensitive issue such as gender identity itself, then this performativity and defensiveness are arguably heightened. And finally, a psychosocial approach maintains that, whether or not this is part of the researcher's conscious strategy, at an unconscious level these processes are going on anyway. A critically reflexive awareness of the impact of these factors should be a part of data analysis when researching sensitive issues with young men.

In terms of my own experience as a researcher, I am reflexively aware that I come to this activity as an older, white man, originally from a working-class/lower middle-class background, but as one who has inevitably taken on a middle-class identity as a result of education and career. I also come to the research as someone who does not identify with many aspects of 'traditional' masculinity: indeed, this has been one of the motivations for my interest in this field of research. Admittedly, all researchers put on something of an act when interviewing: research itself can be seen at least in part as a performance. We choose, either consciously or unconsciously, to bring into play some aspects of our 'self' and not others, or to emphasise some aspects and downplay others.

I am aware that when interviewing participants from disadvantaged backgrounds, my submerged working-class identity, to which I no longer have any real claim, can come to the surface, as I seek connection with participants. One possible danger of this unconscious need to find points of identification with research participants might be the risk of colluding with participants' attitudes, including their strategies for avoiding or diverting from open discussion of sensitive topics. Moreover, as a consequence of seeking to identify with participants, there is a risk of highlighting similarities and overlooking important differences. There is a need for researchers to be reflexively aware of how their own identities and identifications might influence the research process.

Are young men more likely to 'open up' about sensitive issues with a male rather than a female researcher? This is a longstanding debate (see for example, Williams and Heikes, 1993). In our experience, the fact that young men were willing to engage in discussion of these issues at all was a sign of trust that was partly based on a shared gender identity. At the same time, given our earlier discussion of how masculinity operates in all-male settings, it should be remembered that our participants' responses were motivated and shaped, in part, by a need to 'perform' or bolster their masculine identities in front of each other, and in front of us as male researchers.

Methods and approaches

If these are some of the issues that arise when researching sensitive issues of identity and relationships with young men, what can researchers, and particularly male researchers, do to mitigate some of the impact and to ensure that the research encounter is productive, and how can a psychosocial perspective help to frame appropriate strategies? One suggestion is that an open-ended, narrative approach will be more productive in overcoming reluctance and defensiveness in participants, than one based on an interview schedule packed with pre-determined questions. In my own experience, closed and direct questions about sensitive issues are rarely productive, and may lead to brief responses. The language of gender identity, and therefore the way in which questions are framed, may be alien to the discourse of participants. My experience is that asking men and boys direct questions about their 'masculinity' or 'gender identity' is mostly unproductive (see Robb, 2004a). Instead, the aim should be to encourage participants to talk openly about their experiences, with the hope that their perceptions about the issues under review will emerge less directly.

However, as demonstrated here, Hollway and Jefferson (2000) free association narrative interview method may allow participants to avoid the 'sensitive' issues that you would really like them to discuss. Preferable to complete open-endedness might be a semi-structured narrative method in which the interviewer skilfully and sensitively turns the flow of the conversation back to these topics, while also gently disrupting attempts to avoid the topic, or to 'shut down' the contributions of others.

Another consequence of the issues discussed here might be that individual interviews will be more productive than focus groups in encouraging young men to be open about sensitive issues. As suggested in the study by Frosh et al. (2002) cited earlier, a combination of focus groups, which initiate discussion of sensitive issues at a general level, followed by individual interviews, in which participants, are enabled to be more open in a supportive environment, might be an effective solution.

Gender dynamics also mean it is important to give careful thought to the composition of research teams, and where appropriate considering mixed-gender teams, or repeat interviews alternating male and female researchers. There is certainly great value in recruiting a mixed gender team at the analysis stage, so as to compare and highlight gender differences in response to the data.

In addition, it is important to build in time and resource for extended critical reflection on the research encounter. This will involve the researcher making detailed notes after each interview or focus group, followed by supervision or peer review sessions, in which the researcher is enabled to reflect critically on the interpersonal dynamics experienced in the encounter, and how this might have had an impact on the data.

Conclusion

This article has sought to explore some of the complex issues that arise when researching sensitive issues of gender identity and relationships with young men, particularly when the researcher is also male. Based on critical reflections on the author's own experience as a researcher, the article has highlighted some of the issues that arise from viewing the research encounter as a psychosocial process in which the identities and interactions of researchers and participants influence the outcome of the encounter. The article has argued that, because of the nature of masculine identities and the ways that masculinity 'works' in the research encounter, young men are likely to adopt strategies to avoid engaging with sensitive issues, and to actively divert from and defend against the open sharing of feelings and experiences. Finally, drawing on psychosocial insights, the article has suggested some ways in which research teams can mitigate the negative consequences of these factors, and ensure that the research process is productive.

Disclosure statement

No potential conflict of interest was reported by the author.

Funding

The research studies discussed in this article were funded by the Economic and Social Research Council and by Axe-Unilever (via Promundo-US).

References

Anderson, E. (2005). Orthodox and Inclusive Masculinity: Competing Masculinities among Heterosexual Men in a Feminized Terrain, Sociological Perspectives, 48(3), 337–355.
Anderson, E. (2009). *Inclusive masculinity: The changing nature of masculinities.* Routledge.
Association for Psychosocial Studies (undated) 'What is psychosocial studies?' (n.d.) Retrieved 9 September 2019, from http://www.psychosocial-studies-association.org/about/
Benjamin, J. (1998). *Shadow of the other: Intersubjectivity and gender in psychoanalysis.* Routledge.
Bottaro, G. (2018). On the masculine genius. *Humanum: Issues in Family, Culture and Science*, 3.
Butler, J. (1990). *Gender Trouble.* Routledge.
Connell, R. W. (1995). *Masculinities.* Polity.
Dermott, E. (2008). *Intimate Fatherhood: A sociological analysis.* Routledge.
Featherstone, B., Robb, M., Ruxton, S., & Ward, M. R. M. (2017). "They are just good people … generally good people: Perspectives of young men on relationships with social care workers in the UK. *Children & Society*, 31(5), 331–341. https://doi.org/10.1111/chso.12201
Flood, M. (2004). '"Backlash: Angry men's movements". In S. E. Rossi (Ed.), *The battle and backlash rage on: Why feminism cannot be obsolete* (pp. 261–278). Xlibris.
Frosh, S., Phoenix, A., & Pattman, R. (2002). *Young masculinities: Understanding boys in contemporary society.* Palgrave.
Gilligan, C. (1982). *In a different voice: Psychological theory and women's development.* Harvard University Press.
Gough, B. (2003). 'Shifting researcher positions during a group interview study: A reflexive analysis and review'. In L. Finlay & B. Gough (Eds.), *Reflexivity: A practical guide for researchers in health and social sciences* (pp. 146–162). Blackwell, Oxford.
Gunaratnam, Y. (2003). *Researching 'race' and ethnicity: Methods, knowledge and power.* Sage.
Held, V. (2005). *The ethics of care.* Oxford University Press.
Hochschild, A. (1983). *The managed heart: Commercialisation of human feeling.* University of California Press.
Holland, J., Ramazonoglu, C., Sharpe, S. and Thomson, R. (1998). *The male in the head: Young people, heterosexuality and power.* Tufnell Press.
Hollway, W., & Jefferson, T. (2000). *Doing qualitative research differently: Free association, narrative and the interview method.* Sage.
Kittay, E. F. (1999). *Love's labor: Essays on women, equality and dependency.* Routledge.
Mac an Ghaill, M. (1994). *The making of men: Masculinities, sexualities and schooling.* Open University Press.
Nichols, K. (2018) '*Are we missing men's emotions? Re-imagining banter as a form of emotional expression for men*', Discover Society, [Retrieved 5 February 2020], from https://discoversociety.org/2018/11/06/are-we-missing-mens-emotions-re-imagining-banter-as-a-form-of-emotional-expression-for-men/

Redman, P. (2005). Who cares about the psycho-social?: Masculinities, schooling and the unconscious. *Gender and Education*, *17*(5), 531–538. https://doi.org/10.1080/09540250500192751

Robb, M. (2001). Men working in childcare. In P. Foley, J. Roche, & S. Tucker (Eds.), *Children in society: Contemporary theory, policy and practice* (pp. 230–238). Palgrave/The Open University.

Robb, M. (2004a). Exploring fatherhood: Masculinity and intersubjectivity in the research process. *Journal of Social Work Practice*, *18*(3), 395–406. https://doi.org/10.1080/0265053042000314456

Robb, M. (2004b). Men talking about fatherhood: Discourse and identities. In M. Robb, S. Barrett, C. Komaromy, & A. Rogers (Eds.), *Communication, relationships and care: A reader* (pp. 121–130). Routledge/The Open University.

Robb, M., Featherstone, B., Ruxton, S., & Ward, M. R. M. (2017). Family relationships and troubled masculinities: The experience of young men in contact with care and welfare services. In L. O'Dell, C. Brownlow, H. B. Rosqvist, & J. Du Preez (Eds.), *Different Childhoods*. (pp. 72–84). Routledge.

Robb, M., & Ruxton, S. (2018). Young men and gender identity. In H. Montgomery & M. Robb (Eds.), *Children and young people's worlds* (2nd ed.). (pp. 141–156). Policy Press/The Open University.

Robb, M. (2020). *Men, masculinities and the care of children: Images, ideas and identities*. Routledge.

Robb, M., & Ruxton, S. (2017) 'Act tough and hide weakness: Research reveals pressure young men are under', *The Conversation*, (Retrieved 22 July 2019, from https://theconversation.com/act-tough-and-hide-weakness-research-reveals-pressure-young-men-are-under-74898

Robb, M., Ruxton, S., & Bartlett, D. (2017), *Young men, masculinity and wellbeing: Report* The Open University.

Ruxton, S., Robb, M., Featherstone, B., & Ward, M. R. M. (2018). Beyond male role models: Gender identities and work with young men in the UK. In M. Kulkarni. & R. Jainin (Eds.), *Global masculinities: Interrogations and reconstructions*. (pp. 82–98). Routledge.

Ward, M. R. M., Tarrant, A., Terry, G., Featherstone, B., Robb, M., & Ruxton, S. (2017). 'Doing gender locally: The importance of "place" in understanding marginalised masculinities and young men's transitions to "safe" and successful futures'. *Sociological Review*, *65*(4), 797–815. https://doi.org/10.1177/0038026117725963

Williams, C. L., & Heikes, E. J. (1993). The importance of researcher's gender in the in-depth interview: Evidence from two case studies of male nurses. *Gender and Society*, *7*(2), 280–291. https://doi.org/10.1177/089124393007002008

The performance of researching sensitive issues

Carol Komaromy

ABSTRACT

Within sociological and organisational literature much attention has been paid to the emotional labour and emotion work performed by care staff. By contrast, comparatively little attention has been paid to that which researchers perform and how it is shaped by the need to behave appropriately and in ways that are in keeping with the demands of the study setting. Existing literature focuses largely on the need for researchers to be aware of their emotions as part of being reflexive and thus, through acknowledgement, minimising any emotional impact (subjectivity) on research interpretations. In this paper, I draw on two research experiences, an ethnographic study into end-of-life care in care homes and an exploration into the role of the Anatomical Pathology Technologist in a hospital mortuary to explore the tensions between conducting sensitive research and managing emotions. I conclude by drawing on the theories of Goffman and Hochschild to explore the relationship between emotion management and sensitive research.

Introduction, a sociological enquiry

In this paper I explore aspects of what it means to be an ethnographic researcher involved in sensitive research and the emotional nature of this role within the discipline of sociology. I argue that the role is complicated by a number of factors which involve researchers in degrees of emotion management. These factors include being aware of one's emotions and how they might influence data interpretation, and how to conduct oneself in the field. I use two examples of ethnographic research into death and dying to explore and illustrate some of the issues for researchers involved in researching such sensitive topics. Reflecting on the research process in both studies revealed some of the layers of complexity involved in the balance between objectivity and subjectivity demanded of researchers. The 'reflexive turn' describes the need to recognise that the ways in which knowledge is acquired is as relevant as any knowledge claims that are made (Altheide & Johnson, 1994) within the social sciences (Clifford & Marcus, 1986; Denzin, 1989). Certainly, the shift into reflexivity is not straightforward and presents dilemmas in terms of capturing the 'messiness' of reality, not least, as Coffey (1999) highlights, the tension between presenting the author/researcher's self while representing the experience of research participants. Despite such dilemmas, the anti-reductionist approach of reflexivity, which is at least a recognition of the researcher as an embodied, emotional person who brings some- thing more equitable to the qualitative research relationship, is welcomed by researchers who follow social constructionist paradigms. However, thus far much of the focus in the literature on the research process at least, has been mostly on the role of reflexivity on data interpretation. There are exceptions in which the emotional toll on researchers throughout all aspects of the research process is acknowledged (see Young & Lee, 1996; Howarth, 1998; Dickson-Swift, James, Kippen, & Liamputtong, 2007; Lee & Lee, 2012; Johnson, 2009; Woodthorpe, 2007). Here, I extend the focus to cover the process of data collection and the role of the researcher within the field-work endeavour, moving beyond a recognition of the emotional impact to consider what else the emotional demands might include.

In the two studies which I use to illustrate key points in this paper, I drew upon the theoretical perspective of symbolic interactionism to interpret what was taking place. The first study was part of my doctoral thesis (Komaromy, 2005) and was an ethno-graphic exploration into the care of older people in care home settings at the end of life. I used the ideas of Goffman (1990) to argue that death and dying were managed by home staff as performance, in which they had to act appropriately when residents were dying and also what happened when the residents did not die as expected. In the second study, in which a colleague and I explored the role of the Anatomical Pathology Technologist in a hospital setting (Komaromy & Woodthorpe, 2011), we identified the way in which dirty work (Hughes, 1962) and stigma (Goffman, 1963) contributed to an explanation of the lower status of such a highly-skilled and complex role. It is not surprising then, that having recognised the way that performance operated in these roles, I should reflect not only on my emotions but also my own performance as a researcher in these settings.

In the first section of this paper, I discuss the methodological challenges in death and dying research in terms of choosing the most appropriate research method. Next, I explore dimensions of doing sensitive research and identify three key layers of complexity to these dimensions. I then draw on my own research experiences to illustrate these points in more detail. Finally, I discuss what this means in the context of the reflexive turn and how researchers can make sound choices about conducting sensitive research.

Methodological challenges

Care homes and mortuaries are sequestered places to the extent that, despite being places that are occasionally visited by people with a legitimate claim, they are not part of the public domain. Providing an insider view as a researcher involved being able to describe the settings, roles and routines in detail as an important feature of communicating the context of both projects. Researching end-of-life care in care homes meant that the preferred method by which to capture what was happening was to be present in the home as a participant observer and see for myself how this care was delivered to dying residents. Likewise, for the second study, taking an ethnographic approach and being in the setting of the hospital mortuary, which is deliberately concealed from public view, was an essential aspect of conveying the reality of that setting. However, having chosen what appeared to be an obvious research method, there remained many methodological challenges about the extent to which it is possible to represent reality.

Describing the detail by the use of thick description has been positioned as a 'reassurance' of the validity of research by the ethnographic approach. However, the extent to which reality can be captured involves both epistemological and ontological dilemmas and it is something with which researchers have to struggle in order to understand what claims they can make. For example, Clifford and Marcus (1986), take account of the subjectivity of the process when they describe 'realities' as rhetorical devices, and likewise, Atkinson (1990) agrees that reality cannot be directly represented and, rather, is constructed and reconstructed through ethnographic accounts. In a similar vein, Babcock (1980) argues that there is an epistemological paradox in the lack of distinction between what is real and what is fiction. On the other hand, Smith (1984) claims that there are multiple realities – indeed as many as there are people. I was familiar with such debates that reflect the crisis of representation, which is part of the post-modernist paradigm, and how they present a challenge to sociological researchers' (and others') ability to select a method which can present a close and realistic description of social reality. In other words, as I discovered, researchers have to choose where they position themselves on the realism versus relativism continuum and then justify their choice of methodology. Indeed, the further I entered into such methodological debates which have arisen from this crisis of representation, the more I had concerns about the extent to which participant observation could be a 'naturalistic' pursuit that not only would the researcher affect the context, but that all that could be recorded was the process itself – a rhetorical device rather than a reality as Babcock (1980) cautions (see also, Young & Lee, 1996).

Resolving part of this dilemma, I found that Hammersley (1992) presented a middle way through which to convey the meaning of reality. He called this approach 'subtle realism' and argued that research is plausible when 'any truth claim is likely to be true given our existing knowledge'. Recognising that no knowledge is certain, Hammersley argues that a reality exists that is independent of the researcher and about which it is possible to make reasonably accurate claims. This approach suggests that it is still important that the researcher includes, or at least recognises, that he or she is part of the research process. Of further assistance in this quest, Gilbert (1993) described the type of knowledge that researchers derive from participant observation as 'introspective', in that the researcher is involved in making connections between the world of participation and their own personal experience. The stance the researcher adopts in this scenario is more generally referred to as being a reflexive researcher (Steier, 1995) and this reflexive turn as highlighted above, has been part of a different paradigmatic approach to qualitative research since the 1970s (for a full discussion see Foley, 2002).

This was all part of my preparation for entering the field, but what influence should this have on my role while I was in the field? I knew that one way of challenging my own expectations and preconceived ideas was through the way that I documented my field notes. This could be aided, for example, by separating out direct observations in the field, reported speech, and a summary of what people told me, from my own reflections and interpretations of what was happening. From talking to colleagues who used participant-observation methods, I understood that writing up field notes was extremely time consuming and that I needed to prepare for this type of practical demand as well as being available to observe events as they happened. Given all of these qualifications, I felt confident that I could collect data in the homes for the first study according to this approach. Indeed, I conscientiously followed the rule that I should not 'sleep on my notes' without re-reading them and writing up reflections as well as considering what else I needed to see or explore in order to uncover what was really going on. The second study with a colleague in a metropolitan hospital mortuary involved a short intensive period of participant observation; we agreed as researchers to discuss at the end of each day, our experiences in the field and share reflections on our fieldwork experiences.

I was aware that while data would be compromised by my presence, to the extent that people would behave differently than they normally might do, but came to realise that I had not reflected fully on the emotional demands on me in conducting sensitive research into death and dying. I would agree, with Howarth (1998) that for the researcher the dilemma of being sensitive remains difficult to resolve and lies at the heart of any approach that attempts to deconstruct or at least uncover events. However, the initial step in setting off on the first project was to recognise my subjectivity as a valid part of the research and contemplate how to take this into account during the data collection phase of the research process. Part of the preparation was in what special considerations needed to be taken into account in terms of conducting sensitive research and that is what I turn to next.

Sensitive research, subjectivity and emotion

Lee's (1993) seminal work on sensitive research topics identifies what it is that makes research sensitive. He includes such things as the type of threat to researchers and researched alike. Lee categorised the risks of conducting sensitive research into methodological, technical, ethical, political and legal ones. Sociological qualitative researchers (and others) are concerned not to harm participants by their enquiry and the recognition of the unequal relationship of power between the researched and the researcher is central to any consideration of research access; with the need for researchers to demonstrate strategies that minimise potential exploitation. Of course, this is not to position all participants in research as being without power, but sociological researchers need to show that they are following ethical codes of good practice.

In observing death and dying first hand in several different care homes, the sensitive nature of death and dying would call for particular considerations in relation to what sort of data I could and should collect. In her ethnographic study of dying in a hospice and the way in which dying impacts on social identity, Lawton (2000) had to adjust her methods when she was in the field and argued that it was ethically inappropriate as well as practically infeasible to do more than observe when someone was dying. She wrote:

> Formal interviews not only seemed to me to be too obtrusive to many patients and their families; in a substantial number of instances, they were simply not viable.
>
> *(Lawton, 2000, p. 30)*

It would seem to be important that any enquiry into identity, such as Lawton's, would require accounts from those people whose identity was being explored. Likewise, in my exploration into what happens at the time of death, I wanted to hear what those residents who were close to death had to say about the experience, as well as to see for myself what happened. In particular, what did residents understand about what was happening and what had they been told? One of the issues that I was trying to unpack was the arbitrariness of the status of 'living' and 'dying' for people who were already very old, frail and suffering chronic illness and, as I argued, 'unravelling their way to death'. However, as with Lawton's fieldwork, when people were very close to death it would seem to be entirely unethical to question them about what they felt in order to gather data for my study. This is something that could only be judged while I was in the field and which presents a challenge to the appropriateness of research methods. However, as I discuss shortly, the degree to which it was appropriate to explore sensitive issues about death with people who appeared to be close to death is distinct from being there and hearing what people wanted to tell me.

It is also the case, as Lee (1993) argues, that researchers are at risk of harm. His categories of risk cited above include risks to all participants. (See also Howarth's discussion on emotions in health research, Howarth, 1998). Since sociological research has at its core the purpose of challenging taken-for-granted assumptions about society, often correcting misperceptions and challenging negative stereotypes, I would agree with Lee's argument that the researcher is positioned as someone who is potentially vulnerable both during data collection and throughout the dissemination processes. However, I would add that the emotional impact that research can have upon the researcher is also a form of risk. This risk pertains to being exposed to distressing sights and accounts while in the field and afterwards during data analysis when researchers have to become intimately re-engaged with their data and frequently relive experiences. Dickson-Swift, James, and Kippen et al. (2008) used an empirical study into the emotion work of researchers in areas of sensitive research – and acknowledged its embodied nature. They argued for the need for researchers to be supported in their work – though such things as (clinical) supervision. Batchelor and Briggs (1994) also discuss the need for the use of support networks for researchers in the field.

The second dimension I discuss is one that is closely aligned to the first discussed above of the emotional impact of research on researchers; the need to use degrees of objectivity in order to minimise, or at least make transparent, the potential impact of their emotions (and bias) on research interpretations, what has been called the problem of situatedness and partiality (Clifford & Marcus, 1986). No representation is unproblematic and ethnographic writing reflexively involves both a conscious attempt to reveal the writer's assumptions as well as recognising the likelihood of an unconscious contribution made by the author of the text which can present itself through such things as focusing on data that connects with past experiences or an individualised style in writing up. This means that not only is the researcher part of the production of data in the field but also during the writing of the text. Regardless of respect for the embodied nature of the emotional researcher and recognition of them as part of the process of the production of knowledge, researchers who work in sensitive areas are expected to be able to cope with their topic and manage to make academic sense of their data.

This continues to beg the question of what it is that constitutes sensitive research especially within a social constructionist paradigm. Woodthorpe (2011) has argued that within death research the disengagement that allows for critical distance is unworkable. In part, as she argues, this is because death happens to everyone. While, I agree with her points, I would argue that it is possible to explore the subject of death and dying while keeping it at a safe distance *academically*. What I mean by this is that in some ways the 'ordering' of my thesis that was the outcome of the first study kept any personal distress bounded through the process of producing an academic explanation of what was taking place albeit in ways that reflected the nature of the institutional life that I was recording, which also ordered and contained 'death and dying'. However, this distancing did not succeed entirely, because I was emotionally distressed by much of what I saw and frustrated by the way that pain and suffering could be dismissed as a 'normal' part of ageing and dying. And there was always the tendency to pay more attention to difficult, or less common events that disrupted the daily routine. The purpose of social research in health and social care at least, is to attempt to change situations in need of changing, something for which Stacey was a powerful advocate (Stacey, 1991). Therefore, I argue that part of coping with sensitive research in the first study was to make recommendations about how to improve things for those residents who would continue to be treated as docile bodies for whom the trajectory to death was prescribed by the dominant features of the institution of care homes. Indeed, because my thesis was also part of a commissioned study, this was an expectation by the funders. However, the emotional impact on researchers is just one layer of complexity that researchers who conduct sensitive research face.

I argue that the third level of complexity lies in the reality that sociological, ethno- graphic enquiries involve researchers in a form of emotion management; beyond coping at a personal level with subject matter that causes distress, or frustration and anger, as argued above. A researcher who enters the territory of sensitive research needs to be able to conduct her/himself in an appropriate manner according to the setting. Here Hochschild's (1983) notion of emotional labour is useful and is something that has been acknowledged by Dickson-Swift et al. (2008) and Young and Lee (1996) referred to earlier. However, as I discuss later, emotional labour does not fully explain all aspects of emotion management in research into sensitive areas.

In sum, beyond the task of being self-reflective, researchers who investigate areas of sensitivity are required to behave in ways that pay attention to the settings and the people who are the subject of the enquiry (Lee, 1993). Indeed, it is worth noting that sensitive research can include any number of things – and this is something that is played out in ethics committees where individual members fail to agree on the sensitive nature of the research in terms of how participants need to be protected (Hunter, 2013). In this paper I focus on research into death and dying as sensitive by its association with a taboo topic, (for the recognition that all research is sensitive in terms of its process and outcomes could be taken as read). In particular, the way that death and dying research has been described by Lee as being emotionally taxing is of particular relevance to this paper. I also explore the emotional demeanour of the researcher as part of this role and the extent to which this is a performance as much as the management of feelings.

The practice of participant observation and observational research: doing sensitive research

In the first study into end-of-life care for older people in care homes I argued that residents were vulnerable in different ways. Before entering the field, I was aware of some of their vulnerabilities and how tensions between the responses to a series of losses that preceded their admission to homes, and those which resulted from the institutional life, made the role of the institution highly relevant to their experiences. For some residents, institutional life resembled the features of total institutions as defined by Goffman (1961) in that the admission to an institution was a rite of passage to a world in which the process of social control and restrictions removed their self determination, autonomy and 'adult competency'. Further, Goffman argued, the main features of social life that produce and sustain people's identity were lost when they entered 'total' institutions in that 'social arrangements regulated, under one roof and according to one rational plan, all spheres of institutional life' (Goffman, 1961, p. 18). Furthermore, as Willcocks, Peace, and Kellaher (1987) highlight, institutional living structured the routines of daily life in functional, personal and symbolic aspects. Indeed, this was a strong theme in the data analysis and one of the key theoretical components of my thesis.

Part of the institutional life that Goffman and Willcocks et al highlight is the prominence of the hierarchical structure present in care homes. And it is also the case that as a researcher, I needed to be aware of the extent to which institutional practices shaped my access to data and impacted upon my behaviour. For example, in the first phases of the care-home study and during interviews with heads of homes, he or she presented a specific view of what it meant for a resident to be 'dying' in a care home. While this rhetoric is what I wanted to explore, I was also aware that in 'seeing for myself', I needed to be aware of the role the head of home's practice would play in what I observed and how this view might mediate my own observation. In other words, as the gatekeeper to the setting, would they allow me to see everything that I wanted to see, or would certain aspects of care and home life be concealed? While I was in the field, taking an approach that questioned assumptions and shared understandings of social phenomena, was clearly something that I would need to be ever vigilant about. Hammersley's (1992) points about subtle realism relate in part to this, not only is it about being able to question taken-for-granted knowledge, but it is also about approaching the field with an open mind and being ready to adapt one's research plans to what is found there.

As described, the focus of the second study was on what the role of the Anatomical Pathology Technologists (APTs) involved and what took place in the setting of a hospital mortuary in terms of how the space framed their work, the number and type of visitors to the mortuary, the nature of the relationships and what form such encounters took. As well as conducting interviews with all members of the team, my colleague and I each spent three days in the mortuary setting making observations on what happened there. The demands of this setting were different in that that we had to respect the privacy of any relatives visiting deceased people and the anonymity of deceased people – as well as being clear with participants who were all staff members about the purpose of the research and their rights in relation to withdrawing from the project. This contrasted with the comparative freedom of going where I wanted to go in care home (although sometimes this had to be negotiated).

Emotional labour

I argued earlier, that comparatively little attention is given to researchers who need to behave appropriately and in keeping with the setting, insofar as this is recognised as a form of emotional labour. Here, I make a clear distinction between being sensitive to any study participants, and being expected to present the same emotional demeanour as that culturally laid down by the setting worked in. I draw on three examples to illustrate what I mean.

Example 1. In the first care-home project during the negotiation of access to homes, I experienced one of many dilemmas. Seven of the eight heads of homes in which I planned to conduct participant observation, wanted to know how I would introduce myself to the residents and the topic of my study. For example, Rose House (pseudonym) was large private nursing home run by a matron with many years' nursing experience. On my first visit to negotiate the detail of my participant-observer role, she was very concerned about how I would discuss the topic of death and dying with 'her' residents, a topic she clearly saw as being very difficult to discuss. She seemed to be reassured when I told her that I would approach residents very carefully and would let them lead the discussion and thus only take it as far as they wanted it to go. While I recognised the need for heads of home to protect their charges from unethical practice, I was intrigued by the notion that this protection was based on an assumption that death and dying would be an upsetting subject for all residents and thus needed to be raised with great caution. The reality, as it transpired, was that some residents were happy to talk about death and dying and did so freely, while others did not want to discuss the subject at all, refusing to pick up any cues I offered. In this access visit, I wanted to challenge the head of Rose House for being paternalistic; however, I agreed that the subject of death and dying needed careful management. Indeed, the reason for the enquiry into end-of-life care was underpinned by a belief that death and dying were special events and that older people deserved good quality end-of-life care.

By contrast, in Noble House, a large voluntary Catholic care home, when I talked to Sister Margaret she had no problems at all with the subject of the study and on a tour of the home she introduced me to all the residents as 'Carol who is researching death and dying.' Indeed, residents were delighted to talk to me and when word got around, they queued up to discuss the subject of death and dying with me and disclose their personal thoughts about their future demise. Indeed, it took several days for me to hear the many accounts. If it is possible to generalise within homes, perhaps this clear willingness to talk about death was not surprising in a Catholic home where people told me quite openly that they were preparing for the next life.

In terms of researching sensitive subjects such as death and dying, what this contrast between the two homes told me is that death was staged by the home to the extent that the home's philosophy framed the script for death and dying. Further, my task as a researcher in these settings then was to fit in with these different dramaturgical productions (Goffman, 1990) Alongside this and as a sociological researcher, I had to observe, question and challenge my own prejudices and beliefs about death and dying which I discuss later.

Example 2. Negotiating access to the mortuary was a different experience. The process of gaining ethical approval and being questioned by an ethics committee required a different form of emotional management. For example, people on the NHS ethics panel, of whom there were many, were representing different aspects of ethical concern for deceased people and did not ask many of the questions that we had anticipated.[1] In terms of the ethical questions we were asked, the focus of their concerns was on protecting deceased people, and not the staff who work in the mortuary. Even though we wanted to interview technologists and bereavement officers and observe the work in the mortuary, the need to protect staff beyond ensuring that they were fully informed was not an expressed concern. Indeed, most of the questions were focused more on the details of the application form than ethical issues.

Example 3. While the mortuary staff referred to deceased people as deceased patients, challenging the assumptions that underpin seeing death as special and seeing death as an everyday part of their working life presented its own challenges. For example, one afternoon, I accompanied an APT to the radiology department for a series of X-rays on a young baby following a sudden death. She carried the baby in a large covered cot which was clearly very heavy for her and difficult to manage. The appointment had been made for a time when there were no patients in the department, confirming my experience that removing a body from the mortuary had to be concealed in some way. I felt a range of emotions about the tension between death as something special and death as something that is part of life. I thought that I needed to ask why this concealment happened but my questions about the possibility of openly carrying the baby in her arms into the X-Ray department met with some degree of surprise, and I suspect, concerns about my lack of sensitivity to the situation. I really wanted to ask many more questions but I was monitoring and managing my inquiry according to what I considered to be appropriate to the 'culture' of the mortuary. In other words, I was concerned to make what Goffman would call the right impression by conveying sensitivity in the way that participants defined this by their actions.

It is certainly not always the case that my performance was modified by what I was able to challenge. In one of the care homes in the first study, by contrast, one evening when helping with the washing-up I asked two care workers to explain to me what happened when a resident died. They told me that they always opened the window – and even though I knew this to be a tradition in many health care settings and one I had followed myself when I worked in hospitals, and despite the reality that I was concerned about appearing to be stupid, I could not take for granted that the reason was what I understood it to be and so asked why they did this. They then began to disagree with each other about whether it was 'to let something in' or 'something out'. They were clearly embarrassed that they did not know the reason for a practice that they told me was very important to perform after death. I remember that I felt pleased that I had pursued the question and revealed my apparent lack of understanding of their actions. In part, this lack of understanding reflected the quality of their training and development and later I felt sorry for being the cause of their embarrassment. Indeed, this suggests that any challenge is a subtle form of power and that I was more able to exploit the care workers than the APTs. But what is key to my discussion here is that their understanding of my role as a researcher, was so far removed from their common experience of the care assistants that the need to fit in did not affect my demeanour in the same way as in the mortuary where the researcher role was much better understood.

These examples raise the question of what was really happening in terms of the management of my emotions. I would argue that in the first example, I was more concerned with fitting in and being accepted than in the second one – where I was already an *alien* species. I explore this further next.

Power of the researcher

Entering the field, presented an interesting challenge in both studies and begged the question of how clearly the study participants understood the researcher role as well as what would happen to any data that was collected. In care homes, it seemed probable that I would be regarded differently in different homes and also within them by different participants. The issue of role, and the potential power carried by that role, is very pertinent to the culture of care homes. Further, power is a crucial issue in concerns about sensitive research. As discussed above, I knew from the early interviews with heads of homes, that there were clear role boundaries and concerns about what it was permissible for certain care workers to do. I wanted to investigate role, power and status through the ways in which death and dying was produced within an institutional setting. As a methodological point, it seemed that it was going to be difficult for heads of homes to position me within the existing hierarchy and that I was always going to stand out. The notion of research was not particularly familiar to most of the participants in the care homes. There were notable exceptions where residents and staff members asked me lots of questions about the nature of the enquiry and one day, when a resident who was not too enamoured with qualitative research, asked me what I was going to do about the Heisenberg effect. How clearly the study participants understood my role and what I was doing with any data that I collected partly framed my demeanour.

The mortuary study was of short duration and therefore *participant* observation was not feasible. By contrast, research was something that was central to the ethos of the hospital and the mortuary setting. Indeed, in a teaching hospital environment the Pathology Department was central to several research initiatives and projects. It seemed to be less likely that the notion of being a research participant would be misunderstood; however, the notion of qualitative research, which was certainly not the norm in funded research, was seen as something 'quirky' (a second-hand reported description from a senior staff member). But however we were viewed, the APTs were very keen to convey the nature of their role and willing to be interviewed and observed, despite their workload. They were open with us about how they wanted the research to make a difference to the recognition of their role and wanted some of the myths about people who work in mortuaries to be exploded.

The performance of objectivity

In conclusion, there is expectation on the researcher to behave in ways that are true to the values of research, and, alongside this, the sociological researcher (as in other disciplines) has to be able to challenge assumptions that underpin key issues and, at the same time, as participant observers, behave in ways that are in keeping with the setting. In the examples above, I have illustrated how in both settings, I was self-conscious of my performance as a researcher. To some extent, researchers have a script and agree – usually through ethical processes and access negotiation – how they will behave. In sensitive research, the correct demeanour of the researcher is a particular focus of concern. To some extent Hochschild's (1983) essentially Marxist claim that emotional labour is a commodity regulated by social exchange is relevant to researchers who manage their own emotions in order to present what is considered to be the right response. This means that they might need to suppress true feelings in order to produce the right emotional state in another person. This could be by such things as encouraging a research participant to disclose information that might be difficult to hear and to be able to listen to in a non-judgemental way. However, Hochschild's allusion to the notion of the real self, evident in her claim that there are emotions that are authentic and which need to be suppressed, is something I challenge. As a sociologist, I am not convinced that the acting self – however the performance is conducted as deep or surface acting – can be separated from the real self as she implies. The notion of an inner self echoes Freud's theory that individuals have innate drives shaped by experiences in early infancy which are not subject to rational interpretation and which are therefore, polymorphous and perverse. Despite the fact that Freud (see Mitchell, 1988) did not ignore the social context of emotions, he was less interested in their social expression and production than in the barriers to their expression, which he called defence mechanisms. Further, what is also residual here is the Western notion of the ideologically invested self, that is bounded, unique coherent and evident to itself through such things as introspection. It is possible to sympathise with Hochschild's view since, that as a paid researcher, I was in a relationship of exchange, part of which was about my emotional labour. In this sense my emotional demeanour was part of the relationship of exchange. However, I am not convinced that research can be placed directly into a relationship of exchange as analysed by Hochschild when it is not clear to the audience what the researcher should be doing. In these situations, how is the presentation of the right demeanour part of the commodity? I argue that between these two dimensions of the structuralist theory of Hochschild and the psychodynamic one of Freudians sits the integrationist model of symbolic interactionism that offers a more convincing explanation of how researchers manage emotions.

Goffman (1990) used three metaphors of drama, ritual and game through which to explain how people manage the impression they make. He claimed that people have dualistic identities which consist of many loosely integrated social roles as well as a real self. But more than this, the real 'self' that is driving the actions, is produced through performance. In other words, everything is social. He argued that everyone needs to make a convincing impression in their performance, but further, that the notion of performance also extends to the audience. Both audience and performing individuals are concerned to live up to what Goffman called 'the moral standards of the social world' which counters the notion that performances of presentations are entirely manipulative. To this extent, there is a collusion between actor(s) and audience.

I was concerned to make the right impression in the research settings. Not only was I an observer, I was also being observed and, as such, performing front stage. Often, I was unclear about the extent to which I should draw on my professional experience. I had many years' experience as a nurse and midwife, and this role had become what Goffman (1990) would call second nature to me. What he meant by this was that in specific roles people become less aware of the impression they are trying to make, echoing Hochschild's notion of deep acting. The 'reality-making' of roles as the collusion between the audience and the actor, also demands that the audience collude in the 'delusion'. For example, patients want to believe that their doctors have the required attributes of the medical profession and that they are trustworthy and competent. But what of the performance of the researcher? Well, in the care home setting – which at that time was an under-researched area – as I have argued, no-one had any experience of what a researcher did and the staff who talked to me struggled to understand what I was doing. It was easier to some extent, for residents and care workers to understand that I wanted to evaluate the quality of life including end of life and make recommendations for improvements. In the end, for Hammersley and his ideas on realism and the role of research, what seems to be most significant is the extent to which research contributes to existing knowledge and can solve social problems, or at least improve the position of those being researched if they are in some way disadvantaged (Hammersley, 1992). Furthermore, if researchers want their findings to contribute to a change in practice then adding to the information about particular settings will make that a more realistic possibility.

I have described the way in which the mortuary project was a setting where the researcher role was better understood. I gave an example of being aware of feeling awkward about challenging some of the practices around concealment and the impression this might have made. Clearly, it is the case that being in this setting for such a short time, and with the main forms of data collection being conducting interviews and making direct observations, that the need to be accepted into the setting was not as significant. Indeed, in this paper, it has not been my intention to make comparisons between the two studies, but rather to interrogate what it is that researchers do when they conduct sensitive research and how their emotional labour needs to be a more overt part of the process of reflexivity.

It is also the case that researchers need to be able to present the correct emotional demeanour which requires them to meet several layers of expectations; being sensitive to the needs of research participants while also challenging the assumptions that might provide them with forms of institutional protection from the reality of the nature of their role. All of this, I argue, requires a performance which needs to be balanced between the requirement to present the correct demeanour and the separate need of the inquiry itself. This is much more than guarding against the danger of going native, it is a significant part of being reflexive about what is really going on here, which underpins all ethnographic enquiries.

Note

1. We thought it likely that the reputation of the hospital might be one of the concerns in the case of being told something potentially damaging such as examples of bad practice.

Disclosure statement

No potential conflict of interest was reported by the author.

References

Altheide, D. L., & Johnson, J. M. (1994). Criteria for assessing interpretive validity in qualitative research. In N. K. Denzin & Y. S. Lincoln (Eds.), *Handbook of qualitative research* (pp. 485–499). Thousand Oaks, CA: Sage.

Atkinson, P. (1990). *The ethnographic imagination: Textual constructions of reality*. London: Routledge.

Babcock, B. (1980). Reflexivity: Definitions and discriminations. *Semiotica*, *30*(1/2), 1–14.

Batchelor, J. A., & Briggs, C. M. (1994). Subject, project or self? Thoughts on ethical dilemmas for social and medical researchers. *Social Science and Medicine*, *39*(7), 949–954.

Clifford, J., & Marcus, J. E. (eds). (1986). *Writing culture: The poetics and politics of ethnography*. Berkley: University of California Press.

Coffey, A. (1999). *The ethnographic self: Fieldwork and the representation of identity*. London: Sage. Denzin, N. (1989). *Interpretative Interactionism*. London: Sage.

Dickson-Swift, V., James, E., Kippen, S., et al. (2008) Risk to researchers in qualitative research on sensitive topics: Issues and strategies. *Qualitative Health Research*, *18*(1), 133–144.

Dickson-Swift, V., James, E. L., Kippen, S., & Liamputtong, P. (2007). Doing sensitive research: What challenges do qualitative researchers face? *Qualitative Research*, *7*(3), 327–353.

Foley, D. E. (2002). Critical ethnography: The reflexive turn. *Qualitative Studies in Education*, *15*(5), 460–490.

Gilbert, N. (1993). Research theory and method. In N. Gilbert (Ed.), *Researching social life* (pp. 18–31). London: Sage.

Goffman, E. (1961). *Asylum*. London: Penguin books.

Goffman, E. (1963). *Stigma: notes in the management of spoiled identity*. Englewood Cliffs, NJ: Prentice Hall.

Goffman, E. (1990 [1959]). *The presentation of self in everyday life*. Hammondsworth: Penguin.

Hammersley, M. (1992). *What's wrong with ethnography? Methodological explorations*. London: Routledge.

Hochschild, A. R. (1983). *The managed heart: The commercialisation of human feeling*. Berkley, CA: University of California Press.

Howarth, G. (1998). What's emotion got to do with it? Reflections on the personal in health research. *Annual Review of Health Social Sciences*, *8*, 2–8.

Hughes, E. C. (1962). Good people and dirty work. *Social Problems*, *10*(1), 3–11.

Hunter, D. (2013). Participant-led health research and ethical regulation. *Research Ethics*, *9*(2), 50–51.

James, N. (1989). Emotional labour: Skill and work in the social regulation of feelings. *Sociological Review*, *37*, 15–42.

Johnson, N. (2009). The role of self and emotion in qualitative sensitive research: A reflective account. *ENQUIRE*, (4), 23–50, November 2009.

Komaromy, C. (1994) *The performance of death and dying in care homes for older people: An ethnographic account* (Unpublished thesis). Buckinghamshire: Open University.

Komaromy, C. 2005, The production of death and dying in care homes for older people: An ethnographic account. Unpublished PhD Thesis. Milton Keynes: The Open University.

Komaromy, C., & Woodthorpe, K. (2011). British Academy funded 'Investigating mortuary services in hospital settings' (September 2009 – January 2011). Published Report.

Lawton, J. (2000). *The dying process: Patient's experience of palliative care*. London and New York: Routledge.

Lee, R. M. (1993). *Doing research on sensitive topics*. London: Sage.

Lee, Y.-O., & Lee, R. M. (2012). Methodological research on "sensitive" topics: A decade review. *Bulletin De Methodologie Sociologique*, *114*, 35–49.

Mitchell, S. A. (1988). *Relational concepts in psychoanalysis, an integration*. Cambridge, USA: Harvard University Press.

Smith, J. K. (1984). The problem of criteria for judging interpretive inquiry. *Education, Evaluation and Policy Analysis*, *6*(4), 379–391.

Stacey, M. (1991). *The sociology of health and healing*. London: Routledge.

Steier, F. (Ed.). (1995). *Research and Reflexivity*. London: Sage.

Willcocks, D., Peace, S., & Kellaher, L. (1987). *Private lives and public places*. London: Tavistock Publications.

Woodthorpe, K. (2007). My life after death: Connecting the field, the findings and the feelings. *Anthropology Matters*, 9, 1.

Woodthorpe, K. (2011). Researching death: Methodological reflections on the management of critical distance. *International Journal of Social Research Methodology*, 14(2), 99–109.

Woodthorpe, K., & Komaromy, C. (2013). A missing link? The role of mortuary staff in hospital-based bereavement care services. *Bereavement Care*, 32(3), 124–130.

Young, E. H., & Lee, R. M. (1996). Fieldwork feelings as data: 'emotion work' and 'feeling rules' in first person accounts of sociological fieldwork. In V. James & J. Gabe (Eds.), *Health and the Sociology of Emotions* (pp. 99–113). Oxford: Blackwell Publishing Ltd.

Index

abortion 39–41, 43–48, 65, 67–69
Anderson, E. 105
anger 2, 3, 14, 65, 68, 90, 91, 94, 96, 98, 99
anxiety 41, 54, 69, 94, 103
asynchronous internet 39
asynchronous text-based online FGs 40, 42, 43

Babcock, B. 112, 113
Batchelor, J. A. 115
Behar, R. 15
bereaved parents 90, 93, 95–98
black humour 96
Blair, K. L. 44
Bourdieu, P. 2
Braun, V. 56
Briggs, C. M. 115
Brown, L. M. 93

care homes 78, 81, 112, 114, 115, 116, 117, 118, 119, 121
care workers 81, 118, 119, 121
Clarke, V. 56
Coffey, A. 111
collective pressure 104
contract researcher 15
Corbin, J. 91
Cotterill, P. 89
Crenshaw, K. W. 70

data analysis 52–62, 95, 99, 115, 116
death research 75, 76, 80, 81, 115
Denzin, N. K. 78
Dickson-Swift, V. 10, 115, 116
disbelief 47, 90, 94–96, 98
distress 42, 47, 48, 65, 69, 82, 115
Doucet, A. 93

emotional/emotions: expressivity 104; impact 94, 99, 112, 115, 116; labour 82, 84, 89–92, 96, 116, 121; management 89, 98, 99, 111, 116; reactions 11–15, 92; sensitivities 13, 18; wellbeing 10, 30, 95, 103; work 98, 115
emotionally-sensed knowledge 90–92, 99
emotions 2, 3, 13–15, 18, 19, 65, 66, 69, 89–92, 94, 96–99, 120

end-of-life care 76, 78, 80, 112, 116, 117
epistemological significance 92
ethical approval 31, 34, 44, 90, 118
ethics 3, 19, 31, 44, 81, 94, 96; committees 4, 9, 17, 19, 20, 27, 31, 32, 75, 76, 81, 116, 118
Evans, R. 89, 92

feelings 2, 14, 15, 17, 18, 59, 60, 82, 91, 95–98, 104, 105
feminist standpoint theory 67, 69
Finlay, L. 66
focus groups 30, 42, 45, 47, 93, 104, 105, 107, 108; structure 45
Frankena, T. 54
Frosh, S. 108
funding bodies 4

Gallacher, L. 62
Gallagher, M. 62
gender identity 33, 102–108
Gilbert, N. 113
Gilligan, C. 93
Goffman, E. 23, 27, 112, 116, 118, 120, 121
Goodrum, S. 91–92, 95
Graham, H. 53
gratitude 97
guilt 2, 3, 14, 65, 94–96, 98, 99

Hammersley, M. 113, 117
happiness 30, 97, 99
Harding, S. 67
Hartsock, N. 69
HIV 22–26
Hochschild, A. 90, 98, 116, 120, 121
Hollomotz, A. 32
Hollway, W. 108
Howarth, G. 114
Hubbard, G. 90–92, 99

identifications 12–14, 19, 95, 106, 107
inclusive data analysis process 56, 59, 61, 62
inclusive research 3, 52–54, 58, 59
institutional life 115, 116
interaction patterns 46

intimacy 23, 29–34
introspection 78, 83, 84, 120

James, E. 115
Jefferson, T. 108
Jones, K. 90

Kellaher, L. 116
Keys, J. L. 91, 92, 95
Kippen, S. 115
knowledge claims 65, 67, 111
Komaromy, C. 91

Lawton, J. 114
learning disabilities 52–55, 57–62
Lee, R. M. 3, 10, 18, 20, 24, 29, 76, 89, 114, 116
Lee, Y.-O. 10, 18–20
Lesko, N. 31
Letherby, G. 89
LLTCs 29–33

male researcher 106
masculine defensiveness 105
masculine identities 104–106, 108
masculinities 102–104, 106–109
Mauthner, N. 93
McPherson, A. 56
memorialisation 93
methodological challenges 22, 112–114
mind-mapping 58
moderators 39, 42–48
moral voices 104
mortuary 112, 117–119, 121
motivation 3, 12–14, 19, 23, 24, 82, 107
Murphy, S. 90

Nind, M. 53, 54
normal sensitivity 23
normality 3, 22–27

objectivity 16, 66, 69, 92, 98, 111, 115, 120

participant interactions 46, 65, 66
participant observation 78, 79, 92, 113, 116, 117, 119
participatory data analysis 52–55, 61, 62
Peace, S. 116
perinatal bereavement research 94
personal experience 12–14, 19, 80, 95, 113
personal responsibility 78
Plummer, K. 32
postgraduate supervisors 4
posthumous consent 33
potential stigma 25
Powell, M. A. 11, 12

power 2, 16, 17, 26, 53, 54, 57, 59, 61, 105, 114, 119
power (im)balances 61
private message function 47, 48
procedural ethics 77
psychosocial perspective 103, 104, 106
psychosocial research studies 103
Punch, M. 26

qualitative interviewing 90
qualitative interviews 16, 65, 66
qualitative research 69, 78, 98, 99, 113, 119

Redman, P. 103
reflexivity 66, 68, 69, 75–78, 81–85, 92, 111, 121
Relf, M. 66
relief 97
Renzetti, C. M. 76
research: design 4, 17, 54, 81; encounter 13, 23, 25, 67, 102, 104, 106, 108; ethics committees 4; literature 65, 76, 77; projects 2, 4, 17, 23, 26, 65, 67, 69, 90, 92, 93, 95, 99; sensitivities 10, 11; work 58
researcher: emotions 66, 77
researcher vulnerability 75, 77, 80, 83
responsibility 18, 19, 45, 67, 77, 84, 97
Roberts, B. 13
Robinson, C. 19
Roets, G. 54
Rolls, L. 66

sadness 14, 90, 94–96, 99
Schaffir, W. B. 98
Schostak, J. 12
Schwartz, A. 62
Seale, J 54
sensibilities 65
sensitive death studies 76
sensitive issues 2, 3, 11, 14, 39, 40, 44, 104–109
sensitive research 2–5, 9–12, 19, 20, 29, 66, 76, 83–85, 112, 114–116; projects 78, 94
sensitive topics 9, 10, 14, 18, 19, 33, 34, 40, 42, 43, 47, 48, 75, 76, 107; research 16, 19
sensitivities 2–5, 9–12, 16, 18–20, 22–24, 26, 52, 61, 62, 66; internalising 76, 78, 79; issue of 3, 9–12
serodiscordancy 25, 26
serodiscordant relationships 23–26
sex-negativity 31
shame 82, 97
Sieber, J. E. 10
Smart, C. 78, 84
Smith, J. K. 113
social desirability 42
social research 10, 11, 15, 68, 83, 115

sociological enquiry 111–112
Sontag, S. 30
Sparrman, A. 34
Stanley, B 10
Strauss, A. 91
subjectivities 66, 68, 83, 99, 111, 112, 114
supervisors 9, 10, 12, 13, 15, 16, 19, 20, 92, 97

Tates, K. 48
transformative experience 54
transparency 52, 53

Visser, R. C. 15, 99
visual anonymity 42

vulnerability 9, 10, 14, 29–31, 75–78, 80, 81, 83–85
vulnerable participants 20, 75, 76, 83
vulnerable population 39, 40

Willcocks, D. 116
Williams, V. 54
women 30, 40, 67, 69, 93, 94, 96, 97, 99, 104, 105
Woodthorpe, K. 15, 19, 92, 115
workplace issue 40, 43
workshops 4, 54–57; leaders 55, 56

Young, E. H. 116

Ziebland, S. 56

Taylor & Francis Group
an **informa** business

Taylor & Francis eBooks

www.taylorfrancis.com

A single destination for eBooks from Taylor & Francis with increased functionality and an improved user experience to meet the needs of our customers.

90,000+ eBooks of award-winning academic content in Humanities, Social Science, Science, Technology, Engineering, and Medical written by a global network of editors and authors.

TAYLOR & FRANCIS EBOOKS OFFERS:

- A streamlined experience for our library customers
- A single point of discovery for all of our eBook content
- Improved search and discovery of content at both book and chapter level

REQUEST A FREE TRIAL

support@taylorfrancis.com

Routledge
Taylor & Francis Group

CRC Press
Taylor & Francis Group